THE RIVER LIFFEY

HISTORY AND HERITAGE

Christopher Moriarty

The Collins Press

First published in 2018 by
The Collins Press
West Link Park
Doughcloyne
Wilton
Cork
T12 N5EF
Ireland

A CIP record for this book is available from the British Library.

Hardback ISBN: 978-1-84889-354-2

Design and typesetting by Fairways Design
Typeset in Minion Pro
Printed in Poland by Białostockie Zakłady Graficzne SA

THE
RIVER
LIFFEY

HISTORY AND HERITAGE

To Mary
with love

Contents

The Liffey at Ballysmuttan.

Preface: Memories of the Liffey

Thirty-seven years ago Seamus Cashman's Wolfhound Press published *The Book of the Liffey* to mark the Dublin Millennium. Much has happened to the river since then: a great increase in the population of Dublin and the popularity of the Liffey valley, the construction of fine new bridges, the marvellous developments of beautiful and spacious public parks and the spectacular renewal of life in the Docklands. And much remains the same, with subtle but usually positive changes: the wilderness of the river of the mountains, the beauty of the Blessington Lakes and the stateliness of the great houses.

The creators of *The Book of the Liffey* standing by the Samuel Beckett Bridge in April 2011. L–R: the late Jan de Fouw, designer; Seamus Cashman, publisher; Eizabeth Healy, editor, who died in 2018; Gerard O'Flaherty and Christopher Moriarty, writers. Photo by an unknown passer-by.

My first encounter with the Liffey left a lasting memory. It must have been before the Second World War because my father had taken the family by car to the picnic place at Ballysmuttan. Pinkeen-net in hand, I paddled in the shallows until I tripped, fell flat on my face and was rapidly removed by startled parents from the embrace of Anna Liffey. A few years later Barney Flanagan was engaged by the family to build a holiday cottage, down the hill from Blessington, overlooking the new lake and the massive hill called Lugnagun. There we spent Easter and summer holidays and many, many weekends for the next twelve years. And there it might have ended, had I not been awarded a studentship in 1958 to investigate the ways of the fishes of the lakes.

Nearly thirty years later Seamus Cashman was one of two Dublin publishers who conceived a Liffey book. He invited Elizabeth Healy to edit it and Elizabeth commissioned me and others to share the writing and illustrating with her. Her wide knowledge of poetry, painting, legends and song added immeasurably to the charm of *The Book of the Liffey*.

Happily for all concerned, the Liffey book published at the same time by Seamus's friend and professional rival Michael O'Brien, concentrated on the Liffey in Dublin and complemented rather than competed with ours. Illustrated by Stephen Conlin, the text was the work of the engineer John de Courcy, alas no longer with us. Some years before my current effort, he too wrote another Liffey book. Entitled *The Liffey in Dublin*, it is, besides being very readable, an outstanding work of scholarship encapsulating in particular such essential source material as the official records of the city council. Historical details in my city chapters rely heavily on his research.

In 2015 Dublin City Council published a beautiful book entitled *Bridges of Dublin* by Annette Black and Michael B. Barry. Illustrated with superb photographs, historic prints and paintings and detailed technical drawings, its value as a source work is equalled by its readability. I have used it to fill in dates and other occasional details that were not readily available elsewhere. Much of the same information, together with up-to-the-minute additions on temporary closures and such, is available on the website, www.bridgesofdublin.ie.

Shortly before this book was finished no fewer than four very remarkable works with abundant references to Anna Liffey were published. Patrick F. Wallace, who had pioneered and led the great research project on behalf of the National Museum, brought the results to date together in *Viking Dublin: The Wood Quay Excavations*, published by Irish Academic Press. Its 585 pages of scholarly writing and illustrations make a worthy memorial to more than fifty years of study.

The second book, *Dublin: The Story of a City*, is a joint work by Stephen Conlin and Peter Harbison. Stephen Conlin is a well-established illustrator of past people and landscapes based on meticulous research. Peter Harbison, archaeologist and historian, contributed the very readable text. This book, published by O'Brien Press, is a combination of rare beauty and erudition.

In 2016 Irish Academic Press published a new edition of the classic *Irish Stone Bridges* by Peter O'Keeffe and Tom Simington, which had been a collector's item since shortly after its first appearance in 1991. The publishers' decision to produce this in full colour required the editor, Rob Goodbody, to travel throughout Ireland to take new photographs of the 300 or so bridges illustrated.

Rob Goodbody was also the co-author, with Richard Nairn and David Jeffrey, of the superb book *Dublin Bay: Nature and History*, published by The Collins Press, that appeared at the end of 2017. Besides being a comprehensive study of the bay, whose abundant wildlife and architectural history are essentially children of Anna Liffey herself, their book illustrates and explains the complexity of an entity deemed to be of world-class environmental importance.

Any river, great or small, offers sufficient material of interest to fill many books. In a global context, the Liffey, at not much more than 100 km in length and less than 10,000 years old, is puny and infantile. But it is one of the rivers of a capital city, and has contributed in no small way to the development of a civilisation. Many people have written about aspects of the Liffey, none more distinguished than James Joyce, who used it as an allegory of human life itself.

But all writers about the Liffey are confronted by the problem of finding a way to edit the wealth of information about it. My approach has been in part to share the aspects of the river and its immediate surroundings that most appeal to me and in part to dwell on features that are easily accessible to all comers. So I have provided little on the private houses, increasing numbers of country clubs or the multiplicity of golf clubs and other regions devoted to what the planners describe as 'active recreation'. This, together with the constraints of space and time, means that much detail and some entire aspects, such as angling and pleasure boating, scarcely make an appearance. Happily, great scope remains for many more books on Anna Livia Plurabelle.

Acknowledgements

It is a great pleasure to put on record the unstinted help I received from many people who have shared their unrivalled knowledge of particular aspects of the Liffeyside. Mary Eustace, Michael Freeman, Paddy Higgins, John Hussey, Jim O'Brien, Jim Ryan and Glascott Symes took me on tours of their special places. John Hussey read and commented most helpfully on substantial parts of the text. Gerard O'Flaherty allowed me to quote his outline of *Finnegans Wake*, which he wrote for *The Book of the Liffey*. Michael Finn and Richard Nairn very generously provided me with their excellent photographs. Alan McGurdy, Leslie Moore, Peadar Moran, Philip O'Connor and Jim Ryan gave helpful advice. The late David Poole introduced me to the people and devoted work of the Liffey Valley Protection Association. Staff in the National Library and the libraries of Dublin City Archive, the Institution of Engineers of Ireland, the Royal Irish Academy and Trinity College Dublin all gave assistance with their unfailing courtesy and skill.

Permission to reproduce copyright material from Geological Survey of Ireland, National Gallery of Ireland, National Maritime Museum, Greenwich, London, National Library of Ireland and Ordnance Survey of Ireland is gratefully acknowledged. My son Ruairi drew the new maps. Encouraged by Rosaleen Dwyer, South County Dublin Heritage Officer, all five local authorities provided generous financial support for the publication, as did the Dublin Port Company, whose Communications Manager, Charlie Murphy, gave me great help and encouragement.

Mary Pyle – with her dogs – accompanied me on many trips of exploration and her reading of the text led to countless improvements.

Author's Note
In this book, the terms left bank and right bank are from the
viewpoint of a person looking downstream.

1 | Introduction:
The ancient lore of Anna Liffey

The naming of Anna Liffey

While 'Anna' is an acceptable transliteration of the words 'Abha na ...', meaning 'River of ...', an unlikely and implausible origin of the word Liffey may be found in the *Rennes Dindseanchas*, translated by Whitley Stokes and reckoned by him to date to the eleventh or twelfth century. I paraphrase his rather forbidding prose here:

> Life, daughter of Cannan the Pict, married Deltbanna of Drucht, the steward of Conaire the Great, King of Tara. Out of the Elfinmound of Bodb on Femen was he. South of Tara they set up, and because the plain over which she came seemed beautiful to her, she asked that her name might be on it: and Deltbanna dealt out no more liquor for the men of Erin until yon plain was called by his wife's name. Whence *Mag Lifi*. Or maybe *Fea* was the name and *Li-* because what she saw seemed bright to her.

Charming as the tales are, an alternative explanation of the name of the Liffey – and equally of the Boyne, the Shannon and other untranslatable river names – is not only more romantic, but is also favoured by many scholars. It is that the names cannot be translated from Gaelic because they were bestowed, in a language now unknown, by pre-Celtic inhabitants of Ireland. The drastic pressure that Deltbanna exerted on the men of Erin seems excessive for a simple name change. But the strength of feeling may stem from a tradition of reverence for existing place names and a strong reluctance to change them.

The *Metrical Dindshenchas*, edited and translated by Edward Gwynn, has only seven references to the Liffey, all of them brief and all referring to the Liffey of the plain. One mention of the name is in 'Find Life' which, according to a footnote, refers tantalisingly to 'the upper waters of River Boyne'. While the main streams of the two great rivers are distinct and clearly separated, their headwaters lie close together. In the townland of Agher in County Meath, where the Rye Water, a tributary of the Liffey, rises, a nearby stream flows northwards past Summerhill to meet the Dangan River, which joins the Boyne downstream of Trim. In this low-lying country the plains of the Liffey and the Boyne are scarcely distinguishable.

The Liffey of the plains at Leixlip, County Kildare. The dense growth of trees and bushes by the water's edge gives a fair impression of how the greater part of the lowland river would have appeared until medieval times or later.

A number of the early references are to *Mag Life*, the Plain of the Liffey, rather than the river itself. Literary and folk tradition seem to have had less interest in the river than in the land it flowed through. This leads to the question of where the earliest available written records of both the King's River and the Liffey may be found.

Finn McCool and St Brigid

Finn McCool's first name was bestowed in the very waters of the Liffey. Reared in the fastnesses of the Slieve Bloom Mountains by his two guardian women, Liath Luachra and the priestess Bodhmall, he grew up to be a great hunter, able to outrun the deer of the moorland. In his youth, he left the hunting cabin in which they lived and set off to seek his fortune. Lady Gregory tells the tale in *Gods and Fighting Men*:

> So he went away then by himself, and never stopped till he came to Magh Life, and there he saw young lads swimming in a lake, and they called to him to swim against them. So he went into the lake, and he

beat them at swimming. 'Fair he is and well shaped,' they said when they saw him swimming, and it was from that time he got the name of Finn, that is, Fair. But they got to be jealous of his strength, and he went away and left them.

In later life, having taken control of the Fianna, Finn made his headquarters on the Hill of Allen, which rises up from the western edge of the Plain of the Liffey. Neither the date nor, indeed, the existence of Finn as a person are known. Written accounts associate him with more or less historical figures – but these tales were not set down until the eleventh and twelfth centuries. Finn's prowess in hunting and his love of the wild creatures of the forest give scope for speculation that his ancestry lay among the hunter-gatherers of Mesolithic times, predating by thousands of years the Iron Age pastoralists who are the backbone of the Cúchulain cycle. The plain of the Liffey lies between the locations of many of Finn's exploits centred on the Hill of Allen and Glenasmole. Allen and the hills overlooking Glenasmole can both be seen from the riverside and a remarkable number of the latter bear his name: Seefin, Seefingan and Ballymorefinn.

The tenth-century *Liber hymnorum* mentions *Currech, a cursu equorum dictus est* ('the Curragh, said to be a racecourse of horses') and refers to St Brigid as proprietor of the land. The twelfth-century *Book of Leinster* contains a poem on her ownership of the Plain of the Liffey. While these provide written evidence of the antiquity of the traditions of sanctity and horses, there is no doubt that they refer to events centuries before these manuscripts were written. St Brigid's official dates are around 450 to 523. As well as on the Curragh, she is venerated at Kilbride in the upper pastures of our river.

The tradition of horse racing on the Curragh goes back to Celtic times. The gently undulating land has no open water and is therefore used as sheep rather than cattle pasture. It is one of very few surviving commons in the richer regions of Ireland.

The Annals of the Four Masters

The index to John O'Donovan's edition of *The Annals of the Four Masters* lists no fewer than six forms of the name of the river: Life, Liffe, Liphe, Liphthe, Abhainn Liffe, Anna-Liffey. According to these annals, the history of events on the river dates to the Age of the World 3656. 'It was by Tighearnmas also that gold was first smelted in Ireland, in Foithre-Airthir-Liffe. [It was] Uchadan, an artificer of the Feara-Cualann, that smelted it.' In a footnote, O'Donovan says that this was the 'Territory of the Fotharta, to the east of the River Life'. He also provides, from the *Annals of Clonmacnoise*, a little more detail, to the effect that Tighearnmas ordered his goldsmith (Ugden), who dwelt near the Liffie, to make gold and silver pins to put in men's and women's garments about their necks. It is intriguing that the date given, which is equivalent to 1544 BC, does coincide with the Bronze Age and its abundance of gold ornaments.

The mention by the Four Masters of Tighearnmas and the smelting of gold in Age of the World 3656 is followed by a break of 2,088 years in their history of our river, resuming in AD 544 with the death of the great St Mobhi of Glasnevin 'on the brink of the Liffey, on the north side'. Glasnevin today is in the Tolka valley, at least 3 km north of the Liffey and not by any stretch of the imagination on its 'brink'. But the extent of the district referred to by the name may have been much greater in those times and could have extended at least to the summit of the ridge from which both rivers might be seen when houses were fewer and lower.

A silent and deep portion of the Liffey near the Curragh at Athgarvan. The right bank has been grazed to the water's edge; the left bank is wooded. Such a scene of forest and pasture would have been typical from Neolithic times onwards.

One hundred and sixty years later, in 704, comes a somewhat more substantial entry, but, like the ancient one, it refers more to the plain than to the river itself. The passage records a successful expedition made by Congal of Ceann-Meaghair against the Leinstermen. On returning from this expedition Congal composed these lines:

> Bid me farewell, O Liffe ! Long enough have I been in thy lap;
> Beautiful the fleece that is on thee; thou wert safe, except thy roof, O
>   fort of Nas!
> The plain of Liffe was so till now, today it is a scorched plain;
> I will come to rescorch it, that it may know a change.

In 829 the Liffe was plundered by Conchobhar, son of Donnchadh, king of Ireland, but once more the reference is to the plain, rather than the river. In 836 the Four Masters record for the first time an event associated, in no uncertain way, with the river itself:

> A fleet of sixty ships of Norsemen on the Boyne. Another fleet of sixty ships on the Abhainn-Liphthe. These two fleets plundered and spoiled Magh-Liphthe and Magh-Breagh, both churches and habitation of men, and goodly tribes, flocks and herds.'

Another battle on the plain is mentioned in 884, but the watercourse itself appears once more in a line of poetry from the lament for Cearbhall, son of the king of Leinster, in 904. Describing an event that took place 68 years after the first appearance of the Norsemen, it mentions incidentally the development over those generations of the port of Dublin: 'Great grief that Liffe of the ships is without Cearbhall, its befitting spouse.'

After this, both the Liffey and its plains virtually disappear from the Four Masters for 500 years until 1452, when:

> A sure wonderful presage occurred in this year, some time before the death of the Earl [of Kildare], namely, part of the River Liffey was dried up to the extent of two miles.

The nature of this event remains unclear. What is remarkable in terms of climatological history is the evidence of a period of drought, so extreme and rare that it merited special mention.

Birch trees and conifers screen the hills of Knockmaroon and Castleknock from the floodplain of the Liffey. Lord Iveagh's nineteenth-century tower at Farmleigh is a combination of folly and highly functional water reservoir – with the addition of a clock. The high ground commanding a river crossing and a view over valuable farmland generated fortification, historical encounters and legend.

Tales of Castleknock

Michael Herity includes in his edition of the Dublin *Ordnance Survey Letters* a chapter on the place names of the county. This was compiled by The O'Rahilly, less than a year before his heroic death in Moore Street in 1916, and had been first published in Padraig Pearse's magazine *An Claidheamh Soluis*. The entry for Castleknock is a pleasing account of mythical and historic events centred on the hill of the name, which, at 73 metres, is the highest point above the Liffey downstream of St Patrick's Hill near Celbridge. Its strategic importance was marked by the Anglo-Normans, who built a motte and bailey and later a castle there. O'Rahilly wrote:

> This is supposed to be the site of the famous battle where Cumhall the father of Fionn, was slain by Goll Mac Morna. The castle stands on a celebrated tumulus of great antiquity. King Ruadhri O Conchubair occupied it when besieging Dublin in 1171. It was granted to the Tyrrells about 1177. Edward Bruce encamped here in 1316. It was taken by Col. Monk, who executed the garrison, 1642. Recaptured by Owen Roe, 1647. St Bridget's Church and Holy Well adjoin the Castle. Stanihurst avers that there is a certain window in the castle, and that 'though it is neither glazed nor latticed, but open, yet the weather be

stormy and the wind blow boisterously on any side, a candle placed there will blow as quietly as if no puff of wind blew.' Another tradition is that St Patrick tried to convert one Murrishtac, a chieftain who lived there. But in the midst of the saint's exhortations, Murrishtac fell asleep and snored loudly, which so enraged the man of God that he prayed that the pagan might sleep in the same place and posture till Doomsday. And it is said that Murrishtac accordingly still slumbers in an underground chamber of the fortress.

In 1977 James O'Driscoll published a delightful book entitled *Cnucha: A History of Castleknock,* combining details of more than 1,000 years of legend and history of the hill with an outline of its surroundings north of the Liffey. The numerous stories, including a white lady spectre, exploits of Conn of the Hundred Battles and many others – to say nothing of The O'Rahilly's tales – testify to Castleknock's strategic importance. Perhaps its most significant place in the history of Ireland was as the site of King Rory O'Connor's base for a failed attempt to wrest control of Dublin from Strongbow and the Normans in 1171.

The Dublin chronicle

Besides the line of poetry mentioning *Liffe of the ships,* the Four Masters have very little to say concerning the river of the Viking trading post that developed in the vicinity of the *Duibh Linn,* the dark pool made where the Poddle joins the Liffey and provides a sheltered anchorage. At this point the chronicles of the city of Dublin, together with the archaeological record, take up the story.

The *Calendar of Ancient Records of the City of Dublin* was compiled by John T. Gilbert in the latter half of the nineteenth century. Its first volume contains a transcript of the *Liber Albus,* or the *White Book,* and a number of matters relating to our river, under the name of 'Auenlyf' or 'Auenlif'. Most of them are references merely to its serving as a boundary for a grant of land, but a few expand a little on some activity or other.

A curious form of the name appears in 1220 in a letter from King Henry III to his Justiciar Geoffrey de Marisco about the creation of a pool by the friars at Kilmainham. The word used for the river is *Avelith*. 'Ave', or 'river', is common form and comparable with the more usual 'Avon'. The 'lith' is rare – but it may have no more significance than the possibility that an English scribe, who had never heard the river spoken of, misread a letter f.

A thirteenth-century entry refers to a 'Grant to William Dubelday the site of a mill between the gate of the church of St Mary of Dublin and the church of St Andrew. To be held by the service of one hawk yearly'. Another grant, lacking a precise date, is the right to a gate at St Audoen's 'through which a cart loaded with hides and a sack of wool may, when necessary, have passage to the water of

Auenlif'. Then there is a record of a donation of 'the sixteenth fish of the salmon of their fishing hereinafter to be taken in the water of Auenlyf'.

The Annals of the Four Masters tell of 32 men by the name of Aenghus, several of them sovereigns of Ireland or heirs apparent. Sadly, the *Annals* make no reference to Iseult, the fair Isolde, as a daughter of any of them. But her name remains firmly planted by the Liffeyside, in the form of Chapelizod, *Seipéal Iosóid*, the chapel of Isolde, and a massive medieval stone tower on Essex Quay was also named in her honour. Her tale exists in many versions in manuscripts from the eleventh century onwards. The essence is that King Mark of Cornwall sent his nephew Tristan to the court of King Aenghus of Ireland to escort the latter's daughter Iseult to be King Mark's bride. They fell in love and their romance ended in tragedy, as such unions frequently do.

The Liffey as shown on the Down Survey of 1656–8.

A seventeenth-century view

Confusion over the location of the source of the Liffey may possibly be explained by political problems in following the river from the plains to its upper reaches. Sir William Petty's map of County Wicklow, published in 1685, shows the River Liffey flowing from an unnamed point a mile and a half southwest of Lough Bray to 'Cloghoge' and past 'Three Castles' to the county border with Kildare.

The Liffey actually flows from the northeast at the unnamed point, but the Petty map shows it as an almost straight line coming from the southeast from 'The Liffey Head', past the 'Mountains of Cloghoge' through Sally Gap – marked as 'A Glen'.

Evidently the surveyor had seen and recorded the Liffey tributary which flows to the northwest from close to Sally Gap but had failed to observe that this, the Cloghane River, which goes south to Lough Tay, was flowing in the opposite direction. His 'Liffey Head' is somewhere in the region of Lough Tay. This map does, however, give the origin of the 'Liffey Head' a respectable antiquity. The errors strongly suggest that the surveyor had failed to follow the river to its source. This is not very surprising, in light of historical records that the men of the Wicklow Mountains were less than welcoming to settlers in the seventeenth century.

On the same map, the course of the King's River is shown with much greater accuracy. The fact that the King's River valley is the route of a substantial portion of the very ancient 'Pilgrim's Road' from Hollywood to Glendalough could explain this. Access by the surveyor's team, through established farmland, could have been very much less hazardous than in the lonely moorland.

The Liffey in fiction

Sheridan Le Fanu's lengthy novel *The House by the Churchyard*, published in 1863, describes a real house which still stands by the Church of Ireland churchyard in Chapelizod. His story of military absurdities and civilian skulduggery is set in the eighteenth century, but is full of glimpses of the river in his own time. The abundance of trout and the speed and ease with which they were caught has an air of fiction about it. But his descriptions, hilarious in places, of local ferries, ferrymen and salmon fisheries seem soundly based.

Recent fiction includes the novel *The Liffey Flows On By* by Niki Phillips, a true native of the valley who was reared in Chapelizod. Her book, published in 2012, describes the fortunes of the family of a big house in the region of Palmerstown in the twentieth century.

Both before and after he departed from Dublin, James Joyce made abundant use of the Liffey, first as a location and ultimately, in *Finnegans Wake*, as the central character. The Pigeon House and Usher's Island are essential parts of two of the stories in *Dubliners*, and many episodes in *Ulysses* take place by the riverside.

Gerard O'Flaherty and some friends spent a winter long ago unravelling *Finnegans Wake*. He contributed to *The Book of the Liffey* a masterly outline of the great work with a delightful sprinkling of relevant quotations from it. Entitled 'Anna Livia Plurabelle: Joyce's Universal River', this was the first chapter in the book and was illustrated with three beautiful photographs by Jan de

'The House by the Churchyard', scene of eighteenth-century events in Chapelizod in Sheridan Le Fanu's novel of the same name.

The Ormond Hotel which, in the twentieth century, engulfed a former pub in which Joyce set the 'Sirens' episode of *Ulysses*.

Fouw. Gerry has very kindly allowed me to quote from it. His essay begins with Joyce's words 'Softly morning city ! Lsp ! I am leafy speaking' and continues:

> This is the Liffey in *Finnegans Wake* giving a final greeting to the city of Dublin. Those who are familiar with the river can readily recognise the damp overcast feeling that permeates the quays early on an autumnal morning.
>
> It took James Joyce nearly a third of his life to write *Finnegans Wake*, which was meant to be his masterpiece. Unfortunately, when it was published in May 1939 it was regarded by the great majority of the reading public as being incomprehensible because of the dream language in which it was written. However, over the years it has come to be regarded as a great comic novel, having for its principal characters the city of Dublin, standing for all cities, and the Liffey, representing the rivers of the world.
>
> Joyce does not describe the Liffey, his words are the river as, while in exile, he listened to it 'as she bibs us, by the waters of babalong.' He was so obsessed by the river that he had the map of its course woven into a carpet for his living room.
>
> *Finnegans Wake* is the dream of a publican, H. C. Earwicker, in Chapelizod as he lies in bed beside his wife Anna Livia. In the dream, Earwicker becomes the personification of the city of Dublin, beside the Liffey, with his head at Howth and his feet in Castleknock. Earwicker is unreliable, hot tempered, despotic and given to debauchery. He came as a wild Viking rover to establish a city on the banks of the

Riverrun, past Eve and Adam's ... The dome of the Church of the Immaculate Conception, generally known as Adam and Eve's, and the Franciscan friary on Merchant's Quay.

Liffey … 'I laid down by stony battered waggonways, my nordsoud circulums, my eastmoreland and westlandmore, running boullowards and suddenly parading'. [Stoneybatter, North and South Circular Roads, Eastmoreland Street, Westland Row and Sydney Parade.] There is some doubt as to whether or not the Viking married the lady of the river; if he did it would be appropriate that the ceremony should be in a church dedicated to our first parents 'was her bans never loosened in Adam and Eve's or were him and her but captain spliced ?' We will never know.

Anna Livia is not just the Liffey, she is the universal river 'The Log of Anny to the Base All'. She remembers how she was a little cloud in 'My great blue bedroom, the air so quiet, scarce a cloud. In peace and silence … First we feel. Then we fall.' Within the Anna Livia Plurabelle episode there are the names of hundreds of rivers buried or hidden in the text. The narrative opens with two young washerwomen, one on either side of the stream, at the source of the Liffey near Kippure. In the course of their chatter Anna Livia is discussed at great length and she herself thinks back over her life and remembers how she has been a cloud, a shower, a rivulet, a brook before becoming a river.

First she fell as a shower 'little … Anna Rayiny, when under her brella, mid piddle mid puddle, she ninnygoes nannygoes nancing by … Upon Benn Heather, in Seeple Isout too.' [Howth and Chapelizod]. Later she falls 'on the spur of the hill in old Kippure, in birdsong and shearingtime, but first of all, worst of all, the wiggly livvly, she sideslipped out by a gap … while Sally [the Sally Gap] her nurse was sound asleep … fell over a spillway before she found her stride and lay and wriggled in all the stagnant black pools of rainy … and she laughed innocefree wither limbs aloft and a whole drove of maiden hawthorns blushing and looking askance upon her.'

But 'she was just a young thin pale soft shy slim slip of a thing then, sauntering, by ilvamoonlake…before she never dreamt she'd leave Kilbride and go foaming under Horsepass bridge' [Horsepass Bridge is now under the Blessington Lakes].

As the river grows, so too does Anna Livia become a woman, 'ducking under bridges, bellhopping the weirs, dodging by a bit of a bog, rapidshooting round the bends, by … the pools of the phooka and a place they call it Blessington … as happy as the day is wet, babbling, bubbling, chattering to herself, deloothering the fields on their elbows leaning with the sloothering slide of her, giddygaddy, grannyma, gossipaceous Anna Livia.' And 'her muddied name was Missisliffi'.

mid piddle mid puddle, she ninnygoes nancing by . . .

The river flows out of Wicklow and on through Clane, Kildare to the 'strawbirry reds'. The city is reached in the late evening, 'Look, look, the dusk is growing! ... It's churning chill. Der went is rising.' The washerwomen have grown old and in the gathering darkness they appear to be a tree on one bank and a stone on the other, while the Liffey goes 'home slowly now by own way' until it is lost 'Beside the rivering waters of, hitherandthithering waters of. Night!'

Later, the old river is flowing to her father, the sea, and she is yielding place to her daughter who is 'just a whisk brisk sly spry spink spank sprint of a thing' so it is time to 'let her rain now if she likes.' Anna Livia has 'a hundred cares, a tithe of troubles' and she asks, as Joyce did, 'is there one who understands me? ... I am passing out. O bitter ending! I'll slip away before they're up. They'll never see. Nor know. Nor miss me ... A way a lone a last a loved a long the'. And here the book ends, but we know that the narrative loops around to the beginning again to 'riverrun, past Eve and Adam's, from swerve of shore to bend of bay, brings us by a commodius vicus of recirculation back to Howth Castle and Environs.' Yet there is a moment in time between the beginning and the end, be it a second or a million years, which allows the river to become a cloud, a shower, a stream and a river again.

'Anna was, Livia is, Plurabelle's to be ...'

The lie of the land

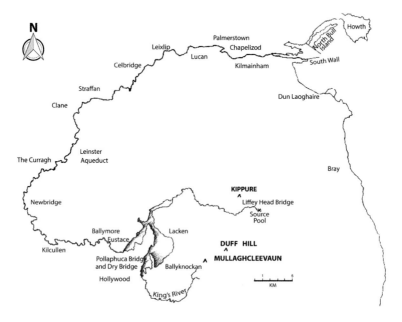

The path of the Liffey. *Ruairi Moriarty*.

The shape and colours of the Liffey valley and the direction taken by the river came about in four phases. The first dates from remote geological time and the next two are prehistoric, though recent in geological terms. The fourth and final period is almost completely contained within the era of written history. The entire valley lies within the bounds of Sheet 16 of the Ordnance Survey half-inch map and this is the scale chosen by the Geological Survey of Ireland for the publication of its latest revision of the geological map. Published in 1994, it shows in traditional bright colours the distribution of the rocks that underlie the soils and buildings of the Liffey valley.

It is likely that global warming, however grim its effects on many human communities, is in terms of geological time a mere blip in a sequence of events which will probably include another cold spell. Geological maps present solid rock. Over the entire Liffey Valley – and the greater part of Ireland – these are more than 400 million years old. Younger strata have come and gone within that immense period of time. The old rocks make an important contribution to the scenery and provide most of the material from which the roads, towns and villages are built. But the details of the prehistoric scene depend mainly on a small fraction of that period, which began less than two million years ago. Known as the Quaternary or Ice Age, it witnessed a succession of cold stages in which much of Ireland was covered by ice fields in the lowlands and mountain glaciers on the higher hills. Their effects on the upper parts of the Liffey Valley are covered by William Warren in his book *Wicklow in the Ice Age*. The moving ice shaped mountains and valleys and covered all the lower slopes with fertile soil.

Water to drink

Water to drink, first for themselves and later for their cattle too, attracted people to the riverside since they first came to live in the Liffey valley. The earliest industrial interest in the water was for the labour-saving power that it provided. The citizens of Dublin have used river water to drink and for power since at least the twelfth century, but their supply of the former came from tributaries such as the Poddle and the Dodder, rather than from the tidal, silty and saline urban Liffey.

There is no reason to doubt that Liffey water has been used for drinking since the Mesolithic people first camped by its banks and speared its salmon, perhaps some 10,000 years ago. But this would have been a casual matter for the greater part of these ages, and historical references to water supply belong to relatively recent times.

Apart from a small number of local schemes using water pumped from the river, the Liffey remained a minor player until the 1940s, when the dam at Pollaphuca was built and the Blessington Lakes created.

Gravel, which formed a delta at the head of Glacial Lake Blessington, is quarried from the sandpits upstream of Ballysmuttan. The green pasture in the foreground shows a well-drained soil with lime derived from the ice field which covered the land to a height of about 300 metres. The darkness of the mountains in the background results from the growth of heather on their granite-based soil.

Water to drive

While surmise, archaeology and mythology hint that Liffey water was used for drinking and bathing for thousands of years, the river as a source of energy also enjoys a long written history. William Dick, in his essay in *The Book of the Liffey*, makes the point that the earliest use of the power of the stream would have come from the flow in its natural bed, without any of the later developments of mill dams or mill races. As the first waterwheels did not demand any alterations to the river or its banks, they make no appearance in the historical record. He suggests that the earliest known watermills on the Liffey were at Islandbridge, and John de Courcy mentions that Hugh Tirrell made over the 'waters and mills, pools and fisheries' in that region to the prior of Kilmainham. That took place before 1220 when King Henry III initiated proceedings against the same prior and his friars, whose commercial operations on the river were causing considerable problems to the people of Dublin.

Electric power, so much less fun to look at but immeasurably more reliable than the slowly turning waterwheels, in its turn banished the steam and diesel engines that had usurped the power of the flowing water. But it brought back the tapping of this energy. In places, as at Straffan, the scale was small and the power was used for farm or domestic purposes. But the Liffey hydroelectric scheme of the 1940s, based at Pollaphuca, Golden Falls and Leixlip, invaded the landscape in an unprecedented way and transformed the Liffey and its valley.

A small book published by the Anna Liffey Power Development Co. Ltd in 1923 gave a detailed outline of the scheme. Its conclusions are interesting for two reasons. First, the lack of any idea of how the demand for electricity would expand in the course of the twentieth century. Perhaps this was not surprising at a time of post-war poverty and net emigration from the newborn state. The writers believed that the Liffey could supply all the power required by the city of Dublin:

> It provides Greater Dublin and the surrounding country with an amplitude of power, sufficient, on the most conservative reckoning that has been adopted in all the calculations of the present Company, for the industrial development of Dublin as far as can reasonably now be foreseen. It is more than probable that the calculations for the present Liffey scheme will prove to fall short of the eventual amount of power yielded by the scheme by a very large margin indeed.

Second, although the thinking was commercial rather than environmental, it was an early instance of enthusiasm for a renewable resource:

> Moreover, whereas under the present methods the consumption of more coal means an increase in the cost per unit of power, under the

Liffey scheme, with water running free, the use of more water means no increase in cost. That is to say, the more power used the less will be the price per unit.

And water to drain

Even though salmon never failed to survive their journey through the heavily polluted waters of the tidal Liffey in Dublin, the human inhabitants became less than pleased with the burden carried by their river. As a transporter of not quite invisible and far from unobtrusive material, the Liffey in the later decades of the nineteenth century was an open sewer.

While the sewage and often filthy surface water may not have impinged on the official conscience until the nineteenth century, Dublin has an honourable position in the history of the control of water pollution. As long ago as 1466 the Corporation passed an order to the effect that 'no tanner, glover nor any other person use limed ware or leather work in the River Liffey on account of the destruction of salmon'. Although the potential damage to fish of limed ware or leather work is not easy to understand – especially if compared with such pollutants as slaughterhouse waste – the order was undoubtedly an important and very early piece of environmental legislation.

Citizens of my age and older remember the river of the city all too well as a frequently foetid watercourse. My great-grandfather Spencer Harty, City Engineer, was one of the pioneers in the cleansing of the Liffey. His eternal reward was to earn mention by name in *Ulysses* – though it must be admitted that Leopold Bloom thought of him in connection with the Vartry and bath taps rather than the Liffey and its less pleasant burden.

Partly by design and partly by chance, great improvements have taken place since those unhappy days. A large, almost unknown but deeply dedicated team of public servants work day and night to guard the purity of our beloved Anna.

In 2005 Dublin City Council published a beautiful book by Michael Corcoran entitled *Our Good Health: A History of Dublin's Water and Drainage*. The author had spent nearly a quarter of a century as a draughtsman with the Council's Drainage Division and, besides his graphic abilities, is a fine writer. Books on water supply and drainage are not always distinguished by their appeal to a wide circle of readers – but this is a very honourable exception.

Shipping

One day in the 1940s my mother took me on my first visit to the quays on the Liffey, just downstream of Butt Bridge. A kindly skipper invited us on board his Guinness barge and took us all the way around the hull of one of the company's vessels that plied the Irish Sea. I held firmly on to a rail, as instructed, little realising that I was one of very few passengers ever to enjoy the privilege of a journey on these splendid craft and that I would remember the adventure fondly for more than seventy years.

Dublin's fair city owes its very existence as a seaport to the discovery by the Vikings that the tidal Liffey provided a safe anchorage for their sea-going vessels. Ferries must have developed at an earlier stage, as had fishing boats. But historical records of these do not appear to predate the Anglo-Normans, the earliest written account of a ferry dating to a royal direction of 1385. Archaeology and history show how the port has been developing ever since Viking times, with bigger and better ships berthing further and further to the east. Towards the west, there is evidence of navigation too. The Vikings successfully brought their boats upstream of the rapids at Islandbridge Weir and made some use of the inland watercourse.

The Liffey, with rapids as far downstream as Chapelizod, never functioned seriously as an inland waterway. As the city grew towards the east, the authorities over some hundreds of years installed low-lying bridges which pushed the port downstream. The ingeniously designed Guinness barges were the only craft which made use of it for the transport of goods. It was not until 2005 that the problems facing cruise operators were finally solved.

The eastward migration of merchant shipping probably came to an end with the building of the Tom Clarke Bridge just upstream of the Alexandra Basin. Developed late in the nineteenth century, the basin

Ships of dimensions beyond the wildest dreams of the Vikings use a port 3 km downstream of the original development at Wood Quay.

continues to provide essential port facilities. The twenty-first century has seen the creation of berthage for gigantic cruise liners just downstream of the East Link Bridge and therefore within walking distance of the city centre.

Dimensions

The length of the river from its source to the top of the tide at Islandbridge is 118 km; from there to the Poolbeg Lighthouse it is 11 km, making a total of 129 km. The original river, before it was lengthened by various engineering works, ended somewhat nebulously upstream of the estuary of the Dodder and was about 5 km shorter than it is at present. But the full length of the watercourse needs to be measured from the source of the King's River on the south side of Mullaghcleevaun, increasing it by 15 km to a grand total of 144 km. A straight line from the source to Poolbeg measures 22 km, and the River Dodder, which rises close to Liffey Head, reaches the sea in Dublin after a journey of only 24 km. The source lies at an elevation of 525 metres.

2 | The sources:
Tonduff, Kippure and Mullaghcleevaun

Upstream of the source, the infant Liffey tunnels through the peat, seeing the light now and then where the roof of its cavern has fallen in.

At the official source of the Liffey on a fine day in May. While it is far from the highest point on the river, the dark pool in the peat is in the position named on maps since 1834. A dramatic piece of micro-landscape, it is a twenty-minute walk from the Military Road.

The shallow pool at the source and the Kippure mast from which the mouth of the Liffey at Poolbeg can be seen. The stream shown in the previous picture flows in a tunnel underneath this pool.

Olivia Moriarty contemplates the source on an August evening in 2015.

The granite

The earliest strata underlying the Liffey valley date to the Ordovician era, which began 510 million years ago. These rocks developed from silt and sand which accumulated as sediments in shallow water, not far from the eastern shores of the Iapetus, an ocean that separated what are now the northwestern and southeastern halves of Ireland. Around 400 million years ago, the movement of tectonic plates squeezed that ocean out of existence. This action was accompanied by the crumpling of the sedimentary rock and the building of the Wicklow Mountains. At the root of this folding of rock strata, high temperatures and pressures changed both their chemical nature and crystal structure from sandstones and mudstones to granite, obliterating nearly all traces of their original stratified form.

The granite was forged deep below the surface of the land, but the results have been revealed by hundreds of millions of years of erosion. This gradual eating away of the uplands has yet to be completed and granite continues to stand out above the plain created by the ancestral Liffey. The chemistry and crystallography of these rocks are of great significance in building the familiar landscape. Granite is an acidic rock which contains insignificant quantities of lime. Few species of plants or animals thrive where lime is scarce and most of those that do are highly specialised and grow slowly. So the vegetation of these slopes is poor. The great majority of the animals are small or scattered and, most important of all, there are no large human populations. Thanks to this acidity today's urban dwellers of Dublin are blessed with wilderness on their very doorstep.

Downstream of the source pool: peat cliff cut away by the stream, revealing stones and boulders enveloped by the peat as it was growing, around 5,000 years ago.

Liffey Head

The point marked on the maps is in the region of a broad, shallow bog pool. In dry weather, a gentle trickle makes its way from this pool to the bottom of a chasm in the peat. In rainy seasons, most of the water flows in a cascade over a ridge of the pool. That statement oversimplifies an extremely complex situation. On a visit on a summer's day in 2013, my hydrologist son Patrick drew my attention to the fact that a gurgling stream just above the broad pool actually burrows down and flows underneath this pond rather than into it.

The shape of the source is continually changing. In 1987, when I visited it with Elizabeth Healy, the shallow pool was clearly separated from a deep, dark pond below it, from which the infant Anna flowed. This pond has since extended upstream, to form the little chasm. The shallow pool in those days was also the point of the first significant appearance of the river on the surface, though its underground track could easily be seen, marked on the slopes of Tonduff by sedges rather than heather. The roof of this natural conduit has fallen away in a number of places so that the first surface water now appears about twenty metres further upstream, issuing briefly, with a pleasing gurgling sound, from a tunnel in the peat, but then returning to its hideaway.

Downstream of the source pool, the infant Liffey has cut itself a channel, between one and two metres deep, with almost vertical walls. These walls are pierced in a few places by the openings of more of the tunnels that have been excavated by streams all over the peatland of Liffey Head Bog. The peat tunnels are too dark and damp for most plants to grow, but the green fronds of ferns appear at the entrances and make a startling contrast against the blackness of the peat.

A new floodplain being created by the wanderings of the infant river.

The stream bursts its banks from time to time and has created a miniature floodplain for itself between the walls of peat, varying in width from one to two metres. At low flows, the Liffey is a stream of clear water, faintly tinged with the brown colouring of humic acids leached from the peat. The bed of this stream, less than one metre wide, is composed of silvery white pebbles of granite. These are the remnants of the rocky surface of the hillside as it was long before the peat grew up. To either side of the stream, where the peat has been carried away by the flow, the surface of the land is green. In very damp parts, mosses are the dominant plants: spongy sphagnum and upstanding *Polytrichum*, which looks faintly like a minuscule fir tree. Elsewhere there are clumps of rushes and patches of deergrass, which in winter turn from green to a pale straw colour.

In places, erosion has cut away steep banks, extending from the surface of the heather moor down to the stream. These banks are between two and three metres in height. The upper one or two metres are pure peat, which rests on a compacted granite gravel that contains occasional large stones. These miniature cliffs record the history of the landscape since the melting of the last glaciers of the Ice Age – a time of global warming that took place about 10,000 years ago. The gravel, dumped by the ice of a mountain glacier, covered the bedrock to a depth of up to a metre. Then the climate changed, plants grew on the gravel and, after they died, came to be fossilised as a blanket of peat which grew thicker and thicker over thousands of years. Ultimately, growth of the peat ceased and the infant Liffey cut its way down through it to the underlying gravel and, in places, to the bedrock once again.

Liffey Head Bridge, visible only as a slight dip in the Military Road with a heap of granite boulders on each side. The ancient granite causeway is pierced by three concrete drainpipes.

Above the miniature valley, the surface of the peat follows the contours and is almost level, before it rises towards the east on the flanks of Tonduff. The moorland that extends for miles between the heights of Tonduff, Maulin, War Hill and Djouce is the watershed of no fewer than three rivers: the Liffey, the Dargle and the Cloghoge. The Dargle plunges down a little way to the east in the form of Powerscourt Waterfall and ends in Bray. The Cloghoge, impeded by natural dams to form Lough Tay and Lough Dan before it joins the Avonmore, makes its way to the Vale of Avoca and reaches the sea at Arklow.

Competition between the sources

The source of the River Liffey, according to the Ordnance Survey, is a spot in County Wicklow some 700 metres to the southeast of Liffey Head Bridge. A lovely, lonely place in the heather moorland, it is hidden away from all overt traces of the hand of man, with one important exception – the television mast on the summit of Kippure. The significance of the latter lies in the fact that the few mortals who have ascended the mast could see the source, the middle and the mouth of the Liffey, a remarkable view of a river that flows for 129 km through three counties.

While its small sister, the Dodder, reaches the same destination in Dublin Bay by a direct route within County Dublin, the Liffey takes a circular path, ending its course close to where it began. This symbol of the proximity of life and death was part of the inspiration of James Joyce in celebrating Dublin's river in *Finnegans Wake*.

But there is an element of myth even in the definition of the source. Far be it from the Ordnance Survey of Ireland to perpetuate mythology, but from their earliest printing in 1838, they followed the decision of some persons unknown to give the name of the beloved river to a particular hole in the bog.

The usual convention for geographers is to identify its highest point as the source of any river. In the case of the Liffey, they failed miserably. The source as designated by the Ordnance Survey lies on the lower slopes of Tonduff at a height of 525 metres 'above mean sea level at Malin Head, Co. Donegal'. But the source of a much more elevated tributary of the Liffey is no less than a hundred metres higher, on the east side of the summit of Kippure. This stream is crossed by a bridge on the access road to the Kippure mast, 200 metres up the hill from its junction with the Military Road. A yet higher tributary rises to the west of the same summit and is called the Sraghoe Brook. Rising at a point a little above the 650-metre contour, it flows for 3 km to join the main stream in the valley of the Coronation Plantation. It must be said that the official source is not only a more impressive opening in the peat than the small streams of its competitors, but also very much easier to reach.

To add further to the complexity, the Liffey is fed by no fewer than four named tributaries rising on the north slopes of Mullaghcleevaun. Of these, the Lugaculleen Brook rises just a little above the 700-metre contour, thereby surpassing Sraghoe on Kippure. From which facts only one thing is clear – that the highest point of the Liffey is neither on Kippure nor at the 'source of the Liffey'.

The infant Liffey leaving the 'source' through a chasm which it has cut in the surrounding peat.

And that is not the end of the confusion. Even the Lugaculleen Brook yields its place to a more exalted partner on the other side of Mullaghcleevaun. There the Annalecka Brook appears at 720 metres, making it the highest visible fountain of Liffey water. There are plenty of invisible ones because the peat bog, especially on Tonduff, has extensive underground drainage, and a subterranean Liffey can be traced for some way up its slopes. More important, the Annalecka Brook is the uppermost part of the King's River, which joins the Liffey at Baltyboys. This so-called 'tributary' is in effect the main river, being not only higher but also 2.5km longer than the Liffey proper.

Liffey Head Bridge

One of the most unobtrusive crossings of any of the rivers of Ireland, Liffey Head Bridge was created in the wake of the Rising of 1798 as a part of the Military Road. Built to protect the inhabitants of the plains from the men of the mountains and scattered with barracks of distinguished architecture, the Military Road has served generations of hillwalkers, cyclists and motorists. Small though it is, the infant Liffey had carved out a broad valley which demanded the construction of a causeway on either bank as well as the bridge itself .

Michael Fewer's book on the Military Road has a picture of the bridge in 1915, which probably shows its original appearance. The construction, of dry stones, appears to be simple but demanded considerable skill. The dry-stone causeway is pierced by a pair of vertical walls which support large granite lintels forming a 'clapper bridge'. The engineers, perhaps under time constraints, preferred this to the beautiful stone arches which were used in the eighteenth century to cross even relatively small tributaries in the valley lower down. The stream bed is paved with hewn blocks of granite which prevent erosion at times of flood.

Crude though the original was, engineers of the 1950s perpetrated something much worse when they repaired the bridge. They filled the gap with three concrete sewer pipes placed one on top of the other and finished the structure with concrete beams. It works – but it is a dismal piece of bridge-building and totally unworthy of the birthplace of Anna Livia Plurabelle.

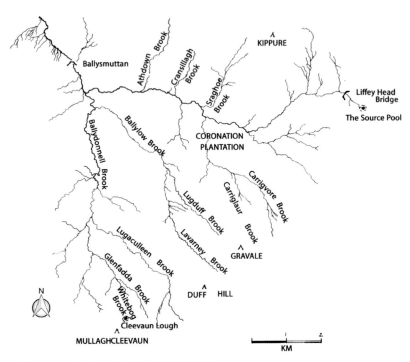

The upper tributaries of the Liffey. *Ruairi Moriarty.*

After reaching Liffey Head Bridge, the river continues its gentle descent until it turns to the left and is lost from view from the road 200 metres downstream. There it begins to take a steeper track, plunging over tiny waterfalls. The point where this happens coincides with a minor geological boundary between the great expanse of granite and an oval patch of granodiorite. The skills of the geologists who delineate such structures are impressive, since the greater part of the boundary lies deeply concealed beneath the peat.

The higher tributaries

Having thus encountered the traditional – and most conveniently accessible – source of the Liffey, we wander the wilderness to view the more exalted points of the catchment. No fewer than twenty named tributaries of the Liffey drain this lonely moorland, which stretches away from Kippure for 7 km to the west and 8 km towards the south. Roads are almost absent from this region of about seventy square kilometres and forestry plantations are not extensive. These hills and rolling moorland make a fair claim to be numbered among the most remote regions of Ireland, although they are a mere 20 kilometres from the centre of Dublin and the ultimate destination of the waters of the streams.

Bridges old and new at Annalecka. The Sitka spruce are self-sown from stray seeds from the plantation in the background.

The Liffey headwaters

On Kippure itself, the bog between the river and the road to the television mast is a special place for botanists, thanks to the large, shallow ponds which are scattered liberally through it. These lakelets add an extra dimension to the habitat, providing living space for a variety of aquatic plants, as well as for dragonflies. The walk up the road to the mast meets a bridge a little more than a kilometre from the Military Road and this crosses one of the higher, but unnamed, tributaries of the Liffey. Three more – the Sraghoe, the Cransillagh and the Athdown Brooks – all plunge southwards from near the ridge which joins Kippure to Seefingan. Another unnamed stream rises a hundred metres to the northwest of Sally Gap and is crossed by the ancient road (R759) between Sally Gap and the Coronation Plantation.

Carrigvore Brook and Carriglaur Brook flow down from Carrigvore Mountain. They join together and are met by Askakeagh Brook. The three together form Lugnalee Brook, which is the pine-fringed river that divides the Coronation Plantation in two. That brings the total of named tributaries to seven.

From Gravale and Duff Hill, Lavarney Brook and Lugduff Brook join to form Ballylow Brook. It flows beneath a bridge named Ballynabrocky after its townland and carries a spur from the road that runs around the nearby Sorrel Hill.

The mighty hill of Mullaghcleevaun is mother to the majority of the streams of this wilderness. The highest on its slopes are named Lugaculleen, Whitebog, Parkbawn and Glencapple, Trent and Tramhongar. The next generation comprises Glenavadda, Boleyhemushboy and Dealbog. They all feed Ballydonnell Brook, which is 2 km long and meets the road at Ballylow Bridge, after which it joins the Ballylow Brook; together they run to the arms of Anna Liffey. These bring the total of tributaries to twenty – and these are just the named ones. All flow to the upper Liffey. One deviationist on the northern slopes of Mullaghcleevaun flows westwards. This, the Ballynastockan Brook, heads away from its companions to flow into the King's River branch of the Blessington Lake.

Cleevaun Lough

The corrie on the north slope of Mullaghcleevaun cradles the tiny Cleevaun Lough, 685 metres above sea level and said to be the most elevated lake in Ireland. *Cleevaun* translates as 'cradle' and very aptly describes the lake which snuggles on the hillside. *Mullagh* means 'summit'.

Sixty years ago I climbed Mullaghcleevaun with my father and first set eyes on its lake. On a bright April day in 2009, with my son Patrick, I visited Cleevaun Lough again. Four kilometres of woodland and moor and 240 metres of elevation separate it from the nearest roadside spot, the car park on the north

Cleevaun Lough.

slope of Sorrel Hill. The only natural lake in the entire catchment of the Liffey, Cleevaun has the added attraction of remoteness. Many of the other lakes of the Wicklow Mountains are displayed in all their beauty to casual visitors. But the view of Cleevaun is reserved exclusively to aeronauts and hillwalkers.

It is defined as a corrie, cirque or cwm, depending on whether you speak Gaelic, French or Welsh, a distinction which it shares with lakes in the neighbouring catchments: Bray, Tay and Nahanagan. Corries in Ireland are confined to the north sides of mountains, where the snow lasts longer and forms bigger local glaciers. The typical form of the corrie is a very steep, high slope to the south and a mound of glacial till in front of it to the north, dug out and quickly dumped by the glacier. A very distinctive feature of Cleevaun Lough is the scattering of great boulders of granite which appear both in the shallow water and on the shore all the way round. The biggest is a magnificent cube of more than two metres perched on the south shore. Even more striking are the black slopes above the lake where the peat is eroding.

Sheet 16 of the geological map joins the lake to a branch of the Glenavadda Brook, but the Ordnance Survey *Discovery* Sheet 56 is more circumspect and separates stream and lake by about 700 metres. Both are correct and you find the explanation when you walk around the lake. On its north side there is indeed an outflowing stream, but this quickly disappears from sight, tunnelling

Erratic boulder of granite, displaced and carried by the mountain glacier of Mullaghcleevaun.

its way through the peat. In places the roof of the tunnel is broken and you can hear the gurgle of the water, which appears briefly at the surface before plunging down again. The highest slopes of its valley are damp and covered mostly with sphagnum moss; lower down, the slopes grow drier and heather takes over. Finally comes a forest fence and a great expanse of Sitka spruce.

Alternating layers of sand and peat silt at the mini-delta where the hill stream enters Cleevaun Lough.

Cleevaun Lough has an inflowing stream, too small to show on a map, at its east end. This stream has created a tiny alluvial fan and a beach of white quartz gravel, streaked in places with black peat silt.

The highest point

The tributaries of the King's River on Mullaghcleevaun's southern slopes, though higher, are fewer – just two. The Ballinagee River, separating Mullaghcleevaun from its western neighbour, Moanbane, is the larger but does not reach quite as high as its companion, the Annalecka Brook. Both cross the R756 Wicklow Gap road by bridges bearing their names. Annalecka Bridge is a recently built structure with white-painted railings, replacing an abandoned older crossing, and there is a car park beside it. The brook descends rapidly through a plantation of Sitka spruce for the greater part of its course upstream of the bridge. But it springs from a remarkable area of gently sloping bog beneath the steep final ascent to the summit of Mullaghcleevaun.

The headwaters of the Annalecka Brook. At an elevation of 720 metres on the south side of Mullaghcleevaun, it is the highest stream in the Liffey catchment.

The southern slopes of this mountain are generously scattered with large granite boulders, liberated from the bedrock during the Ice Age by the same frost activity that bursts copper water pipes and cracks concrete. Sphagnum moss grew, over the course of a few thousand years, among the boulders and, for the most part, smothered them in a blanket of peat. Twentieth-century foresters planted and felled spruce trees except where the Annalecka cut its way down through the peaty soil, revealing the boulders once again and creating a delightful succession of waterfalls and gravelly pools.

The headwaters of the brook are strikingly different. For a long time the peat bog increased in depth over the nearly level higher ground. More recently, perhaps for less than two centuries, the situation changed and erosion of

Huge granite boulders scatter the southern slopes of Mullaghcleevaun and give the Annalecka Brook a character all of its own.

At the highest level of the Annalecka Brook, erosion of the bog is creating an expanse of bare turf liberally scattered with peat hags, protected by caps of deergrass, moss and lichen.

the peat began. The present-day scene is a great expanse of bare brown peat, studded with innumerable moss-, sedge- or heather-topped peat hags. The Annalecka streamlet issues from between some of these, flowing between green banks where sedges are growing rather than being carried away by the erosion.

Birds and beasts of Liffey Head

Because the moorland is so barren, there are few birds and beasts around Liffey Head Bog. Only two species of mammals are to be seen with any frequency: hare and deer. Foxes may forage here now and again, but there is very little food for them, and the small trout of the upland streams are scarcely worth an otter's while. There are almost certainly frogs on the bog, but I have yet to see one.

Red deer have thrived on the heather moor for thousands of years but were probably hunted to extinction in the eighteenth or nineteenth century. The deer that may be seen now and again by the Liffeyside belong to a herd of known ancestry but uncertain species. Red deer from Scotland and Japanese Sika deer from a park in Germany were introduced to the adjoining Powerscourt Deerpark in the nineteenth century. The two closely related species interbred, and now there are few, if any, pure members of either. Whatever their ancestry, an encounter with a group of these splendid and totally wild animals is always a pleasure.

The highest stream in the Liffey catchment, the Annalecka Brook rises on the southern slopes of Mullaghcleevaun and flows down to the King's River. Sedge and moss grow on its banks, in contrast to the surrounding land where the plants are giving way to bare peat.

I never expected to meet a mallard at Liffey Head – until the day in March 2007 when I very nearly walked on the nest of one, on the edge of the source pool. It was a remarkable nesting place: certainly secure because potential predators are scarce; but the shortage of aquatic insects, essential as food for the ducklings, might make life hard for them.

An even bigger surprise was, in May three years later, to see a teal swimming in the same pool. It was a drake and probably had a mate sitting on their eggs somewhere in the heather. Perhaps if I spent more time wandering around moorland lakes I would not have been so surprised. The bird books all agree that this is a typical nesting place for this beautiful little duck with its patch of emerald green on each wing.

Two species of small brown bird nest in the moorland of Liffey Head: the skylark and the meadow pipit. The skylark is the larger, flies higher and has the rich song that inspired Shelley, among others. The meadow pipit has an equally cheerful but simpler song. Both retire to the lowlands for the winter but return in spring to feed on the innumerable small insects that take to the wing with the warmer weather.

A lark in the clear air: the skylark is one of the very few birds that nest and thrive around Liffey Head. The majority migrate to lowland habitats for the winter. *Photo: Michael Finn.*

Two of the birds of the uppermost Liffey are of particular interest. One is the red grouse because of its rarity, which results from its very specialised habitat. But it has no special connection with the river or its tributary streams. The other is the dipper: relatively common but a real bird of the river, most plentiful in clear mountain streams, though appearing from time to time in lowland reaches.

The red grouse is a very special bird, for a number of reasons. Since it is one of few species in Britain or Ireland that is really good to eat, grouse shooting has been a popular sport for generations, although essentially confined to the wealthy and leisured classes. Large populations of grouse on moors in Scotland and England are maintained at huge expense and their management for shooting is a profitable business.

The Irish red grouse is a recognised subspecies, with its own genetic make-up developed over 10,000 years of isolation from its parent continental population. There is no evidence whatever of Irish grouse migrating across the sea or of Scottish grouse coming to Ireland. The species is also very restricted in its distribution because, after a youthful diet of insects, the grouse depends almost entirely on heather shoots for food and on heather plants for cover. All this makes an encounter with grouse particularly pleasing. Such meetings are not only few but usually brief; the grouse spends most of its life concealed in the heather, only revealing itself when an intruder comes close. Then one or two rise with a flurry of wings, followed by a glide and a call of '*go back – go back – go back*'. They fly a little above the heather for a few hundred metres before dropping down to find secure cover once more. A grouse count on Liffey Head Bog in 1991 estimated a density of one bird per square kilometre. At this rate, it is not surprising that you can take a long walk through the heather without ever disturbing one. It's a long time since I saw any on Liffey Head Bog, but I did meet a few on the heather slopes of Mullaghcleevaun in 2009.

Grouse in Ireland have few predators apart from humans and the main constraint on their survival is the encroachment of grazing on the heather. But I still have a vivid memory, after more than sixty years, of witnessing a case of predation. It was on my first ascent of Kippure and, near the summit in the shelter of a peat hag, I disturbed the first peregrine falcon that I had ever seen. It flew away quickly, abandoning its meal, an unfortunate grouse.

While most of the birds mentioned in the preceding paragraphs are very much part of the Liffey valley, they are there because of the terrain and not because of the river. In contrast, the dipper, one of the most delightful and remarkable of all birds in Ireland, is entirely dependent on running water. It shares with the grouse the distinction of being a non-migrant which has developed a distinct Irish subspecies. A dumpy, black bird with a snowy white breast, the dipper feeds on aquatic insects which it often catches on the surface – as many other birds do. But the dipper is unique in being able to walk beneath the surface of the stream and hunt among stones on the bottom. This the bird achieves by holding its wings at a particular angle so that the running water presses it down. Details on the life of the dipper in Ireland can be found in a privately printed monograph by Kenneth W. Perry.

One of the most remarkable of all Irish birds, the dipper is also one of the very few that thrive in the headwaters of the Liffey. *Photo: Michael Finn.*

Plants of the moorland

The flora of the peaty soils of the higher slopes of the valley are almost entirely native Irish plants. This is hardly surprising since the acidity combined with high rainfall prevents the rapid growth of the grasses and crop plants that the human population demands for subsistence, either directly or second-hand through cattle and sheep. Neither farm crops, nor their weeds, nor the garden plants that sometimes establish themselves in the wild were brought to the uplands. The most notable exception to that rule was the planting of Scots pine in the nineteenth century and Sitka spruce in the twentieth. In contrast to the lowlands and even the lower mountain slopes, the variety of plant species on the moorland is small and few of them flower until quite late in summer.

Heather grows over the greater part of the bog. Most of it is ling, the one with small, pale flowers that thrives in relatively moist conditions, as opposed to the more showy bell heather, which has relatively large purple flowers and prefers a drier bog. Bell heather is nonetheless fairly plentiful. Now and again, both of these species produce pure white flowers, always associated with good luck. One more heather, the cross-leaved heath, with pink flowers, completes a trio of common species. It grows as individual stems or in very small clumps in damp patches and, although widely distributed, it is nowhere as plentiful as the two purple heathers.

Three bearers of berries grow in the heather moor. Frochan, with its tasty purple berries, is also plentiful on the lower slopes and is familiar to all. The other two are known only to botanically sophisticated hillwalkers and have confusingly similar names. The crowberry is by far the more common and

begins to appear around the 250-metre contour. A small, straggly plant, its bright green leaves stand out among the darker heathers and it bears shiny black berries.

The cowberry is extra special, rejoicing in an evocative scientific name *Vaccinium vitus-idaea* or 'blueberry vine of Mount Ida'. It has pale pink flowers and strawberry-sized red berries which, sadly, are sour. You have to climb – or maybe drive – to an elevation of at least 450 metres to find it. Its pink flowers are conspicuous, though never plentiful, around the source of the Liffey in June.

Flowers of the cowberry, *Vaccinium vitus-idaea.*

Two species of sedge abound, deergrass and bog cotton: deergrass forming dense tussocks; bog cotton in small tufts or as single stems. Although it gives the impression of growing all over the place, bog cotton demands very strictly defined conditions of moisture. Its cottony fibres have potentially valuable industrial applications, but attempts to grow it as a crop have failed because of its fastidiousness. So it remains a wild plant, its soft, white heads brightening the dark bog.

Deergrass is the dominant plant over a large area of the moorland. In autumn its green, grass-like leaves turn to a very pale straw colour and they persist through the winter. As a result, the hillsides, especially around the Coronation Plantation, are

Bog cotton is one of the most conspicuous and abundant of the moorland plants.

almost white – though giving a pied appearance because of the abundance of patches of heather. In contrast to the deergrass, which covers great swathes of land, heather grows in large clumps and its very dark brown branches stand out against the pale background. Highly conspicuous on the hillsides, the deergrass hides coyly in the botany books. Colgan, in his *Flora of County Dublin*, refused to give it an English name and added to the confusion by using its then current Latin name of *Scirpus caespitosus*. Modern books call it *Trichophorum caespitosum*.

Two beautiful yellow flowers grow in the moorland, tormentil and bog asphodel. Tormentil is a very small member of the rose family, its larger relatives familiar as the numerous potentillas of gardens. The thumb-tack-sized flowers of tormentil stand out against the dark greens and browns of the bog. It grows nearly everywhere, in contrast to the bog asphodel, which is confined to patches of a particular degree of dampness. There are many such patches, some of them quite extensive and providing unexpected pools of colour. Bog asphodel has rush-like stems bearing little clusters of star-shaped flowers.

Mosses and lichens abound in the bog. Mosses, rather than higher plants, grow in the rushing waters of the infant Liffey. The waterweeds of the lowland river are flowering plants and include several species of water buttercup.

Generally speaking, the identification of mosses and lichens is best left to specialists, but a few are conspicuous and known even to casual naturalists. Sphagnum forms soft green, or sometimes pinkish, spongy cushions and is one of the most important constituents of peat. *Polytrichum* is less plentiful but stands out because of its resemblance to minuscule pine trees, all of two or three centimetres in height.

Moorland mosses: *Polytrichum* (left) and sphagnum.

The majority of lichens in the Liffey Head moorland grow on the granite of the stone walls as thin encrustations coloured yellow, blue-green or black. But there is a very special one, *Cladonia*, a small branching blue-green plant which grows on bare patches of peat and would not be in any way noticeable except that it produces pinhead-sized crimson fruits. Resembling paint or sealing-wax, they give totally unexpected little blobs of bright colour among otherwise sombre vegetation.

The lichen *Cladonia*

The Coronation Plantation

At Sally Gap, the Military Road leaves the Liffey valley and heads south towards Glenmacnass. A right turn at the crossroads leads downhill. This road, much older than the early nineteenth-century military construction, connects Kilbride in west Wicklow to Glendalough and follows the valley of the upper Liffey for much of its route. It crosses the river by an unprepossessing structure supported by three stone piers with a parapet of concrete blocks. A little way downstream is an attractive green space with room for parking a car and accessing the Coronation Plantation.

This plantation, of oak and Scots pine, covered the left bank of the Liffey for 3.2 km – with the exception of a clear space around the remnants of a gamekeeper's lodge. This is the site of the monument which describes the purpose of the planting in words which are now difficult to read. Fortunately, they were copied by Weston St John Joyce early in the twentieth century and published in *The Neighbourhood of Dublin* in 1912. They make this proud but sadly unfinished announcement:

Coronation Plantation
Lordship of Blessington
County of Wicklow
This Plantation in the Brocky
Mountains of 500 Irish
Laid out by the
Most Honourable the Marquis of Downshire
The fencing commenced in August 1831
* * *
It was called the
Coronation Planting, in honour of his Most Gracious
Majesty
King William IV
The Most Noble the Marquis of Anglesey being
Lord Lieutenant of Ireland
* * *
And for the future supply of useful
timber for the
Estate
And improvement of the
County and the
Benefit of the
Labouring Classes
* * *
This planting
finished on the
day of 18

The planting was undoubtedly completed, but the most honourable Marquis had died suddenly in Blessington in April 1845 and his heir failed to fill in the blank spaces on his father's obelisk.

The plantation is shown on the 1837 map enclosed by the river and three rigidly straight borders at right angles to each other. The forest covered ten square kilometres, where the land rises gently over the townland of Ballynabrocky to reach, ultimately, the slopes of Mullaghcleevaun. The illustrious marquis who conceived it was proprietor of 100,000 acres (400 square kilometres) of land in Great Britain and Ireland. His primary aim in life was to enhance the value of his property but, as the inscription points out, his way of accomplishing this was by improving the industry and welfare of his tenants.

One or two crops of timber were harvested. Joyce described the early twentieth-century scene as a 'miniature forest mostly of pines and larches' but has a note in the second edition of his book: 'I regret to see that the Coronation Plantation is now (1920) being cut down.' It seems that no replanting followed. The fence was not maintained and grazing deer have effectively prevented any regeneration of the trees. Many stately old pine and oak have survived and these line the valleys of the main river and the tributary streams.

While the original enterprise may have failed, the pattern of ancient trees gives a very pleasing view. Richard Nairn and Miriam Crowley give a good description in *Wild Wicklow* of the state of the forest in the 1990s and point out that there are enough trees to provide nesting places for ravens and crows and also to attract some relatively rare small birds such as whinchat and crossbill.

The Liffey in the townlands of Kippure and Ballynabrocky, joined by a bridge of singular severity.

The plantation, as marked on the 1837 map, kept to the left bank of the Liffey and extended downstream to a point a little way to the south of Kippure House. The same map shows well-wooded demesne lands on the right bank, extending northwards to the road. A police station stands beside the road at the eastern end of the demesne. These developments mark the transition in the Liffey valley from a highland wilderness of poorly drained acid rock with peaty soil to the region of better drainage and richer land that borders Anna Liffey for the rest of her journey to the sea. From this point onwards the townlands along the river are smaller and fields have been fenced. The higher ground on both sides of the valley remains poor and the *Discovery* map of 2010 shows extensive planting of conifers on all the hillsides. The next chapter follows the river through a borderline region: a little too rough to have attracted wealthy residents in times past, but productive enough to make profitable farming a possibility.

3 | The uplands:
Kippure House to Ballyward

Kippure estate

Re-established in 2003 by the scholarly entrepreneur Tim Kyne, this remains the highest developed land in the Liffey valley and was the site of Kippure House, the most elevated stately home. The website https://kippure.com describes the marvellous adventure and social centre that lies discreetly hidden from the road by woodland old and new.

According to the website, one of the earliest references to the estate is in the *Dublin Evening Journal* of 28 April 1778: 'there is a good farm house, stables for ten horses, great Sallow plantations, in fine Sporting Country, and leading to which there are fine Roads lately made from Dublin, Wicklow, Blessington and Naas …'

The property was owned by the Moore family for a century from 1790 to 1890 and in the 1830s they built a large hunting lodge and gardens. The map of 1838 shows extensive woodland and driveways and a circular plantation labelled 'Nursery'. The entrance is a little way to the east of Kippure Bridge, which carries the main road across the Athdown Brook, a tributary of the Liffey.

The sandpits

To the west of the gateway to Kippure House, the 'Sand Pits' marked on the *Discovery* map, in the Townland of Ballynabrocky, come to dominate the scene with their great heaps of silver sand, derived purely from the granite. This means that the sand was deposited by meltwater from the mountain glaciers to the east. The hilly landscape is not an original feature, but results from many years of quarrying. The original surface of the sand and gravel deposit would have been nearly level, the sandpits having been a delta in the short-lived Glacial Lake Blessington.

Downstream of the sandpits, the Liffey created a broad floodplain. The banks of the river are composed of large lumps of granite, its floods having long since carried away all the finer particles. A motte and a graveyard are marked on the map. The former is named Athdown Moat on the 1838 six-inch

Ballynabrocky sandpits exploit the sand cleaned and sorted by the river currents where the Liffey formed a delta in the extinct Glacial Lake Blessington.

map, but only the merest outline remains and archaeologists, not surprisingly, have little to say about it. The graveyard is shaded by a spinney of splendid Scots pines, perhaps as old as 100 years. But from the point of view of a visitor, this burial place is almost as unimpressive as Athdown Moat, being marked above the ground by just one small granite pillar. A plantation of Sitka spruce occupies an area of damp ground nearby, while the lower parts of the hillside have sheep pasture and are divided by a number of massive walls – stones are superabundant in these parts, both on and beneath the soil. In past times, these stones provided a convenient material for farmers making field boundaries.

Athdown glacier and other inroads of ice

The name of the townland to the north of Ballysmuttan is Athdown and it is famous in geological history as the site of a local mountain glacier, whose ice flowed westwards from Kippure and Seefin. At the same time as the ice flowed down from the mountains, more was pushed up from the midlands and from the Irish Sea basin, and all three glaciers fought for supremacy, leaving in their wake a very complicated record of deposits of clay, gravel, stones and boulders. The mountain glacier carried granite down the valley and the two ice fields to the north brought limestone pebbles all the way up the hill to Ballysmuttan. Unlike water, ice can flow uphill as well as down. Ballysmuttan is a good place from which to look at some aspects of the effects of the Ice Age on the Liffey valley.

The Liffey at Ballysmuttan with Seefin and the townland of Athdown. There is gorse and broom on the riverbank, enclosed sheep pasture on lower slopes and spruce plantation on deeper peaty mountainside, extending up the hill to shallow soils and exposed rock.

It is likely that global warming, however grim its effects on many human communities, is in terms of geological time a mere blip in a sequence of events. The Ice Age in which we live and move and have our being is known overall as the Quaternary and has two divisions. The first was the Pleistocene, which began 1.7 million years ago when cold conditions first moved towards the equator from the two poles. The second is the Holocene and dates to between 11,000 and 12,000 years ago, when the last cold period came to an end.

There were several great advances of the ice, each followed by an 'interglacial' lasting for tens of thousands of years. While it is possible that the Ice Age has actually come to an end, its demise perhaps accelerated by the accumulation of greenhouse gases, the general opinion amongst geologists is that we are enjoying the warmth of an interglacial and Ireland may once more be overwhelmed with ice – though perhaps not for quite some time.

Whatever the future may hold for us, the effects of past glaciations on the form of the Liffey valley have been profound and continue to influence most aspects of the landscape. William Warren, in his book *Wicklow in the Ice Age*, gives a detailed account of conditions around the upper Liffey, which happens to run entirely within the county. For the most part, traces of the earlier glaciations have been swept away by the last one. The ice and snow in that period persisted for more than 60,000 years and the final remnants of the glaciers disappeared around 10,000 years ago. Through the ages since then, the vegetation developed gradually from tundra through coniferous forest to the broadleaved woodland that would cover much of Ireland to this day – if it had not been replaced with pasture by farmers in the course of the last 5,000 years.

During the glaciation, the lowlands of Ireland, together with the Irish Sea basin, were covered by an ice field resembling that of present-day Greenland. The concept of an ice field is a little misleading because fields stay in one place, whereas ice fields in the northern hemisphere travel slowly southwards. The higher ground of the Wicklow Mountains had its own local glaciers, in which the ice flowed slowly downhill. Moving ice plucks pieces of rock from the surface beneath it, carries them along and subjects them to grinding and crushing. The process is self-feeding in the sense that the rocks being carried along act like sandpaper, rasping away and smoothing the surfaces beneath them.

The stones by the riverside at Ballysmuttan were brought to the valley by a succession of glaciers, held in a mass of clay. The river carried the clay away and released the stones. They include granite, limestone and greywacke. The granite came from the higher hill slopes, the others from the lowlands.

When the ice finally melts, its burden of rocks, pebbles and clay remains in place, creating a new land surface. Known as 'glacial till', this material fills many of the pre-existing valleys and the Liffey and its tributaries have been engaged ever since in cutting themselves new ones.

Before the glaciation, the valleys of the Wicklow Mountains meandered and had V-shaped cross sections. The glaciers straightened out the bends by cutting off the rock spurs that formed them. They also steepened the sides of the valleys and flattened their bottoms, resulting in a U-shaped rather than a V-shaped cross section. This form is more strikingly developed on the eastern slopes of the mountains, away from the Liffey. But it can be seen in the region of the Coronation Plantation and most splendidly in the upper reaches of the King's River. Another type of glacial feature that is more plentiful towards the east is the corrie (as described above under Cleevaun Lough).

Perhaps the most striking of all the relics of the glaciation in the Liffey valley is the sharp horizontal line that separates a landscape of enclosed green fields, with their pattern of stone walls or hedges, from the unenclosed and brownish or purplish moorland above them. The depth of the ice in the region of the Wicklow Mountains was about 275 metres. This great glacier carried pebbles and gravel of limestone from the north and covered the acid rock of the uplands with it. Good soil therefore developed much higher up the slopes than it would otherwise have done and the distribution of glacial till, rather than the divisions between types of the solid rock, came to divide rich land from poor.

Glacial Lake Blessington

For a moment of geological time – about eighty-five years – the margin of the midland ice in the region of Saggart made a dam with a crest at around 275 metres. This dam created a large lake which extended from Crooksling in the north to Hollywood in the south and inundated the Liffey valley eastwards to the Athdown region. The water covered the lower slopes of Ballynatola, the hill to the west of Ballysmuttan, extended as far as Ballydonnell and was the origin, as we have noted, of the sandpits upstream.

Ballysmuttan

An ancient ford and a nineteenth-century bridge provide a picnic place of singular significance in my family. Early in the twentieth century, my grandfather Hastings Draper used to cycle there on Sundays from Rathgar and fish for the minuscule brown trout that inhabit the pool below the bridge. In the 1930s, my parents brought their two young children there more than once and it was there in 1939 that I made my first intimate encounter with the river, as mentioned in the preface to this book. Of considerably greater importance is its place in history, together with Straffan, as the *locus classicus* for basic research on the brown trout.

Ballysmuttan Bridge at a time of low flow on the Liffey, exposing the assortment of lumps of granite originally deposited by mountain glaciers.

At times of low flow, the stream at Ballysmuttan is confined to the north side of the river bed. To the south there is a white beach, with fine sand on its upper side and fist-sized lumps of granite and other rocks on the lower. Between the beach and the road is a sward of green grass, shaded by birch trees. Such a beach is an unusual feature of a river and it owes its existence to the way in which the bridge has narrowed the channel so that pebbles carried downstream are swept to the side. The opposite bank is a steep one, being slowly undercut by the river and bearing a luxuriant growth of gorse which blooms as early as March. Later in the year, broom by the bank comes into flower and supplies additional splashes of yellow.

Ballysmuttan Bridge

The map of 1838 shows a road on the left bank leading from the hamlet of Ballysmuttan to the bend in the river where it takes a sharp turn to the west and where the bridge would be built. A track on the right bank winds its way up the hill to meet the ancient road from Sally Gap to Kilbride. The river was forded at this point. Drowning tragedies had taken place at the ford and the local landlord and owner of Kippure House instigated the building of the bridge.

Kathy Trant, in *The Blessington Estate 1667–1908*, gives an account of the beginning of the undertaking, based on the diary of Elizabeth Smith of Baltyboys. The foundation stone was laid by the Marchioness of Downshire and the event was attended by a large crowd, who were subsequently invited to a banquet at Kippure House. They walked there accompanied by four horn players and such tunes as Handel's 'Hail the Conquering Hero'. The Great Famine, then at its height, seemed far away – which it was to some degree as few of the west Wicklow tenant farmers depended on the potato.

The date 1848 is carved in bold letters a little above the water on the upstream side of the stone pier nearest to the right bank. The bridge is a tribute to the ideas of railway engineers and iron-masters and the skills of local stonemasons. The two piers, with angular cutwaters, and the decking were very neatly built of granite ashlar. The walls were lattice girders.

The bridge stood for more than a century and a half until the flood caused by unusually heavy rainfall on the night of 24 November 2011, when in a few hours' downpour more than the monthly average rain fell. Tragically, Ciarán Jones, a young garda who lived nearby, was swept to his death while trying to warn approaching traffic of the danger.

The bridge was rebuilt with great care for its appearance – and with impressive speed – and the damaged pier was replaced with a granite replica of the original. But this time concrete rather than stone was used for the abutments. At the opening, on 16 May 2012, the repaired bridge was named in honour of Garda Jones.

The fishes of Ballysmuttan

In the 1930s government Inspectors of Fisheries had engaged in pioneering work on the food and growth of trout and, to a lesser extent, salmon in the Liffey catchment. A subject of increasing interest in those days was the difference between the growth rates of trout in streams with acidic water and the much larger trout found in habitats that were rich in lime and were therefore alkaline rather than acid.

Efforts were being made at the time to develop sport fishing in Ireland and studies of the basic biology of the trout were of great significance. Above all, the effectiveness of artificial stocking of particular waters was an unknown quantity. The seemingly logical idea was that, if you hatched trout or salmon eggs under artificial conditions and released the young into the wild, you would have more to catch. This was widely accepted over many generations, but relatively recent research has shown that, except in a very limited number of special cases, the natural runs of breeding trout and salmon provide rivers and lakes with as many young fish as they can support.

The proximity of the Liffey to Dublin and the headquarters of the fisheries administration may have influenced its choice as the place for the research. But more important was the fact that the same river contained both acidic and lime-rich stretches. It was well known that trout in different rivers attained different sizes: if they could be shown to vary in different parts of the same river, some of the basic questions would be answered.

The studies were begun by Rowland Southern, a senior scientist in the Fisheries Branch of the Department of Agriculture. But the greater part of the work was done by two young assistants from England, Arthur Went and Winifred E. Frost. Both would go on to become international leaders in fisheries science, Went settling in Dublin and Frost returning to England for a career in the newly established Freshwater Biological Association in the Lake District. They chose two Liffey sites: Ballysmuttan on the edge of the peaty upper reaches; and Straffan, where the mature river drains land that is rich in lime.

Southern began the study in 1929, with Frost as his assistant, but he died in December 1935, before any results were published. Known to all as 'Wef', the redoubtable Winifred eventually saw to the publication of no fewer than six papers on the Liffey, its fishes and their food and growth, in the course of the next sixteen years. The final one was 'River Liffey Survey VI. Results obtained from investigating the food and growth of brown trout (*Salmo trutta*) in alkaline and acid water'. Published by the Royal Irish Academy in 1945, it gives a comprehensive overview of the work. The most significant discovery was that the Straffan trout, particularly in their first year, grew much more quickly than their Ballysmuttan neighbours, and that early start in life enabled them to attain much greater sizes.

The researchers discovered that the various insects that formed the staple diets of the trout were as numerous at Ballysmuttan as at Straffan and that the fish appeared to be equally well fed. But, while the numbers and the quantities of the insects were much the same, the species were generally different. Surprisingly, Wef attached little significance to this – but then it has to be remembered that hers was indeed a pioneering study and all those involved believed at the outset that the chemistry of the water had a direct effect on the growth rate of the fish. So, while Southern, Frost and Went provided the facts for later people to use and come to different conclusions, they themselves seem to have missed some of the most important points, above all that the individual insects eaten by the Ballysmuttan trout were smaller and less nutritious than those in the diet of the Straffan fish.

Trout habitat at Ballysmuttan: the deeper, slow-running stretches provide food, cover and spawning beds. It is possible that the ancestral trout of the Liffey here, upstream of the Pollaphuca waterfall, were artificially introduced, although there is no historical record of such a project.

Seefin and its cairn

On the right bank, the land climbs gently at first, towards the steeper slopes of Seefin. The lower ground is sheep pasture, enclosed in fields by dry-stone granite walls. In the past, the stones were scattered over much of the ground. When farmers came to clear the land, the walls, as well as acting as field boundaries, provided a convenient place to dump the stones.

The abundance of small stones and gravel, in spite of the shortage of lime, makes for reasonably good drainage of the soil and so allows for pasture. Higher on Seefin, the slopes are covered by a blanket of peat and the vegetation of the more acid soil contrasts sharply with the green of the lower slopes. Heather and sedges were the natural vegetation, but large areas of the hillside have been planted with Sitka spruce, one of the very few species of tree that actually thrives in such soils. Close to the summit of Seefin is the cairn which was built around 5,000 years ago by employees of the Neolithic cattle barons who had had the primeval forest cleared to create pasture for their herds.

The structure is a passage grave. Compared with Newgrange, this one is a modest achievement. Because of the relative poverty of the grazing and the absence of salmon, the community must have been less affluent than the dwellers in the bend of the Boyne and that might go some way towards explaining the difference. But, while Newgrange is on a low hilltop, Seefin is high up a steep mountain. Carrying large stones to its summit is unlikely to have appealed to the Stone Age residents of the upper Liffey.

Nevertheless, Seefin Cairn is an impressive piece of work, demanding the input of a thriving and well-organised community. It may have been no more than a tomb, as the archaeological term 'passage grave' implies. There can be no question that its position commands a marvellous view: down over the pasture which provided food and wealth for the people. It is also clearly visible from the valley, confirming for those who looked up to the hills the power and influence of the people who ordered it to be built. The view is not merely of the valley immediately below the mountainside; it extends across the fertile plateau where the Brittas River flows and away to the hills of Silurian age that confine the upper Liffey valley.

Cloghlea

The right bank to the north of Ballysmuttan Bridge forms the border of the townland of Scurlocks Leap. The family of that name is known to have lived in the region since the twelfth century, but which Scurlock leapt, why and when, remains a mystery. River and road run close together towards the northwest here for the next 2 km, between spruce plantations on the hill slopes on each side and sheep pasture lower down. The beautiful granite church of Cloghlea stands between river and road and occupies the site of an ancient place of worship marked on the 1838 map. Built in the 1830s, the present church overlooks the deep valley of the stream of the same name, whose banks were planted ornamentally in the nineteenth century. Some details of the history of the area are provided by Jim Corley in his excellent website article on Rev. Ogle Moore, a profligate nineteenth-century incumbent of the parishes of Blessington and Kilbride, St John's at Cloghlea being the church of the latter (see http://blessington.info/history/historypage15.htm).

Cloghlea Bridge on the Shankill River.

Cloghlea Church, surrounded by the descendants of ornamental trees, is the centre of a community in the sheep-pasture lands of the upper Liffey.

For a while there was a little car park at Cloghlea Bridge, but it has been closed and roadside parking is required for a visit to the church, the elegant single-arched bridge with its stone balustrade and the woodland in the valley of the Shankill River which joins the Liffey a few hundred metres downstream.

By 1838 a small plantation had been established on both sides of the road in the Cloghlea valley. The descendants of these trees survive in the form of a bright and beautiful beech wood, with a scattering of exotics including Spanish chestnut and horse chestnut.

The road runs northwest after Cloghlea and stays close to the Liffey, where it flows through a steep-sided valley for the next 500 metres. Then road and river part company, the road continuing towards the northwest until it meets the village of Kilbride beside the Brittas River. The Liffey heads westwards, its character changing from hill stream to a meandering lowland river. Access to this section is difficult because the only roads run through a relatively built-up area, with houses and their gardens occupying the riverside. The river's next public appearance comes at Ballyward Bridge. But this is so much a part of the lake drive that we will leave it to the next chapter.

4 | The lakelands

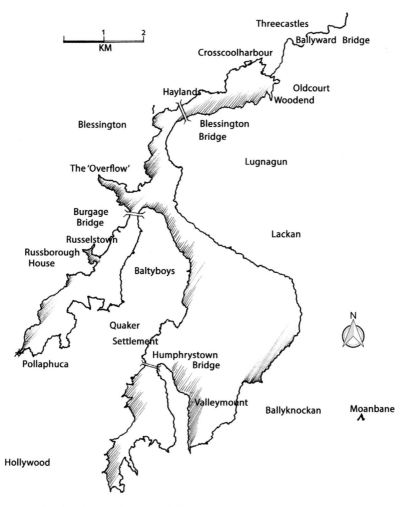

Features of the Blessington Lakes. *Ruairi Moriarty.*

The most dramatic change to the Liffey valley in historic times began at 10 o'clock on the morning of 3 March 1940. The concrete dam in the Pollaphuca Gorge had been completed and the sluice gate on the channel that diverted the Liffey around the construction site was closed. The concrete dam replaced a higher natural barrier that had been deposited by a glacier 10,000 years earlier and carried away not much later by the prehistoric Liffey. There were personal and aesthetic losses in the shape of the destruction of farmsteads and picturesque stone bridges and in diverting the water from the cascades at Pollaphuca. But incomparable gain came in the restoration, if on a smaller scale, of the earlier Lake Blessington. The idea of creating the lake first surfaced in 1918 and the building of the dam began just twenty years later.

Power from the Liffey

To celebrate fifty years 'on the Liffey', in 1994 the ESB produced an excellent little book on their achievements. The book includes an interesting collection of contemporary photographs and an all-too-rare tribute to the individual members of the workforce who created lakes, electricity and drinking water. The editor was Liam Kenny and a substantial part of the text was the work of the late John Godden. They were colleagues in the remarkable and remote office building above Lough Nahanagan in Wicklow Gap, a short step over the mountain pass from the headwaters of the King's River. John, besides his abilities as writer and administrator, had a deep knowledge of all environmental matters relating to the Liffey and the rivers of Wicklow Gap – which he shared most willingly.

The Turlough Hill complex is a spectacular 'pumped storage' power station but, although it operates in the neighbouring catchment to that of the Liffey, its impressive engineering details do not concern us. Where there is a real connection between Wicklow Gap and the Liffey hydroelectricity is that all three Liffey stations are controlled by engineers and others in the centre at Turlough Hill. Under normal circumstances there are no people at the Liffey dams apart from visiting security staff or maintenance engineers.

The conception of the Liffey scheme

Sir John Purser Griffith, born in Holyhead in 1848, graduated in engineering at Trinity College Dublin in 1868 and made his first professional connection with the Liffey three years later. That was when he became an assistant to Bindon Blood Stoney, engineer to Dublin Port, another of the individuals whose schemes have had a permanent benign influence on the river. Griffith, who was appointed chief engineer to the Port Authority on the retirement of Stoney in 1898, retired in 1913 to become an extremely active consulting engineer. A man of boundless vision, energy and political skills, he served on numerous public committees and had a particular interest in the generation of electricity – from peat as well as from water. In 1918 he became a member of the Commission on the Water Power Resource of the United Kingdom and, most significantly for the future shape of Anna Liffey, chaired the commission's Water Power Resource of Ireland Sub-Committee from 1919 to 1921.

This committee in 1921 proposed the erection of a dam in the gorge of Pollaphuca to form an immense storage reservoir and power source. It also identified sites for dams downstream at Golden Falls and Leixlip and upstream at Cloghlea on the Upper Liffey and at Lockstown on the King's River. The latter two were not pursued – but otherwise the scheme put forward by Griffith and his colleagues was the one adopted. Conceived at a time of warfare between Great Britain and Ireland, it took some years to come to fruition. In 1922 a Commission of Inquiry into the Resources and Industries of Ireland published its report on water power, which included the words:

> The Liffey powers are of immediate national importance owing to their proximity to the city of Dublin, and should, therefore, be especially investigated at once.

Griffith was an enthusiastic lobbyist for the Liffey scheme, but his hopes of rapid development were dashed by an equally enthusiastic and talented engineer, T. A. McLoughlin, who had a much more ambitious plan. While Griffith concentrated on the needs of the capital city, McLoughlin was thinking nationwide. In the event his daring proposal for harnessing the Shannon won the day as far as priority was concerned and the turbines at Ardnacrusha began to turn in 1930.

While the larger Shannon Scheme took precedence, work continued on planning for the Liffey. In 1922 a water-level gauge was installed in the Pollaphuca gorge and daily records of the height of the river were maintained until 1938. The average flow for the twelve years 1922 to 1934 was 9,459 litres per second. The river was described as 'flashy', the extremes of flow ranging from 1,000 litres per second in a drought to 300,000 litres per second in a high flood.

These flow calculations confirmed that the upper Liffey and King's River catchments had more than enough water available both for generating and for water supply. But there remained the crucial question of whether that water could be held in the valleys by a dam at Pollaphuca. There was no problem concerning the impenetrable granite core of the mountains to the east. But the nature of the low range of hills to the west, with their superabundant gravel, was far from promising. In the words of the Commissioners:

> Unfortunately, it is doubtful if a considerable portion of the hill, which would form the northern side of this reservoir about half a mile above the dam, would be watertight. The surface indications all suggest that this portion of the hill is an old watercourse filled with gravel and sand.

If so, it would not be watertight, and serious leakage would occur …
This point cannot be decided until trial borings should be made.

They may have been concerned, among other factors, by the fact that the original Geological Survey map marks an area of 'Fine grey Rabbit Sand' in Bishopsland, across the river from Tulfarris.

Accordingly, a large number of borings, trial pits and trenches were made under the guidance of geologists Dr J. Hug of Zurich and T. H. Hallissy, Director of the Geological Survey of Ireland. These trials extended from Blessington to Golden Falls and the geologists expressed themselves satisfied with the results. The information provided by the water gauging and by the test drillings confirmed that the entire project was viable, and planning began in earnest.

About the same time as the geologists were making their report, Dublin Corporation was applying pressure on both the ESB and the government to develop the Pollaphuca dam as a source of domestic water for the growing city.

Sand and gravel deposited by meltwater in the final centuries of the Ice Age have provided raw materials for building since the nineteenth century. The planners of Pollaphuca reservoir feared that they would prove too porous to contain the water. Trial drillings showed that the bedrock beneath the gravel would prevent serious leakage.

The Liffey Reservoir Act

The early 1930s saw intense work by planners within the ESB, Dublin Corporation and the Department of Industry and Commerce of the Free State government. This appeared in public in the form of the Liffey Reservoir Bill which became law in 1936. The Act contains an Agreement:

made the 18th day of June 1936, between THE RIGHT HONOURABLE THE LORD MAYOR, ALDERMEN AND BURGESSES OF DUBLIN (Hereinafter called 'the Corporation' ... of the one part and the ELECTRICITY SUPPLY BOARD ...

This agreement set out the details of how the land was to be prepared, what water levels were to be maintained and how much water the Corporation was entitled to draw off. The ESB was required, among other provisions, to:

(i) Cut down and remove from the site of the Reservoir all growing timber and undergrowth to the satisfaction of the Corporation:

(ii) Remove all dwelling-houses, sheds, stables, cow-byres, and piggeries; and shall render sanitary the sites of the same by sprinkling the site with chlorate of lime to the satisfaction of the Corporation:

(iii) Subject to obtaining all necessary ecclesiastical and other permissions, remove from any graveyard which may be flooded by the Reservoir the bodies buried therein and inter the same elsewhere ...

(iv) Remove and level down, or partly remove and level down as far as may be reasonably necessary, all mounds, fences, ditches and obstructions upon that part of the Reservoir which shall lie over five hundred and seventy five feet.

The land and people before the lake

In 2008 the Stationery Office published a very remarkable book on the valleys of the 16 km of the Liffey and 13 km of King's River that were inundated in 1940. Edited by the archaeologist Christiaan Corlett, *Beneath the Poulaphuca Reservoir*, in addition to an account of the origins of the hydro scheme, presents the findings of a survey made in the summer of 1939 by a number of specialists in the fields of folklore and archaeology.

Corlett records slightly conflicting accounts of how the survey began, but it appears that Eoin McNeill, Liam Price and the teacher at Lackan National School, Michael O'Connor, were among the instigators. Liam Price, a district justice whose spare-time activities established him as the authority on place names and other aspects of the heritage of County Wicklow, planned the survey. Most of the field workers would later occupy top positions in their respective professions. Sadly, the various authors did very little to bring their results together. Happily, their material was preserved and, thanks to Corlett and the Stationery Office, much of it is now available as a unique snapshot not just of life in the valley but of the ways of a community of small farmers in Ireland at the end of the 1930s.

The creation of the Blessington Lakes

The final scheme was more ambitious than the earlier proposals. Pollaphuca remained the chosen site for the dam, but the top level of the water was fixed at 618 feet (188.4 metres) rather than 600 feet. The low-water level is 177 metres. Between 177 and 187.5 metres, the water storage capacity is 148 million cubic metres, equal to half the annual inflow to the reservoir.

Planning of the joint hydropower and water supply scheme was carried out in parallel by the ESB and Dublin Corporation. Although substantially smaller than the Shannon Scheme, the Liffey Reservoir Scheme, as it was officially known, was as complex as its larger predecessor. The Shannon required two dams and the spectacular headrace canal that carries the water from Parteen to Ardnacrusha at a high level. Besides its three dams, the Liffey undertaking entailed the construction of a water treatment plant at Ballymore Eustace and a pipeline to bring the water from there to Cookstown and across the Liffey to consumers on the north side of the city. Engineering works in the upper valley included building three large bridges and two small ones, to say nothing of extensive replacement of the roads that would be inundated. Above all was the legal and social problem of acquiring 5,500 acres (2,256 hectares) of land and destroying 76 homesteads.

The agreement also required that the entire reservoir and the land that surrounded it should be enclosed, and the fence is 51 km long. Concrete

The granite hills to the east of the lakes: Black Hill; Mullaghcleevaun, from which the highest Liffey tributaries spring; and the two-headed Moanbane.

posts were used with barbed wire in places, but mainly with five strands of plain galvanised wire: a happy choice that facilitates entry to the forbidden ground. Furious notices, neatly printed on enamelled steel, were erected at all convenient access points, telling the public that they were forbidden to enter, boat, bathe in or otherwise enjoy this, their property. That was, perhaps, part of wartime austerity but also reflected the utilitarian thinking of the times. Much would change over the years in the public enjoyment of the lakes.

As the law required, the farmsteads were demolished and disinfected. Human bodies exhumed from Burgage Cemetery were removed, resuming their peaceful rest at a more exalted site nearby. Trees, shrubs and fences were cleared. In spite of the fact that there was plenty of saleable timber, no acceptable offers were made for the removal of the trees by contractors, so they stayed where they fell until the valley was flooded, when they could be floated to suitable gathering places. Some of the timber was removed in this way, but by no means all. This I discovered in the 1950s when the nets I used in fishery research were all too frequently snagged on submerged branches.

Compensation was paid to the owners of the 76 farm houses and labourers' cottages in the doomed area. Besides the dwellings and farms that were completely destroyed, the rising waters occupied substantial portions of farms whose actual buildings stood on dry land. Major works were undertaken to restore their fences and to replace water supplies where wells and boreholes had disappeared.

Clearances of the peasantry by landlords in Ireland in the nineteenth century had in some cases been on an even larger scale. But there was the profound difference that the Liffey Reservoir was being created for the benefit of hundreds of thousands of citizens, rich and poor, not the pleasure and profit of already wealthy individuals. But whatever the purpose and whoever the perpetrator, loss of home and land is a bitter experience. While the victims did indeed receive compensation, it was far from generous. For the 50 farms that were flooded, the ESB was empowered by the Liffey Reservoir Act to pay only the current market value of the land. Although some of this land was of good quality, much was poorly drained and unproductive. This meant that the price paid for an average farm was not sufficient to allow the farmers to establish themselves elsewhere. Some of those whose land was only partly flooded saw their holdings reduced to an uneconomic size and the cash payment they received could not make up for the loss. Numerous protest meetings were held, but it seems that little material improvement was achieved and the dispossessed, as in earlier times, were left to their fate. By the end of 1941, the land had gone and the protests had come to an end.

The landscape of the lakes

The official name bestowed on the lake was Poulaphuca Reservoir. This title is still honoured by the Ordnance Survey – except that they spell it Pollaphuca, as they have done since the 1830s. Lieutenant Alexander Taylor in 1783 used two 'l's and an 'f', Pollafuca, a good phonetic attempt; but it hides from English speakers the name of the Pooka. While 'Pollaphuca' sounds appealing, 'reservoir' is a deadening technical term, so it is not surprising that tourism interests baptised the waters as Blessington Lakes, a term I am happy to apply.

The fact that there is only one lake loses significance when its appearance, both from ground level and on the map, is considered. The reservoir is divided by the hills into five parts, one large and four small, each portion effectively screened from its neighbours. Three are on the Liffey: the first from the river's inflow to Blessington Bridge, the second from Blessington Bridge to Burgage Bridge, and the third from Burgage Bridge to Pollaphuca. The other two are on the King's River: a smallish one from the inflow at Lockstown to the Valleymount peninsula and the magnificent large water from the peninsula to the confluence with the Liffey. Man-made or not, they form far and away the greatest lake in the entire southeast quarter of Ireland.

The maximum level of the lake, dictated by the crest of the dam, is 188.49 metres OD (ordnance datum). The dam is 31 metres high, so that is the greatest depth of the water. The foot of the dam is 157 metres above sea level, meaning that the entire valley is, by Irish standards, high in the hills. The *Discovery* map has brown shading over the greater part of the valley of the lakes, indicating that it is almost completely surrounded by hills of 200 metres and higher. The only stretch at a lower level is near Pollaphuca and happens also to border the only part of the lakes in County Kildare.

Perhaps the most surprising feature of this impoundment is the fact that it so closely resembles the structure of many of the large lakes of Ireland. In particular, the underlying rock of one side is granite, which yields an acidic soil, while the other lies on basic sedimentary strata. This explains the contrast between poor moorland to the east and rich pasture to the west.

The history of the landscape

The discipline of geology calls for a very remarkable combination of interests. The geologist must have a profound knowledge of chemistry, physics and biology. The basic skills include surveying, hacking off large pieces of rock and reducing parts of them to slices so thin that a hundred piled up would reach the thickness of a thumbnail. All this and much more combine with the learning of a couple of centuries to allow the interpretation of events that took place hundreds or thousands of millions of years ago – as well as happenings in the geologically 'recent' times of the last few thousands or tens of thousands of years. An account of the geology of the entire Liffey valley was published in 1994 as Sheet 16 of the Geological Survey of Ireland. It is accompanied by a readable handbook by Brian McConnell and Michael Philcox entitled *Geology of Kildare–Wicklow*.

Bedrock

The oldest rock strata in the valley of the lakes are of Ordovician age. They pre-date the granite of the mountains and underlie the glacial till, mostly along parts of the eastern shores. Named the Aghfarrell Formation, they are described as thinly bedded greywacke, siltstone and slate.

The greater part of the King's River section of the lakes is surrounded by granite. Deep below the ancient land surface this was intruded in a molten state into the Ordovician strata some 405 million years ago. When it cooled, it crystallised, forming, among other constituents, the shining mica that makes the stone sparkle.

The rock beneath the western and part of the eastern shores of the lake, the Pollaphuca Formation, is Silurian, belonging to the age that followed the Ordovician. Towards the south, however, it is bordered by a narrow strip called the Slate Quarries Formation. The latter is of vital importance in the landscape, explaining the whole incongruous course of the upper Liffey – how and why are described below under 'The Pooka and his pool' (page 96).

The base of a cliff composed of glacial till. Stones of all sizes are held together by a mass of clayey material, all scooped up from the rock surface and mixed by the flowing ice. The cliff stands above the lakeshore, where the action of waves has carried the clay away and left clean sand and stones.

Glacial Lake Blessington

In the course of the hundreds of millions of years after the Ordovician and Silurian strata were formed, the land was covered over by many types of rock which were washed away again, revealing the ancient ones once more. Then, about one million years ago, came global cooling and the Ice Age, whose effects in the upper reaches are outlined on page 47.

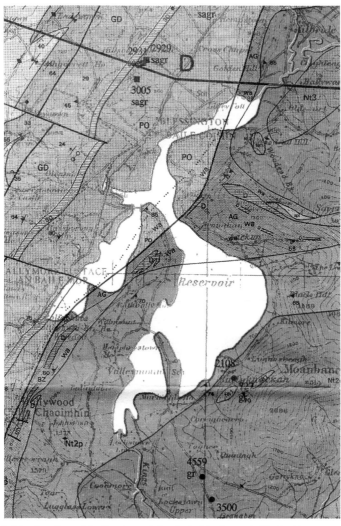

Solid rock geology of the Blessington Lakes: Ordovician in purple, Silurian blue-green, granite orange. *Courtesy Geological Survey of Ireland* Sheet 16.

In preglacial times, the Liffey and the King's River had cut their valleys between the eastern granite and the western Silurian strata. These came to be filled by a forked tongue of the ice field during the cold spells. For some hundreds of years, as the climate improved and the glaciers receded at the end of the last cold snap, the ice in the valley melted, but the Slade of Saggart and Hollywood Glen, where the meltwater should have escaped, were blocked by ice dams, formed by the larger ice field to the north and a smaller mountain glacier to the south. A magnificent lake filled the valley between the two, extending from Hollywood Glen all the way to Crooksling. Evidence for the existence of this lake remains in the form of 'varves', deposits of grey clayey mud which often shows a layered structure. This mud is a partly consolidated mass of lake-bed sediments. Each layer represents the accumulation in the calm lake water of one season of silt carried by the torrential streams of meltwater that flowed when the ice and snow melted every summer.

Lakeland fishes

Before the inundation, the River Liffey in its valley near Blessington provided good trout fishing. Indeed, it is likely that sizeable trout were plentiful from a point not far downstream of Ballysmuttan, where the river flows slowly and where drainage through limestone gravel provides the vital element for a productive trout habitat. The broad meandering river gives space and comfort for the successful trout – those that had eaten most of their siblings, as trout and other fishes usually do. When the valley was flooded, these trout enjoyed a bonanza. The lakes made a vast living space free from competitors and predators. At the same time the insects, and other creatures that the trout eat, multiplied.

It was wartime, the variety of food in the shops had been severely reduced and there was plenty of demand for the delicious trout that the lakes offered. Angling, the only permitted means of catching them, became very popular. And the trout were fine ones: in 1942 the average weight of a sample of 150 fish was 2 lb (0.9 kg) – more than double the weight of those that lived in the river. Great catches were recorded and a number of the anglers fished to make a living. But in the following year, 1943, disaster struck. The big trout succumbed to an infestation of tapeworms.

An investigation was conducted by two unusual anglers and lovers of trout. Maurice Hickey was the State Pathologist, more familiar with the sudden death of people than of fish. J. R. (Dick) Harris was a talented amateur naturalist who would win renown as the author of the classic *An Angler's Entomology*. Hickey and Harris identified two species of tapeworm that had spent an earlier phase of their lives in the stickleback on which the big trout were feeding. By 1947, most of the big trout had died – the smaller ones survived by not eating stickleback. But the future was far from rosy for the trout.

In 1948 Frank Richardson, a lakeside resident, recorded the presence of perch in the lake. Frank was an enthusiastic angler who helped supply Hickey and Harris with the specimens they needed and would later provide me with help and hospitality when I came to study the fish. My work showed how the prolific perch virtually obliterated the slow-breeding trout. In the 1960s persons unknown released pike into the lakes and, in the next decade, roach were introduced. The newcomers prospered and a unique population of native fish was brought close to extinction.

Far from being a fish in zoological terminology, the white-clawed crayfish is an important and remarkable member of the fauna of the lakes. Resembling a very small, finger-length lobster, it is widely distributed throughout Ireland, but only rarely abundant in lakes. The reason for this is that most Irish lakes have eels, and eels eat crayfish to such a degree that the two are seldom found in the same habitat. But the Blessington Lakes are virtually eel-free and so the crayfish thrives in them. The species is not native to Ireland. Julian Reynolds, who has studied crayfish for many years, believes that they were first introduced to Ireland by continental monks, possibly the Cistercians, who first came here in the twelfth century. This may very well be the case, but it does not solve the mystery of who introduced crayfish to the Liffey catchment upstream of Pollaphuca.

Lakeland birds

The creation of the lakes formed a habitat new not just to Wicklow but to the southeast quarter of Ireland, an area formerly devoid of large lakes and the water birds associated with them. A few species that thrive in lakelands had been present: mallard probably lived in the Blessington–Ballyknockan valley since prehistoric times. They need calm, open water for their ducklings, but there were – and still are – many ponds and stretches of still water in the valley that gave them sufficient nursery space. The same may be said of the moorhen. The damp pasture provided a living for small numbers of lapwing and curlew throughout the year and for larger numbers of these, together with golden plover, in winter. But the new lakes led to an invasion of wintering waterfowl.

Greylag goose, whooper swan and a variety of species of duck gathered in the valley. Of these, wigeon and teal, shoveler and many more mallard feed to a greater or lesser extent on the dry land or in the shallows, but they demand open stretches of water for refuge. Tufted duck and pochard feed under water and spend most of their time in or on the lake itself. The delta that is extending the already flat land at Threecastles makes a significant addition to the pasture where curlew and plover can feed.

The heron – one of a number of bird species whose habitat was greatly increased by the creation of Blessington Lakes. *Photo: Michael Finn.*

Visiting the lakes: an eastern circuit

The first three chapters of this book followed the Liffey from her source to the lake; the last four will resume the trail from lake to sea. Other than looking at their valley as a whole, such an orderly treatment would not do justice to the convoluted Blessington Lakes. So we will explore the valley by two lake tours: a large eastern circuit of 32 km and a smaller western one measuring 20 km. A single great circuit might reveal much, but would pass by a number of spots that are particularly interesting or beautiful or both. The logical place to begin a visit is the seventeenth-century foundation of Blessington, once the administrative centre of a great estate, now a delightful dormitory suburb. A popular spot for visitors to the valley for more than a century, it remains the most easily reached from the outside world by public or private transport.

The roughly eastern circuit takes the traveller from Blessington to Baltyboys, Valleymount, Ballyknockan and Ballyward and back to Blessington, crossing the water at two points by the ESB bridges. The western circuit visits Russborough and Pollaphuca and goes to lesser-known regions of the King's River valley.

Watercolour by Denis Moriarty of his holiday home, built in the 1940s in a former sand quarry which he bought from the ESB. The wooden hut in the background was the medical quarters at Pollaphuca during construction work. The cottage was a concrete block construction by local contractor Barney Flanagan. The haycocks above are on the farm owned by William Gyves. The cliff was occupied for many years by a colony of sand martins, but they were displaced by subsequent growth of grass.

Horseshoe arch dated 1852 on the main street of Blessington.

Blessington

Now a large and prosperous dormitory suburb, Blessington has succeeded in retaining something of the essence of its charming old-world appearance. The seventeenth-century church, overlooking the Liffey, still stands, but the original manor house to the west, destroyed in 1798, was never rebuilt. The eighteenth-century village was virtually replaced after 1798 by a single broad street on the main road which led from Dublin through Ballymore Eustace to Baltinglass, Carlow and Waterford. This broad street, flanked by neat two-storey houses, has survived and screens from view the twentieth-century housing developments. While the main street and its houses were and remain in County Wicklow, many of the newer dwellings are on the far side of the border with Kildare.

Samuel Lewis, in his 1837 *Topographical Dictionary of Ireland*, gives a generous entry of a page and a half to the state of Blessington, including the following:

> This place is situated on the river Liffey, and on the high road from Dublin, by Baltinglass, to Wexford, Carlow, and Waterford. The town occupies a rising ground on the north-western confines of the county and was built by Archbishop Boyle in the reign of Chas. II. It consists only of one street, and contains about 50 houses, which are mostly of respectable appearance, and a good inn or hotel. Considerable improvement has taken place since the construction of the new turnpike road from Dublin to Carlow, by way of Baltinglass, in 1829, by which the Waterford mail and the Kilkenny day mail, and several coaches and cars to the counties of Wexford and Carlow, have been brought through it. The celebrated waterfall called Poul-a-Phuca, about three miles distant on the road to Baltinglass, and described under the head of Ballymore-Eustace, is generally visited from this place ...
>
> The inhabitants were incorporated by charter of the 21st of Chas. II. (1669), granted to Michael Boyle, Archbishop of Dublin and Chancellor of Ireland, and certain forfeited lands assigned to him were at the same time erected into a manor, to be called the manor of Blessington ...
>
> The corporation was styled 'The Sovereign, Bailiffs, and Burgesses of the Borough and Town of Blessington;' and consisted of a sovereign, two bailiffs, and twelve burgesses, with power to a majority to admit freemen and choose inferior officers, and the archbishop was authorised to appoint a recorder and town-clerk. The borough returned two members to the Irish parliament till the Union, when the £15,000 awarded as compensation for the loss of the franchise was paid to Arthur, Marquess of Downshire; the right of election was vested in the corporation at large, which from that period has been extinct ...

The parish, which, previously to the erection of the town and church in 1683, was called Burgage, comprises 17,570 statute acres. The land is chiefly under tillage and pasturage, and there are some large tracts of mountain waste, on which are turf bogs; the state of agriculture has considerably improved. The subsoil is chiefly limestone gravel; and the mountains abound with granite, which is quarried and sent to Dublin for public buildings. The Marquess of Downshire had a handsome mansion and demesne of 410 statute acres, with a deer park of 340 acres, all surrounded by a wall, and situated on the right of the road from Dublin: the mansion was originally built by Primate Boyle, the last ecclesiastical chancellor of Ireland, who held his court of chancery here, and built houses for the six clerks, two of which yet remain; the interior was burnt by the insurgents in 1798 and has not been restored; the demesne is richly embellished with fine timber ...

A neat building, the upper part of which is used as a girls' school, and the lower as a court for holding the petty sessions, with a house for the master and mistress, has been erected at an expense of £800 by the Marquess of Downshire, who allows a salary of £20 to the master and £10 to the mistress the latter of whom also receives the £5 payable by the incumbent: there are about 20 boys in the school, who are taught in a school-room a short distance from the building, and 30 girls. There are also five hedge schools in Blessington and Burgage, in which nearly 150 children are taught.

The Blessington Estate

Such was the situation in 1837. The story of Blessington and the surrounding Downshire property is taken up by Kathy Trant in her excellent book *The Blessington Estate 1667–1908*, which uses, among other sources, the voluminous Downshire papers preserved in the Public Record Office of Northern Ireland. The great manor house to the west of the village, burned in 1798, was never rebuilt. Boyle's village was also destroyed in '98 and the third Marquis began restoration and rebuilding in 1809. G. N. Wright, who visited Blessington about 1822, describes it as having only 'a few large and well-built houses'. The 50 houses that Lewis described were built a little later.

In the 1940s, when I first saw Blessington, there was little more than those buildings of the early nineteenth century. Kathy Trant gives details of the trials and tribulations of building the present market house between 1838 and 1845 – a date which suggests that the courthouse described by Lewis prior to 1837 may have been replaced. The Marquis died in 1845 while riding nearby on a tour of inspection of his property. Inheriting huge debts on his coming into the inheritance, he had been totally absorbed in the maintenance and development of his vast properties and the welfare of his tenants. His heirs were less energetic and the Blessington Estate was finally sold to the Land Commission in 1908. The road that Lewis mentions had been built in 1835, only two years before his publication.

The inscription on the drinking fountain in the square – which has an irreverent local designation unsuitable for printing in a respectable book – has suitably abject words on three of its four faces in honour of the Marquis and his progeny:

ERECTED
ON THE
COMING OF AGE
OF
THE EARL OF
HILLSBOROUGH
24th DEC. 1865
***

THE WATER
SUPPLIED AT THE COST OF
A KIND AND GENEROUS
LANDLORD
FOR THE BENEFIT
OF HIS
ATTACHED AND LOYAL TENANTS
***

A TRIBUTE OF RESPECT
FROM THE TENANTRY
ON THE
WICKLOW KILDARE
AND KILKENNY ESTATES
OF THE
MARQUIS OF DOWNSHIRE

By the 1940s the village had begun its existence as a dormitory suburb of the city of Dublin, with commuters availing of the number 65 bus during the Second World War when private cars were forbidden. The Catholic church at Cross Chapel, two miles to the north of the centre of Blessington, was built in 1861 on the site of an earlier place of worship at the crossroads in use since 1771. Once a conspicuous part of the scenery, but now hidden by trees, the church was in the centre of a community which, in the course of time, moved to the village. The building of a more convenient church in the 1950s coincided with the beginning of a period of expansion to north, south and west.

The majority of the houses lining the eighteenth-century main street have twentieth-century shopfronts on the lower storey but the upper storeys remain more or less intact and a good few dwellings retain their original front doors with fanlights and granite surrounds. On the left, as you head south, the line of terrace is broken first by the toll house from turnpike days, then by the bright modern church of 1982 which stands beside one of the four schools in the village.

Besides the numerous pubs and shops, some very old, one of the old two-storey houses has been opened as a delightful combination of bookshop and restaurant – food for body and mind, including a stock of books on local history.

The northern row of houses ends at St Mary's church and churchyard, dating from the seventeenth century and the days of Archbishop Boyle. In his time, a broad tree-lined avenue led northwestwards from the church to his splendid house. This space is today occupied by the nineteenth-century fountain and courthouse – now the Credit Union – and the late twentieth-century development of shopping centre, public library and school. Next to the church, the Downshire House was built for the Marquis's agent in the 1820s.

The line of shops and dwellings beyond the Downshire House is broken by a left turn that leads down to the lakes, passing 19th century school buildings on the left. After this turn-off, the line of houses is resumed and is broken just once by a handsome granite horseshoe arch bearing the date 1852 on its keystone. It was the entrance to the smithy which was later moved to the west side of the street.

Burgage and leisure

South of Blessington a diversion from the circuit of the lakes is required since the main road runs some way to the west of the Liffey valley. The diversion follows an older road leading to a medieval settlement where a castle commanded first a ford and, in due course, a bridge. The 1838 map shows, 2 km south of Blessington, the King's River flowing northwest and joining the south-flowing Liffey, which then runs eastwards until it meets the ruined castle and church of Burgage. There the river takes a U-turn to meander in a southwesterly direction for 5 km to Pollaphuca. A photograph in *Beneath the Poulaphuca Reservoir* shows the bridge, which had a level surface, supported by four stone segmental arches. Like its companion upstream at Blessington, it was probably eighteenth-century work and in June 1940 it, too, met its fate at the hands of military engineers (page 91). Not long afterwards, road and ruin were submerged.

The *Discovery* map uses the name Burgage, but the townland is often referred to in writings as Burgage More, and that is the older title. 'Burgage' is a term for a form of land tenure at a yearly rent, so the single word would mean little as a place name. A 'big burgage', on the other hand, is quite intelligible and the old form of the name is one of many mixed Irish and English place names to be found in west Wicklow.

Meeting of the waters: King's River on the left meets the Liffey in foreground, both flowing to Pollaphuca on the right. The distant hills are the granite slopes of Black Hill, Mullaghcleevaun and Moanbane. The parkland with beech trees is on Baltyboys Hill; the spruce plantation is in Russelstown.

The old road to Burgage from the south end of Blessington leads to one of the few major developments of accommodation to be built within easy reach of the margin of the lake after the valley was flooded. The Avon Rí Blessington Lakeshore Resort and Outdoor Adventure Centre provides luxurious accommodation with all the usual country club facilities and is, not surprisingly, a hub for water sports, happily restricted to quiet enjoyment: power boats, jet skis and other such intrusions are forbidden. The resort's brochure lists kayaking, sailing, windsurfing and canoeing. Good food is available in a bar with a beautiful view over the lake.

Across the road from the entrance to the Centre is the Burgage Cemetery, created in the 1940s to accommodate mortal remains and stone memorials transferred from the former burial ground that dates from monastic times and now lies beneath the waters of the lake. At the south end of the burial ground is St Mark's Cross. This tall granite twelfth-century sculpture has a ring connecting the four arms, but otherwise minimal decoration. Fine headstones from the eighteenth century and onwards stand among the modern graves.

The old road comes to an abrupt end a little way south of the cemetery and there is no public access to the castle. A turn to the west before the cul-de-sac sign leads to the main road, which, a little way to the south, crosses what was once a small tributary stream. It flowed through a broad, straight valley to join the Liffey and formed the county border between Wicklow and Kildare. After the dam was closed this valley created one of the most beautiful of all the aspects of the new lake. The former valley now forms a bay with pasture to the north and the ruined castle of Burgage romantically sited in the distance. The 1940s road that replaces the old turnpike at this point was built on a causeway pierced by concrete pipes.

The causeway divides the bay in two and for many years allowed car parking with a view towards the east, where the noble mountains of Black Hill and Moanbane sweep down to the lake. In the more distant background, the head of Mullaghcleevaun – whence flow all the highest source streams of the Liffey and King's River – peeps over the shoulder of Black Hill. While walkers and cyclists can continue to enjoy this view in safety, the high kerb makes it impossible for motorists to stop there.

Closer to hand and still accessible to motorists is the green hill of Baltyboys, which we shall meet after crossing the Burgage Bridge built by the ESB. To the west of the causeway the head of the bay forms sometimes a large pond and sometimes a grassy swamp, depending on the lake level. It is known as the Overflow by the angling fraternity.

The bridges

A left turn, south of the Overflow, leads to Burgage Bridge, the longest of the three large viaducts built by the ESB to join the roads on either side of the new lakes. Since childhood, I have loved and admired their simple functional design and considered them objects of beauty, even though some have made disparaging remarks about them. Though severe and functional, they are quietly elegant in their way and deserve better than to have been omitted from more than one recent volume on the bridges of Ireland.

The bridges were required to give headroom of six feet (1.8 metres) above the surface of the water. The possibility of round arches, as had been used in the old bridges, was considered and dismissed for two reasons, one practical, the other aesthetic. The conglomeration of clay, stones and large rocks that covered the bedrock in the valleys would have made foundations for true arches difficult and expensive to build. And the changing water levels would affect the shape of the arches in an unpleasing way. So the decision was taken to use paired piers.

Baltyboys Lower

Burgage Bridge leads to the lovely long hill, usually known as Baltyboys, the more convenient form of the official names of the adjacent townlands Boystown, or Baltyboys Upper, and Boystown or Baltyboys Lower. The names have an intriguing history and etymology. In the Talbotstown volume of his *Place Names of Co. Wicklow*, Liam Price dates their origin to 1531. The name Baltyboys originates from James Boys, Constable of Maynooth Castle, who received the land from the Earl of Kildare. 'Balty' derives from *Bailte*, the plural of *Baile*, and Price considered that this referred to the two divisions of the property.

Baltyboys House, originally built high above the river, has been transformed to a lakeshore dwelling.

Baltyboys House stands, surrounded by trees and parkland, a little way up the hill from the eastern end of the bridge, where there is a car park and beach. The original building was a typical two-storey Georgian country house, but it was later enlarged by the addition of a long wing towards the west. The house has a distinguished history, having been the home of a talented nineteenth-century writer and social commentator and of a supreme dancer and promoter of classical ballet.

The writer was Elizabeth Grant, a Scottish woman who, in India, married Henry Smith, a colonel and later a general in the imperial army. Smith inherited a rather run-down Baltyboys House and the couple moved there, improved the house and farm and lived in considerable comfort. Elizabeth established a school and kept diaries that give a detailed and valuable picture of life, high and low, in mid-nineteenth-century west Wicklow. They include the Famine years, when the family took its responsibilities to the destitute very seriously. Ten years of her activities have been made available by Dermot James and Séamus Ó Maitiú in *The Wicklow World of Elizabeth Smith 1840–1850.*

The dancer, born in Baltyboys as Edris Stannus in the summer of 1898, became better known as Dame Ninette de Valois. She lived at Baltyboys until the age of seven, when her father died and the family moved to England. There, having achieved fame as a child dancer, she came to have a profound influence on ballet throughout the world. W. B. Yeats invited her to come to Dublin in 1927 and establish the Abbey School of Ballet, which she directed for six years, returning to London in 1933, where she remained until her death in March 2001 at the age of 102.

The lakeshore at the west end of Humphrystown Bridge. The glacial till has been eroded to form the little cliff to the left; sand and gravel left behind by the waves form a beach. Willows grow on the damp clay soil.

A little way past the east end of the bridge, a laneway leads to the lakeshore and a very pleasant picnic place. When the water level is low, a broad sandy beach appears and it is possible to walk for many miles along the margin of the lake. At the northern tip of the Baltyboys headland, the action of the waves has cut away the soil and created a cliff all of two metres in height. This cliff provides a particularly good specimen of the glacial till which covers all the lower parts of the Liffey valley. The greater part of the material is a brown clayey mass. But many kinds of stones, large and small, stick out from it. The clay is carried away by the waves, but the stones fall out and the beach is liberally scattered with granite, greywacke and others. There are two interesting minor elements among these. One is a little patch of tarmacadam – all that remains of the surface of the pre-1940 road. The other is small pieces of slate, from a narrow vein in the Silurian strata which provided a small industry to the northwest of Blessington. Much more importantly, the hard slate created the natural dam and the Pooka's pools and the ideal site for the concrete barrier that contains the lake.

A profile of the glacial till soil that covers the margins of the lakes. It is being eroded by wave action and water currents, which carry away the fine clay particles and deposit stones and sand to form a beach. The roots of the grasses tie the soil so that it overhangs the cliff – but the grasses die because the soil cannot hold enough water to sustain them.

A little way up the hill above the cliff, a row of mature beech trees follows the curve of the headland. Much older than the lake, they had been planted along the side of the road that skirted the demesne of the big house. That was the road that had crossed the River Liffey by the former bridge at Burgage before being replaced by the higher ESB road that now divides the demesne parkland in two.

Humphrystown or Valleymount Bridge
From the picnic place the road goes around the headland and suddenly offers a view of the magnificent Lackan Lake – the name by which the great King's River portion of the reservoir is known. Side roads go up the hill to interesting places which we will visit on the western circuit (page 105), while the main road goes to cross the lake by way of Humphrystown or Valleymount Bridge.

The foundation stone to the left of the main entrance to Valleymount Church.

It replaces an earlier road which plunged down into the valley to the King's River. The western end of the bridge is in the townland of Humphrystown, which lies south of Boystown or Baltyboys Upper. To the east is the village of Valleymount.

Picnic places, furnished by the ESB at both ends of the bridge, are beautifully situated, giving a view of the Lackan Lake and looking across the water to the lofty but very damp-topped Moanbane and, beyond its left shoulder, the summit of Mullaghcleevaun from which Liffey tributaries flow northwards and King's River tributaries flow south. On the lower flanks of Moanbane is the quarrymen's settlement of Ballyknockan. To the north is the long shoulder of Lugnagun, which, although a relatively low spur rather than a high mountain, dominates much of the lake. Its lower, glacial till-covered slopes are green and divided by hedges. The summit ridge was planted with Sitka spruce which, when mature, bore a remarkable resemblance to a Mohican haircut. But they were clear-felled in 2012 and will take some decades to grow again.

The lakeshore at the east end of the bridge has more space, but its western partner is more interesting as a landform. A little way back from the lake, the Humphrystown park is mostly green pasture, though with a grove of willow, which grows on a patch of clayey material that does not drain as easily as the more gravelly soil nearby. At the top of the shore, the clay has been undermined by the action of the waves and forms a low yellow cliff. This clay is part of the lake-bed deposits of the original Glacial Lake Blessington, which disappeared 9,000 years ago. Perhaps the most interesting point about all this is that it is in one way a natural development of landscape, but in another artificial because the lake which makes the waves is man-made and, at the time of writing, less than seventy-five years old.

While the clay has been in place for millennia, the sandy beach is an entirely new phenomenon. The sand and nearby small stones have been left behind where the finer clay particles were carried away by the waves, to settle in deeper parts of the lake where they, in their turn, are making new sediments.

The shore at the east end of the bridge is similar to that on the other side. But the approach is different: where an open car park has been provided close to the road at the west end, the approach to the east is by a narrow pathway between stands of natural woodland. Willow and alder dominate the wood, making it a safe haven in summer for willow warbler and other small birds. In winter it provides food and refuge for long-tailed tit and redpoll.

Valleymount

Before the valley was flooded, the King's River flowed to the west of the village of Valleymount, passed beneath a former Humphrystown Bridge, meandered in a northeasterly direction towards Lackan and then northwest to join the Liffey to the north of Baltyboys. The King's River's wanderings between Humphrystown and Baltyboys, aided and abetted by torrential streams coming down from the granite mountains, created the broad valley below Ballyknockan and Lackan now covered by the Lackan Lake. Valleymount, by a happy chance, developed in the early nineteenth century on the 190-metre contour, about the same elevation as the top of the gorge at Pollaphuca, the highest practicable level for the surface of the reservoir. So the lake could be given its maximum depth and storage capacity without inundating the village. The other communities in the valley, Kilbride, Blessington, Lackan and Ballyknockan were all safely above this level.

Neither the village of Valleymount nor the townland are mentioned by Lewis, but the 1838 map shows the beginnings of a community there, even though it does not provide a name, in the label 'R. C. Chapel' to the east of the road. Built in 1803, the chapel continues to serve the faithful to this day. Just to the north of the chapel, the map shows a road leading off towards the east but it disappeared beneath the waters when the lake arrived. In addition to the chapel, the map shows two long roadside buildings to its south. They could have been single dwellings or terraced houses. About eleven other buildings are marked, nearly all of them to the east of the road.

The 25-inch map of 1881 shows a very much more substantial settlement. The chapel has become 'St Joseph's R. C. Church'. Two separate schools replace the long buildings and, down the road from the second school, is the Star Inn and then 'Valleymount House (Post Office)'. St Joseph's Church, within and without, remains the outstanding feature of the village.

Two pages on its history are pinned to the noticeboard inside the church. They are probably the work of former parish priest and outstanding local historian Father Richard Cantwell. He recounts a local legend that the numerous pinnacles that decorate both the church and the wall in front were inspired by returned emigrants from New Mexico in the 1830s.

After passing Valleymount, the road around the lake crosses an unnamed stream by a small ESB bridge. The valley of this stream to the north has an alder and willow swamp similar to that at the Humphrystown Bridge. As the road climbs, the landscape begins to show the influence of the acid soil derived from the granite of the Wicklow Mountains and the peat that grew to cover it. The

Built in 1803, the church of Valleymount is unique in style and its exterior was lavishly decorated by the quarrymen of neighbouring Ballyknockan.

pasture is poor and the fields small, hedges are few and trees are scarce, with the exception of a rectangular plantation of spruce on the flank of Moanbane. Stone walls rather than hedges mark the field boundaries and these are distinguished by the fence posts that have been placed in them. The posts are hewn from granite – the first indications that we are approaching the quarrying settlement of Ballyknockan.

Ballyknockan

Bits of Ballyknockan are scattered far and wide throughout the Liffey valley and much further afield. Granite quarries were established there in 1824 and the beautiful grey stone, flecked with black and white crystals, was cut and shaped to grace many of the finest buildings of Dublin in the course of very nearly two centuries. By the Liffeyside, Ballyknockan granite is particularly well displayed as the facing of the Civic Buildings completed on Wood Quay in 1994. The village is one of very few in Ireland that developed around a local industry rather than as the centre of a farming community. The history of the settlement, its quarrymen and their achievements may be read in *Ballyknockan: a Wicklow Stone Cutters' Village* by Séamas Ó Maitiú and Barry O'Reilly.

In contrast to the rigidity of the landlord-designed village of Blessington, the dwellings of Ballyknockan seem to have grown wherever a quarryman or stonecutter could find a patch of hillside with space for a cottage and garden. The result is a road system of baffling complexity serving a delightful collection of stone dwellings, some basic and simple, others with decorated details.

Some have been abandoned, providing the visitor with a feast of indigenous architectural detail. Others are very much alive. The quarries, now almost silent, are at the north end of the settlement.

The stone lion that guards a roadside of Ballyknockan. Known as the 'Stormont Lion', one story tells that it was carved to embellish the Northern Ireland Parliament building. But the more likely derivation is from the name of an estate across the valley to the west.

The Madonna of Ballyknockan stands in a little enclosure, overlooking the Lackan Lake, the Valleymount isthmus and Baltyboys Hill. She was created n 1864 by Ambrose Freeman, a member of the quarrying community.

Lackan to Oldcourt

After Ballyknockan and its quarries, the landscape of the lakeside reverts to the eighteenth-century pattern of scattered holdings and farmhouses with fields divided by hawthorn hedges. In the peaceful past, the badlands – steep hills with sheep pasture on granite-based soil – began just a little way to the east of the lake. In the centuries when the Pale existed, the descendants of the Anglo-Norman conquistadors had used the Liffey and the King's River as boundaries and left the land to their east to the dispossessed. To defend the fertile region they built the fortresses at Threecastles and Burgage. In more settled times, Blessington had come to serve as the market town for both the fertile green valley and the sheep from the hills. But Blessington was quite a long way from the hillside community above the King's River and a village with church and school grew up in the townland of Lackan to serve their needs.

Lackan Church east window. The foundation stone beneath the central pane reads 'AD 1811'.

A left turn in the village leads down the hillside to the beautifully situated church dedicated to Our Lady of Mount Carmel and built before Catholic emancipation. Further down the hill, on the shore of the lake, is a shrine to St Boden, who had other connections with the Liffey (see page 130). The saint was Bishop of Glendalough in the 1640s and the name commemorates his blessing of the well. Christiaan Corlett gives some details of remarkable happenings in its vicinity in the days before the lake drowned the holy well. Even more remarkable was the resuscitation of the well in more recent times. In 1978 the lake level was lowered to an unprecedented degree and the well reappeared. The ESB installed a pipe to lead to a patch of land on the shore together with a hand pump to raise the water from the depths.

From Lackan the road runs northwest towards Blessington, following the lower slopes of Lugnagun. Then it leaves the King's River portion of the lake to follow the expanded Liffey and meet the ESB's Blessington Bridge, built to the same design as those at Burgage and Valleymount. Measuring 146 metres, it is the shortest of the three.

Lackan Lake looking northwards to Lugnagun and Sorrel Hill.

The road continues eastwards, keeps close to the lakeshore for a kilometre, crossing a small inlet of the lake by the little Rundle Bridge and then moving away from the shore, which becomes hidden by woodland planted in the 1960s. In the townland of Woodend, an old stone-arched bridge crosses Woodend Brook, which enters the lake through a narrow bay just downstream. The name seems to imply the survival of trees going back for some centuries and a portion of Woodend Hill was covered with trees long before the post-war afforestation began in the Liffey valley.

After Woodend the road turns towards the northwest and the hamlet of Oldcourt. Oldcourt townland includes a broad stretch of gently sloping fertile land before it begins to rise steeply towards the east. The lowland was part of the floodplain that Anna Liffey had carved for herself. A laneway to the left at Oldcourt is the last remnant of a road which led to a ford on the river not far from the castle that commands the right bank.

Ballyward

A kilometre to the north is the classical Ballyward House, clearly visible from the road at the bridge of the same name. It is the furthest upstream of several 'big houses' in the setting of the green pastures and gently sloping land of the upper valley. Its neighbours downstream have been transformed to lakeside demesnes.

Downstream of the bridge at Ballyward, the river takes a double U-bend and then turns sharply from west to south where it forms part of the boundary of the townland of Threecastles and runs for a little at the bottom of a picturesque larch-clad hill. The sole survivor of a group of three stone custodians of the Pale stands by the roadside, looking across the river to the once hostile mountains.

Ballyward House. In the foreground is green pasture on the limestone-rich floodplain of the Liffey; background hills have granite soil and have been planted with Sitka spruce.

Ballyward Bridge.

At this point the Liffey is still flowing as a lowland river, and has not yet been swallowed up by the lake. Ballyward Bridge, opened in 1815, had three round-headed stone arches, a small one on each side and a large central span. The latter was swept away by the floods resulting from Hurricane Charlie in September 1986 and for the next twelve years the gap was filled by a Bailey bridge. According to its nameplate, the replacement was officially opened in November 1998. Faced with neat granite stonework, the three arches have been replaced by a graceful single concrete span.

Threecastles

A left turn shortly after Ballyward Bridge leads back towards the lake drive, crossing the Brittas River and passing through the village of Manor Kilbride to run, for a little, high above the Liffey where it flows at the foot of a steep slope. At the bottom of the hill, a small roadside parking space gives a view of ancient castle and modern lake.

An entry for the year 1547 in the *Annals of the Four Masters* tells a grisly tale of the end of an attack centred on one or more of the three castles of the townland's name:

> The rebels [Fitzgeralds] sustained a great defeat at Baile na dtri gCaislen from the English and from Brian-an-chogaidh, the son of Turlough O'Toole, in which the two sons of James, son of the Earl, namely, Maurice-an-fheadha and Henry, with fourteen of their people, were taken prisoners. They were afterwards conveyed to Dublin, and all cut in quarters, excepting Maurice, who was imprisoned in the King's castle, until it should be determined what death he should receive. Thus were these plunderers and rebels dispersed and scared; and although their career was but of short duration (one year only), they committed vast depredations.

The 1838 survey marks 'Site of a Castle' a little way to the east, but the third fortress seems to have disappeared by then. The surviving castle is a solid structure, the walls mainly of greywacke and limestone blocks, but with neatly carved granite surrounds for the doors and windows. Broken stonework indicates that the present-day west wall and doorway were built originally as indoor partitions and the castle was evidently very much bigger in the past, perhaps as long ago as the sixteenth-century skirmishes. Restored and repaired now, it stands with doors and windows barred to keep out both cattle and people. It was once accessible to both and, on more than one occasion, I climbed a wall to the doorway on the first floor which gave access by a spiral staircase to the roof.

The tower house guarding the Pale at Threecastles. Broken walls show that this is the remaining northern portion of a much larger original.

The view from the top is magnificent, commanding the valley of the Liffey for miles upstream and downstream. The importance of the castle lay in its position close to the Pale, on the eastern frontier of the fertile land of west Wicklow and Kildare. Across the Liffey the poorer, acid land was not worth the colonists' trouble and expense to annex. There dwelt the O'Tooles and O'Byrnes and other dispossessed Irish clans. They lived, as have mountain men the world over, to some extent by pillaging travellers and the descendants of land-grabbers of the lowlands. Hence the castle, from which it was possible to spot musterings on the far side of the river. A road ran past the fortress down to a ford on the Liffey and was abandoned when the lake was made. It can still be traced, lined by hawthorns which once formed hedges on each side but have since grown into straggly trees.

Between road and river lies a great, nearly level, area of land that drains badly and remains moist throughout the summer. This has

Window and door surroundings are of decorated granite, walls of greywacke.

made space for the development of a reed bed on a scale never before seen in the Liffey valley. In Ireland, reed beds provide a habitat for two small bird species, the reed bunting and the sedge warbler. Reed bunting remain throughout the year, never plentiful because they demand large territories. Sedge warbler are summer visitors, also territorial and well spread out, making a cheerful, if untuneful, chattery noise from the time of their arrival in spring until their departure in autumn. The grass that dominates this jungle is the giant fescue *Festuca arundinacea*.

Reed bed of *Festuca arundinacea* at Threecastles. Woodend Hill and village of Oldcourt in background.

Crosscoolharbour and Haylands

Two townlands lie between Threecastles and Blessington. The northern one, Crosscoolharbour, contains a large area of flat, slightly boggy fields, but the land rises in Haylands to the south and was a delta which developed in the course of the brief life of Glacial Lake Blessington. This delta consists of fine sand, washed and sorted according to grain size by the water as it entered the long-vanished lake. For the greater part of a century the sand has been quarried on a grand scale to provide the basis of the concrete used in the buildings of Dublin and its suburbs. Viewed from the road at the Blessington Bridge, the hillside to the west for the most part looks much the same as it has done since the enclosures of the eighteenth century: green pasture divided into patches by hedges, mainly hawthorn. The soil is rich in lime and is a home for a number of specialised plants, above all cowslip, pink-flowered centaury and yellow-wort; and the very scarce bee orchid. The untouched appearance of the landscape is something of an illusion. On the far side of the hills the sand and gravel have been removed by major quarrying works and much of the ground has been levelled.

Old Blessington bridge and mill

The old maps show no watermills on the main Liffey upstream of a 'Corn Mill' marked beside the bridge below Blessington. Perhaps, in the eighteenth and nineteenth centuries, when large-scale mills were being developed, those upper regions were a little too far away from civilisation and serviceable roads.

The head of water from the rather gently descending river in the Blessington valley was generated from a weir upstream which created a substantial millpond. This supplied a mill race which ran for 1.5 km on the right bank of the main river. The course of this mill stream was nearly a straight line and an aqueduct is marked on the 1838 map where it crossed the path of a small unnamed tributary of the Liffey. Although slightly less than half the length of the mill race at Palmerstown, this was the second longest in the Liffey valley and a very substantial undertaking.

Christiaan Corlett gives an account of the history of this mill. Owned by a gunsmith early in the nineteenth century, it was acquired in 1822 by William Merry, bailiff for the Blessington property of the Marquis of Downshire, who established a needle-making factory. This does not seem to have enjoyed a long life and in 1836 the premises was described as a 'corn mill in good repair', with an undershot mill wheel 12 feet (3.6 metres) high. For many years after the valley was flooded, the chimney of the mill building remained standing above the lake waters.

Photographs of the old bridge in Corlett's book show a graceful structure with a gentle curve supported by eight segmental arches with cut-stone surrounds. It was probably an eighteenth-century construction. Large fields in pasture slope gently down to the broad river and the banks are totally free of bushes of any kind. The mill buildings stand on the right bank.

The bridge was demolished by army engineers in September 1940 and Corlett provides photographs of the event, together with a report from the *Irish Press*. The action was accomplished with considerable ceremony, in the presence of senior officers. Whether there was any need to remove the bridge in the interests of reservoir management remains unknown. But a redundant bridge provided the soldiers with a rare practical opportunity to demonstrate their destructive skills. They applied three different techniques and also built a temporary tank trap on the shortly-to-be-flooded road.

The road to Blessington through Haylands, after the bridge, rises to pass a little pocket of beech woodland, overlooked on the right by the rectory, a substantial nineteenth-century building with a generous allowance of land. On the left, closer to the village, is the dispensary, evidently designed by the same hand and now partly hidden by a more recent health centre. A Downshire landlord contributed with these two old buildings to the spiritual and physical welfare of his tenantry.

This completes our 'Great Circuit', which makes a delightful day's outing for a Dubliner. Blessington offers a pleasing variety of hospitality. Sadly passed away is the charming Downshire House Hotel, presided over for decades by its owner, the delightful Mrs Byrne. The house on the main street happily remains, now an art gallery. This tour, however, omits some of the most notable features of the lakelands, which we cover in the next section. The Blessington Book Store deserves special mention, a welcoming café which also sells books and wool.

The steam tram: a diversion

For 52 years from 1888, a locomotive with a tall smoke stack hauled two double-decker carriages on a track along the edge of the main road and brought passengers and goods from Terenure to Blessington and, from 1895, to Pollaphuca. Its fortunes are described, with a fine collection of photographs, by Aidan Cruise in *The Dublin and Blessington Steam Tram*. The tramway died a natural death in 1932, by which time buses had developed sufficiently to provide a more effective form of public transport. In particular, the buses allowed a considerable extension of the route to such faraway places as Valleymount and Annalecka Cross.

Visiting the lakes: a western circuit

Having passed Burgage, the Liffey meandered towards the south through fertile pastureland dominated by big houses: Russborough and Russelstown on the right bank; Tulfarris and Baltyboys on the left. Baltyboys remains in private hands; Russborough is the centre of a great and glorious piece of public property; Tulfarris flourishes as a hotel and golf resort; and Russelstown is no more. Since 1941 the three survivors have changed from riverbank demesnes to lakeside neighbours. All this thanks to the creation of a band of slate in ancient geological times and the ingenuity of twentieth-century engineers. Tragically, the central hub of gorge and dam at Pollaphuca are intransigently barred against enjoyment by the people of Ireland who, at least technically, are its owners. Happily, much remains to be seen of this part of the Liffey valley and access is easy.

Russelstown

A large sign on the right-hand side of the road 3 km south of Blessington invites the visitor to enjoy the many splendours of Russborough – an invitation we will accept in the following section. An unobtrusive turn to the left at the same point leads to a secluded lakeshore car park, screened from the road by a delightful forestry plantation. About twenty years after the completion of the waterworks the ESB decided to plant conifers over much of its lakeside property, following a period of renting it for grazing. Russelstown Wood is the most easily accessible of these and has the added attraction of a footpath leading through it to an even more secluded reed-fringed inlet and then to the lakeshore itself with a distant view of Baltyboys House. Now about fifty years old, the spruces – Sitka and Norway – and some other conifers have reached maturity. The canopy is high and plenty of light penetrates, so the understorey is bright and open and abounds in wild flowers.

The bay at Russellstown, populated by reed beds and fishermen's boats.

Russborough

Often described as the most beautiful of the great country houses of Ireland, Russborough spreads to the west of the road in the townland of Russelstown. Looking across the Liffey valley, it also enjoys one of the finest settings, from the point of view both of people in the house and of passers-by. When Russborough was built and the demesne planned in the mid-eighteenth century, neither road nor lake had been conceived. The main road ran behind the house to its north and west. The front looked to the east, over parkland and the valley to the distant blue mountains of Moanbane and Black Hill. The river itself flowed at the foot of a steep bank and was hidden from aristocratic view.

The situation and outlook changed with the construction in 1829 of the turnpike from Dublin to Carlow that provided a new route from Blessington to Pollaphuca. This road passes in front of the house, but is kept well away from it by the demesne lake. The walls around Russborough are as high and forbidding as those of any grand Irish house; but Russborough's were lowered in a direct line with the house so that travellers on the road have a wonderful view of the mansion, standing on a green hillside overlooking a great expanse of pasture with some fine old trees. Rocque's map of 1760 shows a very much bigger pond than exists today and many more isolated trees. But otherwise little has changed.

The view from the road is of a central block with wings on each side, connected by curved colonnades. Beyond the wings are arched gateways leading to the coach- and stableyards on the left and kitchen quarters on the right, screened by low walls. This style, which became very popular in eighteenth-century Ireland, dates to the vision of the sixteenth-century Venetian Andrea Palladio. The entrance gate to Russborough is away to the right as you face the house and the driveway is marked by an avenue of lime trees.

Russborough owes its origin to the success of a family of brewers in Dublin. Joseph Leeson, heir to the founder of the firm, inherited a fortune on his father's death and decided to invest in a magnificent country house. A Member of the Dublin Parliament from 1743 to 1756, Joseph remained an important public figure, ultimately ennobled as First Earl of Milltown.

In 1741 he engaged Richard Cassels, the German architect, to design the house. Cassels, who settled in Ireland in the 1720s and changed his name to Castle, was responsible for a number of the finest buildings in the land, among

The north colonnade of Russborough.

them Leinster House and Carton – where he died in 1751 while still working on all three commissions. Russborough was completed about 1756 under the direction of Francis Bindon.

Great houses built in the first half of the eighteenth century had strict classical lines on the outside, with well-proportioned but very uniform windows. The main pediment above the door is supported by massive pillars, but otherwise there is little enough ornament. Russborough has more embellishment than usual in the form of classical sculptured figures in the colonnades, but these are invisible from a distance and the simple design is what meets the eye.

Within the house, the scene is very different. The fashion in Ireland at the time was for baroque plasterwork, and this has rarely been developed on such an exuberant scale as in Russborough. All the ceilings are richly decorated and the main staircase has a magnificent display. Two of the greatest artists of the time were the Italian brothers Paul and Philip Francini and the work in the saloon, the library and the music room is believed to be theirs. The plaster reliefs on the stairway have hunting scenes and include a portrait of the First Earl.

The stucco work is generally confined to the ceilings, but in the drawing room it extends down the walls and forms four oval surrounds made specially to frame four pictures. These scenes of harbours and shipping, by Joseph Vernet, were bought for the Earl in Rome in 1750.

The first two of Lord Milltown's three wives died young but the third outlived both the earl and his heir, dying in 1842 at the age of 100. Meanwhile, the Second Earl inherited the estate and, at the end of the eighteenth century, Russborough suffered its first and only serious damage in its 250 years as a family home. In 1798 first the United Irishmen and then English troops occupied it. The Irish treated the house with respect, but the English pulled down some of the roofing for firewood and ruined the outer buildings. Fortunately, the fine work of the main block survived.

The original family connection ended in 1931 when the estate was sold to Captain Denis Daly. The Dalys were able to repair much of the deterioration which had taken place over a long period of neglect. But, apart from being something to admire from the road, to the public it was essentially a private house.

Then came the change that transformed Russborough to one of the treasure houses of Ireland, with a welcome for anybody who is willing to pay a modest fee for admission. It was bought in 1952 by Sir Alfred Beit, who was looking for somewhere to live and in which to keep the fabulous collection of paintings and sculpture begun by his uncle and to which he had added.

Sir Alfred established the Beit Foundation, under which both house and paintings have become the property of the people of Ireland. Following two robberies, the most valuable of the paintings are now kept in the National Gallery, but there are a great many superb works still in the house, among them an interesting eighteenth-century view of the Liffey at Islandbridge. The special attraction of Russborough is that you see these masterpieces of several centuries hanging in surroundings which, although large and elaborate, have a feeling of being in a home rather than in an impersonal gallery.

Today's visitors to Russborough can enjoy light meals in refurbished servants' quarters and view the interior of the house on guided tours of the apartments with their notable collections of furniture, paintings and sculpture. The greater part of the parkland that surrounds the house is fenced off to contain a tenant farmer's cattle. But a walkway has been provided around this fence and there is plenty of open space for casual wandering, in contrast to the necessarily supervised experience within the house.

Bishopslane and Bishopsland

In days gone by, the Liffey a little way south of Russelstown formed the county border for about 2 km. The flooding of the valley resulted in County Kildare being presented with a short stretch of lakeshore. This lies in the extensive townlands of Bishopslane and Bishopsland – testimonies to the good old days when the Church and its princes enjoyed very substantial temporal wealth and lands. A large car park close to the road, 2 km to the south of Russborough, gives easy access to a view of the lake and over Baltyboys hill to Mullaghcleevaun and its companion mountains. Pedestrian access to the lake from the car park is barred by a formidable green chain-link fence.

Built to protect wayfarers from the perils of the adjacent geographical features, the footpath beside the fence does ultimately lead to a more welcoming part of the shore. The cliffs, invisible from the path, are composed of the glacial

Cowslips abound on the lime-rich soil around the lakes.

A warning to wayfarers at Bishopslane car park.

till which is being eroded by the action of the waves when the lake level is high. This leads to a constant risk of the occasional landslide and other hazards listed on a helpful notice. Those who keep to the straight and narrow are rewarded by a very pleasant walk among cowslips and other wild flowers.

The pooka and his pool

Pookas live in hollows, known by a number of variations of the Irish *poll* in many parts of Ireland, but the Liffey's Pollaphuca remains the most splendid and was even more so in the days before the dam was built. The dam itself is a very imposing structure and one which has served the people of Ireland well for more than seventy years. But, even though relatively few visitors now living have set eyes on it, there is still a feeling of nostalgia for the times when a great cascade plunged down through a series of three pools. The middle one was the home of the Pooka himself, a protean sprite whose preferred manifestation was that of a coal-black stallion.

One memorable day in 2015, not many months after the preceding paragraph was written, I went with the surviving members of the *Book of the Liffey* team, Elizabeth Healy, Seamus Cashman and Gerard O'Flaherty, to visit the gorge. It was a mild November day, following a very wet weekend. We walked with some difficulty down the slippery track towards the river to a background noise of rushing water. Turning a corner near the bottom of the slope we were rewarded with the expected view of the arch of the bridge.

But there was very much more to it than that. The cascade was there again, as large as it had been in its past life: one of the most splendid sights in the entire Irish landscape. The falling water event is rarer than in former times when the unrestricted river descended the slaty cliffs. The appearance of the torrent, since the building of the dam, has required a combination of high reservoir level and excessive rainfall.

The waterfall of Pollaphuca in the very wet winter of 2015–16. The photo shows the lower two of the three cascades, with the water flowing from the Pooka's own pool.

The ancient and recent geology of the gorge is complicated. The Liffey takes a sharp turn to the right, to head briefly west, then south and gradually north towards Ballymore Eustace. Most of the rock strata are sandstones and greywackes of Silurian age. But a narrow strip of slate running from north to south separates the two. It is part of a stratum once quarried in the townland of Slate Quarries a few miles north of Blessington. Much harder than its neighbours, the slate formed a natural dam, which would in time be enveloped in concrete by the ESB. Besides causing the triple cascade, this dam had the effect of making the upper Liffey behave very much like a lowland stream, meandering gently through a broad valley. It also prevented salmon and eel from ever reaching the upper waters.

For centuries, the gorge forced the main road from Dublin to Baltinglass and towns further south to divert through Ballymore Eustace. The route was straightened in the 1820s when Alexander Nimmo built a bridge across it – which was constructed so well that it has comfortably taken nearly 200 years of increasingly heavy traffic.

Born in Kircaldy in 1783 and educated in Scotland, Nimmo, polymath and engineer, came to Ireland in 1811 to make a study of bogland. He was subsequently employed to survey the fisheries of the west coast and to design harbours, great and small. Nimmo built a home for himself in Connemara but also had a town house, not far from the Liffey, at 78 Marlborough Street in Dublin. There he died tragically early in January 1832 at the age of 49.

A formidable engineering achievement, his bridge at Pollaphuca is also a work of art. The pointed arch may have been the best practical solution to the

The parapet and arch of Nimmo's magnificent bridge at Pollaphuca viewed from downstream on a summer's day.

The former tram – and later bus – station at Pollaphuca.

problem of crossing the gorge, but he added decorations to it in the form of battlemented parapets. Built to be admired, as well as used, views of the bridge today are less easily obtained than they were.

The gorge had a long history as a beauty spot. Early in the nineteenth century, G. N. Wright was an enthusiastic admirer. His *Guide to the County of Wicklow* was published in 1822, before Nimmo's bridge and the present road were built. So he sets out from Ballymore:

The celebrated fall of the River Liffey, called Pol-a-Phuca, or the Demon's hole, is about one mile from the village of Ballymore Eustace. In rainy seasons, when the river is much swoln, the fall is calculated to be 100 feet in height. This is to be understood as combining the altitudes of the three stages constituting the cascade. The chasm through which the water rushes is only forty feet wide, lined on each side with perpendicular masses of Greywacke rock. The centre fall is an extraordinary and terrific object. Here the whole body of water composing the stream of the Liffey rushes down with the utmost impetuosity into a circular basin of stone, worn perfectly smooth, the form of which imparts to the water a rotatory motion, which Seward compares to the eddy on the coast of Norway, called the Navel of the Sea, a vortex whose power of ingulphing is so great, that no vessel dares approach it. Across this chasm a bridge is now about to be thrown, to continue the new line of the road to Enniscorthy; the span of the arch will be 60 feet, the altitude of the chord above the upper fall 48, and from the battlements will be had a direct perpendicular view into the whirlpool just now described, and which gives name to the waterfall. When this work of difficulty will be completed, the beauty of the scene will certainly be increased, and the execution of so bold a design will most assuredly stamp a high degree of professional reputation on the undertaker, Mr Bergen.

The scenery on each side of the fall might be made very interesting and beautiful by a very trifling expense in planting. One side was planted, some years since, by the late Earl of Miltown, whose property it is; but the other side of the glen, belonging to Colonel Wolfe, is quite naked and barren, unproductive to the landlord and ungrateful to the eye of the picturesque tourist. It is said that the late Earl had actually agreed with the landlord of this bank for the fee-simple, and resolved upon planting and improving it, but that destructive blight to all the best hopes of Ireland, the last rebellion, disgusted him with any farther attempts to improve. Upon Lord Miltown's side of the glen there is a care-taker, who receives visitors, and points out the beauties of the place with great civility and attention; and pretty cottages, summer-houses, grottos, banqueting room, &c., are scattered through the hanging wood; seats, too, are placed in the most advantageous places for viewing each particular inclination in the waterfall, and many circumstances conspire to render the grounds at Pol-a-Phuca a very pleasing retreat to while away part of a midsummer's day. Its distance from Dublin, 16½ miles, is just that limit which permits a party, leaving town early in the morning, to dine in a summer-house on the river's side, and after amusing themselves in admiring the sublimity of the waterfall, to return in the evening to Dublin.

About ten years later, in the *Topographical Dictionary*, Lewis described the completed bridge and an element of improvement in the landscaping:

Immediately over the basin, on the line of the new turnpike road from Blessington to Baltinglass, is a picturesque bridge of one pointed arch springing from rock to rock, built in an antique style from a design by the late Alex. Nimmo, Esq. at an expense, including the land arches and approaches, of £4074.15; the span of the arch is 65 feet, the altitude of the chord above the upper fall is 47 feet, and the height of the keystone of the arch above the bed of the river is 150 feet. The late Earl of Miltown took a lively interest in this picturesque spot, which he embellished by planting one side of the glen forming part of his estate, making walks, and creating rustic buildings in various places, besides a banqueting-room, 45 feet long by 25 wide, from which there is a delightful view of the falls and the bridge, with the perpendicular rocks partly planted, and the upper moss seat appearing through the arch; but owing to the disturbances of 1798 he went abroad, and some time after sold it to Col. Aylmer, who is now the proprietor, and has appointed a person to take proper care of it, by whom accommodation has been prepared for the numerous visiters that resort hither from Dublin and elsewhere, and seats have been placed in the most advantageous situations for obtaining different views of the fall; a rustic seat above the head of the fall commands an excellent view of the cataract, bridge, lower rustic seat, and banqueting-hall, with the windings of the river.

The beauty of Pollaphuca, as Wright and Lewis saw it, owed nearly as much to the behest of the Earls of Milltown as it did to Mother Nature. That bounteous lady indeed created the steep rock faces and the outcrops which forced the water to hurl itself down through the gorge. But nowadays there is such a luxuriant jungle of mostly native woodland that the gorge and the river are very difficult to see. In the past, the steepness of the banks and frequency of flooding effectively prevented grazing and the valley was well wooded. The slope of the land on the Milltown side is generally less than on the property of Colonel Wolfe, on the left bank, which remains too steep for much tree growth. The Milltowns, whose estate ran by the riverbank from Russborough to the gorge, apparently had most of the trees and bushes felled to create the romantic garden of the nineteenth century. This is a case where deliberate landscaping undoubtedly enhances the appearance of the land and where wilderness hides its beauty.

Access to the gorge nowadays is very restricted. The walls of the bridge are so high that anyone under six feet tall is unable to get a view of the defile. Even the tallest person can see little more than the tops of the trees that hide the water. The only public approach is through the grounds of the Poulaphuca House and Bar. A gap in their wall leads to an overgrown path which winds its way down the bank and gives the best, if limited, view of this once spectacular gorge.

Poulaphouca House and Bar, the remnant of past teahouses and dancing rooms of the nineteenth century. The avenue gives a fine view of the Dry Bridge and a faintly perilous path leads from near the house to the bottom of the gorge and a view of Nimmo's bridge and the (usually dry) waterfall.

The 1838 map marks a 'Ballroom' close to the riverbank on the inside of a U-bend 300 metres to the west of the bridge. This, and other buildings, have long since disappeared. A survivor of a later phase in the tourist trap is the tram station, now a private house with a well-kept garden on the steep right bank. The owners have carefully preserved, on an ornamented gable, a sign informing the public that 'G. S. R. motor bus stops here'.

Work for the water: the Pollaphuca dam

The ESB's book *50 Years on the Liffey* tells of how, from March 1940, when the process of filling the reservoir began, engineers

> ... walked the fields around Ballymore checking for springs which would suggest that the hills towards Bishopsland and Russborough were not holding back the water. The stability of the hill barrier was further tested by the fact that the dam was not filled to completion in one continuous process but was partially filled and dropped over a period of nearly eighteen months. But there were no tell-tale signs of leakage and the lake water never emerged beyond the perimeter fence.

The Pollaphuca dam is 31 metres high and 79 metres wide at the crest. Nearly 10,000 cubic metres of rock were excavated for the foundations and 18,000 cubic metres of concrete were used to build the dam. There is a second, much smaller, dam in the townland of Britonstown, a kilometre to the east over the hill from Pollaphuca. It closes off the Dry Valley, the prehistoric course cut by Anna Liffey, but abandoned by her in favour of the Pooka's gorge. Until the lake was created, this valley hung incongruously, high above the river bed.

The crest of the principal dam can be glimpsed from the road to the north. It is surmounted by engines which drive winches to raise and lower the sluice gates to adjust the level of the lake. Across the road from them stands the octagonal Valve House which contains the control system for diverting water for the use of Dubliners from the lake to the treatment plant nearby in Bishopsland.

The main dam was made in a narrow part of the gorge, at a point upstream of the waterfall. The usual arrangement for hydropower is to have the turbines close to the foot of the dam. At Pollaphuca it was possible to get a greater head of water by placing the generators further down the valley, so they are installed in a turbine house about 400 metres away from the dam.

The water is brought there under the road through a concrete-lined pressure tunnel, 5 metres in diameter. Excavating it through the hard slate and sandstone was a formidable task and progress was limited to 8 or 9 metres a week. The upper end of the tunnel is protected by a screen and can be closed by a steel door, operated by a switch far away at Turlough Hill in Wicklow Gap.

When the water rushing down the length of this tunnel is shut off, its momentum makes it want to react violently, putting a tremendous strain on the system. This energy is allowed to dissipate itself by surging into a special tank at the lower end of the tunnel. This 'surge tank', the most impressive construction at the power station, is a colossal tower, 36 metres high and 20 metres in diameter, made from riveted plates of steel. When the turbines are shut off, the water in the tank can surge to about 8 metres above the level of the

The surge tower and adjacent turbine housing at Pollaphuca.

reservoir nearby. The top of the tank is 9 metres above the maximum lake level to allow a margin for safety.

Underneath the surge tank the roof of the pressure tunnel is open so that the water is free to escape into the tank. The tunnel forks into two conduits which slant slightly downhill to a valve house where the water can be held or released by butterfly valves. These valves command the entrance to the two penstocks, steel pipes 3.6 metres in diameter, through which the water rushes in its final descent to the turbines. The penstocks bring the water down a further 29 metres.

The turbines at Pollaphuca and at Leixlip are based on the principle developed by Viktor Kaplan in Austria in 1920. The water is led through a snail-shaped tube to the turbine, which has a vertical axle and rotates in a horizontal plane 300 times a minute. The pitch of the blades can be adjusted from within the hub, to allow the turbine to rotate at a constant speed no matter how high or low the lake surface may be. Each of the two units generates 15 megawatts under a head of 47 metres. At full load, 40 tons of water pass through the system every second.

Pollaphuca began to generate electricity in 1944. The power is transmitted at 110 thousand volts to Inchicore, where it joins the national network. The output is about 30 million kilowatt hours per year.

The Dry Bridge

Perhaps surprisingly, neither Wright nor Lewis mention this very remarkable structure a couple of hundred metres to the south of Nimmo's creation. On the road southwards from Pollaphuca the Dry Bridge crosses the more accurately but equally unusually named Dry Valley. There is no reasonable doubt that it was a path of the Liffey in times long past, before it cut its way down through the Pooka's slatey gorge. In wet weather a mere trickle flows beneath its bridge and in times of drought no water whatever can be seen. The road crosses the valley by a causeway with a central portion pierced by a barrel vault, looking as if the structure might have been inspired by one of the neighbouring castles of the Pale. The roadside parapets are undecorated stone walls, so you drive over the bridge and valley without any indication of the extraordinary structure or landform beneath. The avenue of the Poulaphuca House and Bar gives a good view and mildly difficult access. O'Keeffe and Simington provide a date of the early 1820s and suggest that the designer was John Killaly, who worked closely with Nimmo.

The Dry Bridge from downstream.

Baltyboys Upper

The first turn to the left after Pollaphuca gives a good view of the Dry Valley and then the road heads eastwards with occasional glimpses of the Pollaphuca portion of the lake whenever breaks in the hedges permit. It leads to where the former stately home of Tulfarris now offers leisure in country club style. After passing the entrance to Tulfarris the road continues to the northeast. The first turn on the right takes a very narrow route to the ancient Pilgrim's Way to Glendalough. A tempting diversion would extend the trip to pass through the splendid Hollywood Glen where Glacial Lake Blessington once made an exit. But that belongs to the Slaney catchment and is therefore unmentionable in a Liffey book. The second right turn leads to two very remarkable burial grounds, both giving beautiful views across the Lackan Lake to Ballyknockan, where the water laps the lower slopes of Moanbane.

One lies beside the road and is the last resting place of generations of quarrymen, stonemasons and their families. Still in use, it contains a great variety of memorial stones. Some possibly never bore inscriptions, and some have beautifully carved lettering from the eighteenth century. Two features are of particular interest. The first is that the cemetery is divided in two by a granite outcrop that thwarted the last wishes of the quarrymen by making the soil too shallow to accept their bodies. The second is the neat boundary wall, with well-made gateposts, a final tribute to the work of the community of stone carvers.

Granite walls surround the burial ground of Baltyboys where the bodies of generations of quarrymen rest.

The second burial ground is hidden away on the edge of the golf club nearby, which is signposted at a junction to the south of the first. Cleared of scrub and furnished with a new gate by the local community in 2014, it is notable for the absence of memorials of any kind, other than a pair of modern wall plaques.

One of these announces that it is a Quaker burial ground. The other pays tribute to the enthusiasm of local people, encouraged by the parish priest and historian of Valleymount, Father Richard Cantwell. Needless to say, all the stonework is of granite. The left-hand plaque notes that the last interment was in 1810. This date explains the absence of memorials: Quakers in Ireland forbade their use for more than a century until the 1860s.

The first Quaker birth recorded at Baltyboys was that of Jeremiah Peisley, born to Peter and Ann in 1679. Members of the Society of Friends had settled there in the 1670s and existing deeds record the sale to them of 297.3 acres of land in 1678. The small community of thirteen families prospered throughout the eighteenth century. Records of their births, marriages and deaths virtually ceased from 1798, and only one family seems to have stayed there after the Rising. Between 1801 and 1804 John and Mary Williams had four children, but there is no record of what became of them. In 1809 Ann Eves died and hers was the last named interment in the burial ground

The Quaker burial ground at Baltyboys.

John Hussey, who has a profound knowledge of the region, believes that Quakers settled in Baltyboys as agents in the wool trade. As we have seen, the King's River and the Liffey in these parts divide rich land to the west from the poor mountain pastures to the east, and in the seventeenth century Blessington became the major centre for marketing wool from the highlands. The movement of sheep to Dublin was a feature for centuries and the Blessington sheep fair in

September persisted into the 1950s before giving way to trading centred on marts. John has found evidence of 'booleying' – the movement of sheep to the upland pastures for the summer, together with their shepherds – on the road over Sorrel Hill, among other places. His book, *The Quakers of Baltyboys, County Wicklow, Ireland, 1678 to 1800s*, was published in 2017.

Heading back to Pollaphuca, the road downhill and southwards from the Quaker Burial Ground leads by way of Humphrystown Bridge towards Valleymount, Ballyknockan and the long way back to the Liffey and Blessington. A shorter route may be found by taking the right turn before the bridge to go through Humphrystown by a little-used road which zigzags up the hill for about a kilometre, passing a Coillte car park and then returning to Pollaphuca – where the lakes began and where we finish our visit.

5 | The farmlands

The greater part of the Liffey valley upstream of the lakes is hilly moorland. Nobody lives or has ever attempted to live on the highest ground: too much rain and too little lime in the land. In the distant past it was a place for hunting the native red deer, which thrive on the heather and poor grasses. Eventually sheep were introduced and, given very large land holdings or common grazing, a community of mountainy men prospered – up to a point. Dwellings were few and small until the late eighteenth-century establishment of Kippure House on the outermost edge of the productive farmland.

The lower parts of the upper valley, those covered by the limestone soil deposited during the last long cold period of the Ice Age, were fertile. They came to be protected by the Pale and they extend beyond the valley far to the north and west. But the point of plunge of Anna Liffey at Pollaphuca brings her firmly into the land of farms, mostly large and, with the remarkable exception of the Curragh of Kildare, bearing all the traces of the enclosures of the eighteenth century: many hedges and horses, few forests, some large towns and villages and a considerable degree of comfort and prosperity.

The pattern of the agricultural landscape from Ballymore Eustace all the way to Leixlip is of large and small fields almost indiscriminately scattered. The fields are bounded mostly by hawthorn hedges and are given to grazing rather than tillage for the most part, although there are extensive wheat and barley crops and an increasing area of maize. The great tradition of use of the fertile lowlands, beginning 5,000 years ago with the arrival of the first farmers of the Neolithic period, was rearing cattle. In the Iron Age cattle were the foundation of wealth and the prize in the many battles between clans, epitomised in the Táin, the cattle driving of Cooley, delightfully translated by Thomas Kinsella in the 1960s.

But there was also something of a pattern of those who were enriched by their cattle spending their profits on horses – some becoming even richer, others falling by the wayside. This worship of the horse has a long history in the Liffey valley, with evidence that the Curragh had already developed as a racetrack in the Iron Age, perhaps 2,000 years ago. The wealth generated by bloodstock is clearly displayed in the contrast between the immaculately clipped hedges of the stud farms and the rather less regimented boundaries to cattle pasture.

Water for the Dubs

Something of a roadside memorial to a revolution in the supply of water to the people of Dublin stands in the form of a tall white octagonal building, across the road from the crest of the Pollaphuca dam. Above its door the letters DCWW in bold Roman script indicate that this is the property of Dublin Corporation Waterworks. Beneath this Valve House lies the deeply buried pipe which carries water from the lakes to the treatment plant just over a kilometre to the northwest.

The Valve House – an expatriate property of Dublin City Council.

A little to the north of the Valve House, a road leads through Bishopsland to the gate to the treatment plant and a view of the great concrete settling tanks where the water rests before being led off to sink gently through the sand filters. Before filtration, the water is dosed with alum, which flocculates the humic acids that give it a pale brown colour. Flocculation and filtration allow the citizens of Dublin to enjoy crystal-clear water. The water also receives chlorine, to kill a host of bacteria – both harmless and harmful to humans – and fluorine to save the consumers from tooth decay. In the good old days, the abundant brown soupy slimy sludge was permitted, from time to time, to befoul the Liffey. Since 1987 it has been collected, compressed and removed for recycling as a solid fertiliser.

The Pale and the church

The greater part of Bishopsland is something of a plateau, bordered on three sides by a U-bend of the Liffey. To the east the river plunges down through the Pollaphuca gorge. The southern border is less steep and the valley since the 1940s has been partly filled by the Golden Falls Reservoir. To the west Ballymore Eustace lies in the valley. The water treatment plant occupies much of the western edge of the plateau, standing high above the village. The Pale ran along this edge and a plaque on the wall to the left of the gate of the treatment plant draws attention an earthen ridge nearby. This is one of the very few remaining pieces of the original earthworks of the great defensive structure. Most of the earthen part has long since disappeared. Towers such as those of Burgage and Threecastles are the principal survivors.

The Pale Ditch at the gateway of the Ballymore Eustace Water Treatment Station. The structure probably had a covering of trees in its functional days but the stone wall looks like a modern addition built to preserve the bank.

Surrounded by trees, the Protestant church stands on an ancient religious site. Two Celtic crosses in the churchyard imply Early Christian presence. The church building that was there in 1798 was destroyed during the Rising and replaced in 1820 by the present one, dedicated to St John. Protestant worshippers from the village faced a steep climb to the church every Sunday. Their Catholic neighbours, since shortly before emancipation in 1829, have enjoyed a more convenient site at a lower level.

Golden Falls

The Pollaphuca turbines normally run only at peak periods of electricity demand and then close down. The water driving them at full power flows so quickly that if left to its own devices it would cause serious flooding downstream. This is prevented by the dam just upstream of Ballymore Eustace at Golden Falls, 1,500 metres down the river from the main power station. Anna Liffey danced over rocky rapids there, a fine sight according to the old photographs – but less impressive than the Pooka's cascade. Wider and lower than the barrier at Pollaphuca (15.5 metres high and 90 metres wide), the ESB dam created a smaller reservoir in the little valley upstream. This can hold all the water from a sustained three-and-a-half-hour flow through Pollaphuca and that is quite enough to give the desired safety margin.

The water from Golden Falls is released much more slowly, through a propeller turbine which produces four megawatts and a smaller 'house generator' with an output of 250 kilowatts. The house generator supplies the power needed for heat and light to control the machinery that operates both power stations. The Golden Falls turbine uses 30,000 litres of water per second and this flow is acceptable in the river downstream.

The secluded reservoir that the dam created is the home of the Golden Falls Waterski Club. Directions to the centre are provided on its website and the path leads to a peaceful lake, surrounded by very traditional affluent parkland.

The Golden Falls Reservoir, a safe haven for waterski enthusiasts.

Ballymore Eustace

J. N. Wright recounts the past glories of this village, but is less enthusiastic about its state in the 1820s:

> The village of Ballymore Eustace is distant about two miles from Lord Miltown's seat of Russborough, the road lying through a rich vale, watered by the River Liffey. The name Ballymore Eustace means the great town of Eustace; it was once a place of some consequence, and founded by the Eustaces, an ancient and respectable family, shortly after the English invasions. The Eustaces are descended from Maurice Fitzgerald, to whom the cantred or barony of Naas was granted by Henry II, to Eustace, fourth son of a branch of that family …
>
> Ballymore Eustace is now reduced to complete insignificance; formerly the great southern road passed through it, but that being turned through Kilcullen, the village is much decayed and neglected. It is, however, a market and post town, and fairs are held there on the 26th Aug. and 29th Oct. The Liffey passes through the town beneath a handsome stone bridge.

By 1837 there had been some improvement and Lewis refers to the 'large manufactory' that Christopher Drumgoole had erected nearby, which employed 700 people. The village stands – or perhaps wanders – in marked contrast with the landlord-designed Blessington and its broad, straight street. Established nearly five centuries earlier, Ballymore just grew, with houses built wherever they might fit. The result was a charming, rambling collection of dwellings and shops with roads squeezing in as they could, a church on the hillside nearby and the six-arched 'handsome stone bridge' built to carry the trunk road over the Liffey.

The 'large manufactory' and mill pond at Ballymore Eustace.

Lewis gives a little more detail than Wright on the bridge, mentioning its six arches. Marked on Taylor's map of 1783, it was already old by Lewis's time and continues to be in use. Construction is of random rubble, but with cut-stone finish to the piers, the six segmental arches and the parapets and triangular cut-waters on the upstream side.

The handsome stone bridge of six arches crosses the Liffey at Ballymore Eustace, immediately downstream of the ruins of the woollen mill.

The Eustace family had built a castle in medieval times, but this was completely demolished not long before the survey made for Lewis. It seems likely that the castle stood in a commanding position above the ford where the bridge would be built in the eighteenth century. Downstream of Golden Falls, the Liffey takes a sharp U-bend towards the west and the village was built on high ground within the bend, protected by the river which makes its way onwards through a broad floodplain.

The hydro dam, built upstream of the old bridge at Golden Falls in 1940, dominated the view of the valley for more than one generation but now, after 80 years, is almost completely hidden from the road by the trees that have grown up below it.

Ballymore Eustace today is a thriving village again, greatly expanded thanks to its position within commuter range of Dublin and Naas. Just upstream of the bridge, on the right bank, the substantial ruins of the woollen mill still stand – with a major restoration project in place in 2015. A little way back from the

Mill workers' cottages and other nineteenth-century buildings in Ballymore Eustace.

river and up the hill from the bridge a neat row of mill workers' cottages is a reminder of nineteenth-century industry and an element of concern for the well-being of the employees.

There is public access to the riverside on the right bank of the Liffey, above and below the bridge. The upstream bankside was until 2014 something of a park by default: nobody had made any serious attempt to develop it, but neither did anyone assert ownership. Access was via a rusty gate beside the bridge. This is the site of the great woollen mill that provided employment for hundreds in the nineteenth century and was described briefly, but enthusiastically, by Lewis.

The extraordinary mill race, almost making a circle, began at a weir immediately upstream of Golden Falls and flowed northwards, nearly parallel to the river. Its elevation is marked as 416 feet, while the river downstream of the falls is 397 feet, giving a head of some 4 metres. The mill race curves eastwards, away from the river, and then takes a U-turn to the southwest, to reach the woollen factory. The reason for this unusual course lies in the landscape at Ballymore Eustace. Downstream of Golden Falls the Liffey swings towards the west and runs at the bottom of a steep hill that follows the curve. The mill race was cut into this hillside to maintain a high level. A weir is marked on the 1838 map opposite the mill and may have carried water from the tail race to power another turbine downstream.

Harristown and neighbours

Between Ballymore Eustace and Kilcullen, Anna Liffey wanders from side to side of a broad floodplain. The roads on both banks run well away from her and the houses are built on high ground on either side of the valley. Before 1940 and the building of the dams, floods were uncontrolled and farms, roads and houses kept out of reach of the rising waters. The descent of the river is so gentle that there is little head of water and, consequently, very few mills. The first was in the townland of Mullaghboy, 7 km downstream of the great woollen mill of Ballymore. It had a very long weir, extending nearly parallel to the riverbank for 220 metres and creating an island. The water provided power for Rochestown corn mill.

The greater part of this valley is the property of a small number of landowners who live in splendid houses, keep their estates in beautiful order and devote much of their holdings to the nurture of superb horses. The right bank, just downstream of Ballymore Eustace, is so steep that it would be beyond the powers of any beast other than a goat to graze and this has been abandoned to nature. The result is an area where something resembling a pre-agricultural habitat survives. It is of considerable botanical interest but, because of the dense bushes, rather inaccessible.

Most of the estates are private property, but Harristown opens to visitors from time to time. It continues to be a family-owned dwelling and farm. The big house, secluded from the outside world, is surrounded by rolling green pasture screened by a fringe of mature woodland – an idyllic spot. The house, on relatively high ground overlooking a bend on the Liffey, was built to the order of the Huguenot La Touche banking family after they purchased the estate in 1768.

A fire in 1891 destroyed the original three-storey classical mansion, which was then rebuilt on a slightly smaller scale and with only two storeys. The designer was the local diocesan architect James Franklin Fuller. He followed

Harristown House, built for the La Touche bankers in 1768, stands safely above the floodplain of the Liffey.

the classical style but introduced a central lantern, not visible from the outside, which brightens the upper storey. Fuller was an enthusiast for revival architecture and applied Hiberno-Romanesque design to two Church of Ireland churches in the Liffey valley: nearby at Carnalway and further away at Millicent.

The La Touches' ownership ended in 1921 and 25 years later Michael and Doreen Beaumont, from Buckinghamshire, bought the estate and set to work on an exciting scheme of renovation and furnishing. The interior is beautiful and full of curiosities, such as the use of one-time spinets as tables. One room displays exquisite sixteenth-century Chinese wallpaper with brilliantly coloured birds. The current owners, Noella and Hubert Beaumont, conduct tours of the house and regale their visitors with tales of the very remarkable previous owners and their employees, among them John Ruskin. Opening times are restricted.

A corn mill is marked on the 1837 map, 1.3 km downstream of Rochestown, but neither mill race nor weir are shown and it may have been supplied from an artificial lake in the grounds of the demesne.

Below the house the river is crossed by the Old Bridge. Both banks of the Liffey upstream are densely wooded, mainly with beech trees. Downstream, the left bank is similarly wooded, with a large island. On the right bank open parkland, dotted with specimen oak trees, extends from the riverside to the house on the hill. On Taylor's map of 1783 the road from Naas leads southwards through Harristown, crosses the river, takes a sharp turn to the right and

The Old Bridge at Harristown.

continues briefly south and then west in the direction of Kilcullen. There was no sign at that time of what is now the R412, running from Carnalway to Brannockstown crossroads. The 1838 map shows 'Old Bridge' crossing the river and leading into the wood on the left bank, but the road on this side had disappeared from the scene. The 1937 map shows the existing avenue leading from Carnalway, past the big house and over the old bridge to join with the main R412 at the crossroads in Brannockstown.

The Old Bridge has seven segmental arches of roughly hewn greywacke on tall piers, the same stone being used for the voussoirs and for the angular cutwaters. Granite is used to decorate the walls, both in the flat coping and in a series of broad pilasters above the piers. This is evidently the bridge shown in the 1783 map. It was repaired and repointed early in the twenty-first century.

La Touche Bridge

This bridge, marked on the maps as 'New Bridge', is less than a kilometre downstream of its senior partner. Its plaque tells us that:

In° La Touche Esqr
Built this Bridge
A D 1788

La Touche Bridge in summer.

As might be expected from the family of Huguenot descent who commanded the Bank of Ireland, it is an elegant structure. In common with the Old Bridge just upstream, the fabric is the local greywacke, roughly hewn. It has four broad segmental arches on relatively low piers. The soffits are of ashlar, the cutwaters angular, with pyramidal tops. The gently sloping flat-topped, rather than curved, walls meet at a point in the centre of each side, giving it a very pleasing angular appearance.

Kilcullen

Kilcullen spans the Liffey at the southernmost point reached by our river. The name of the village comes from the monastery situated 3 km to the southwest. Now known as Old Kilcullen, that settlement was on the southern member of a pair of isolated hills that rise from the plain. Both of them were of great importance in ancient times. But they are a little way removed from the Liffey and that is the only good reason for making no more than a passing reference here. Marked on the map as Knockaulin, the northern hill is also known as Dun Ailinne. It flourished in the Iron Age as a ritual site and there is archaeological evidence of great seasonal gatherings over a period of some hundreds of years.

Tradition tells that the monastery of Kilcullen on the neighbouring hill, the name translating as 'the Cell of the Holly', was founded by a particularly obscure companion of St Patrick, St Isserninus. Remnants of a round tower and of a beautiful Celtic cross, with panels illustrating scriptural subjects, combine with references in monastic annals to testify to its importance over a long period. The cross is the only one with scenes from the scriptures to have survived in the Liffey valley.

Lewis describes the development of a substantial walled town at the monastic site and the building of a castle by the Fitzmartin family on the river. He goes on:

> Previously to the year 1319, the town was surrounded with strong walls and defended by seven gates, but Maurice Jacques having in that year built a bridge over the river Liffey, about two miles from this place, the town of Kilcullen-Bridge began rapidly to increase, and the ancient town to decline.

In the 1720s the Fitzmartin castle was replaced by a classical house. Serving as government headquarters in 1798, it was seriously damaged and subsequently rebuilt. Meanwhile, the old town came to be virtually deserted and, by 1837, the new town on the Liffey had taken over. It merited a separate entry by Lewis, under the heading 'Kilcullen-Bridge':

This town had its origin in the erection of a bridge over the river Liffey, in 1319, from which period it continued gradually to increase, and has now totally superseded the ancient town of Kilcullen, of which the market has been removed to this place. It is two miles to the east of the former town, and within a short distance of the great Bog of Allen, and consists of one principal street containing 112 houses; it lies chiefly on the western bank of the river and is well supplied with water; the bridge has a venerable and interesting appearance, and not far from the eastern end of it is a large rath.

In common with Ballymore Eustace, which also developed close to an Anglo-Norman castle, Kilcullen grew in a haphazard fashion. But, while the castle of Ballymore Eustace eventually disappeared, the Fitzmartin fortress retained its importance when it was transformed from a military bastion to a comfortable big house. For more than forty years the demesne was the property of the entrepreneur Sir Anthony O'Reilly, who rescued it from decay. Commemorating the name of the warlords as Castlemartin, the estate spreads over the land on the left bank, to the west of the town. The house stands at the end of a magnificent avenue of lime trees, visible from the road that leads to Athgarvan and the Curragh. Taylor's map of 1783 shows the house surrounded by extensive woodland, but with no sign of the avenue that is clearly shown 50 years later in the 1838 Ordnance Survey map.

Twentieth-century riverside development of Kilcullen.

Kilcullen is today one of the centres of the bloodstock industry, notable for saddlers' shops and the offices of leading horse dealers. The development of riverside walks and small parks is an indication of a notable degree of civic pride among the townspeople.

Athgarvan

Between Kilcullen and the next ancient crossing place at Athgarvan, the Liffey continues to meander through parkland and passes beneath a thoroughly modern bridge on the M9 motorway. At Athgarvan outcropping rock and consequent rapids made first for a ford and, a long time later, for a mill and a bridge. Access to the banks upstream of the bridge is firmly fenced off by the owners of opulent dwellings and by the mill complex. Overlooking the weir is a great white house with multiple Tudor chimneys.

A bend of the Liffey downstream of Athgarvan. Pasture on the right bank allows for easy access by anglers, cattle and others. The woodland on the left bank shows how unkempt nature keeps people away from the rivers of Ireland.

An undefined mill is shown on Taylor's map of 1783. It has an extensive footprint and is labelled 'Corn Mill' on the Ordnance Survey map. Evidently powered directly from the Liffey, it stands at the northern end of a long weir, 150 metres, running from south to north along a section of the river 100 metres wide. Today a four-storey mill building stands a little way back from the road. Attached to its front is one of a pair of oast houses, tall, windowless buildings designed for processing barley to make malt.

Athgarvan corn mill and oast houses with the typical pyramidal slate roofs, topped by wooden ventilation structures.

Taylor marks the mill, the present-day road and an island upstream of it, but no bridge. The 1837 map shows 'Athgarvan Ford' and indicates its path by a dotted line downstream of the mill dam. By that time the stone arch which crosses the tail race of the mill had been built – but not the main bridge. When it came to be built, a traditional style was used, resulting in a pleasing structure of four segmental arches, with ashlar voussoirs, angular cutwaters and a string course above the arches.

The Liffeyside, on the left bank at Athgarvan, is accessible through the elegant housing estate close to the M7. A narrow tarmacadam footpath leads from the estate along the tail race, fringed by alder and willow, to a more open bank where tall grasses grow by the water's edge. The grasses and footpath extend downstream until the river turns to the right and a fence prevents access to the woodland that lines the left bank.

On the right bank sheep graze and their pasture looks like a lawn. But on the wasteland of the park, the grass is mown from time to time and the result closely resembles a traditional hay meadow – what ecologists describe as 'unimproved grassland'. This term means that no fertiliser has been spread and the great variety of wild flowers that used to be a feature of meadows still thrive there. Among the grasses, colourful flowers bloom: red and white clovers, yellow bird's-foot-trefoil, white- and pink-flowered yarrow, cream-coloured meadowsweet and many other species, making it a perfectly delightful spot on a summer's day.

The Curragh

The left bank of the valley upstream of Athgarvan is part of the boundary of the Curragh – in old writings *Curragh na Life* . Much of the rainwater that falls on the Curragh ultimately reaches the river, but not by way of visible streams. The sandy soil of this great expanse of land allows easy drainage at the surface and movement of water through the underlying soil. This constitutes the 'Curragh aquifer', a great mass of water-holding gravel and one of the largest of its kind in Ireland. Cattle need to drink water and the scarcity of ponds and absence of streams makes the pasture inhospitable to them. Sheep, on the other hand, can get all the water they need from the grass they eat. The unsuitability of the soil for cattle may be part of the reason why the Curragh continued to be a pasture held in common when the proprietors of the surrounding land enclosed their fields in the eighteenth century.

The army 'camp' – a permanent assemblage of barracks in red brick, with two tall towers, successor to a real tented settlement in Napoleonic times – is screened by planted trees, mostly birch and pine. The only other conspicuous human feature on this marvellous landscape is the racecourse with its grandstands and associated buildings. Contemporary homes and farmsteads stand on the periphery of the commonage, which is therefore a wide open space, free from banks and hedges and with fencing confined to the racecourse, a golf links and the army establishment. Close-cropped grass, with invading gorse, covers the ground. The land is not quite flat, but its gentle undulations

The memorial to the prize fighter in Donnelly's Hollow at the edge of the Curragh. Gorse encroaches on the grassland. It restores nitrogen to the soil and gives the land a respite from the sheep grazing.

are not enough to interrupt the distant views in all directions. Man-made structures are far from absent, though, and the plain is dotted with ring forts, the remnants of Iron Age farm and dwelling compounds. Even in those far-off times, the Curragh was famous as a centre for horse racing.

Not far from Athgarvan, one of the deepest dips in the landscape makes for something of a natural amphitheatre. This was the scene of bare-knuckle prize fighting and has long been known as Donnelly's Hollow, in honour of the renowned victory of the Irishman Dan Donnelly over the English champion George Cooper on 13 December 1815.

Greatconnell

Downstream of Athgarvan and the Curragh, the river makes an S-bend which leads to a weir built upstream of one large and several small islands between the townlands of Walshestown and Greatconnell. The weir diverts water to a mill race just 1 km in length, which led to a 'Flour Mill' marked on the 1837 survey, changed to 'Corn Mill disused' on the 25-inch map, close to the ruined 'Greatconnell abbey'.

The warlord Myler Fitzhenry introduced Augustinian monks to his property and in 1202 they built a priory at Great Connell dedicated to Our Lady and St David. The Welsh connection persisted for many generations as the 'mere Irish' were not admitted. The priory was closed in 1541, four years after King Henry's Act of Confiscation. In its heyday one of the greatest and wealthiest of the religious houses of Ireland, the buildings of the abbey have disappeared, almost without a trace other than a cemetery.

Newbridge

The Liffey was fordable in ancient times at the point where a new bridge would be built in 1308. Long years before that the Anglo-Normans had established a motte and bailey to control the ford. Its mound stands in a field across the river from the Dominican college, a little way downstream of the present bridge.

Although no town worth speaking of existed in medieval times, there had been a considerable settlement by the Liffeyside at least since the Norman occupation. The earliest known new bridge had been replaced by the seventeenth century and that one was destroyed by a flood in 1798. The unsettled times of that year and the consequent Act of Union were celebrated by the building of a cavalry barracks, completed in 1816. It is said that the ruins of the priory were used as a source of building stone for the military men.

A garrison establishment with accommodation for 800 men and 536 horses needed support and the arrival of the troops led to the building of shops and dwellings across the main road from the barracks. They form the nucleus of the town. The need for a school was met by the Dominican Order, who founded Newbridge College by the riverside in 1852. Its most distinguished building is the church of 1966, dedicated to St Eustace, patron of the Eustace family which, generations earlier, had supported the Dominicans. The church's crowning glory lies in the brilliance of the windows. The work of John Murphy, they throw a shower of colour on the altar and its surroundings. The church also contains beautiful sculptures in bog yew by the Dominican priest Father Flanagan, who was a teacher at the college.

The modern town was in its infancy in Lewis's time – but he certainly foresaw its future development:

> This place is of very recent origin, and appears to have arisen from the erection of extensive barracks for cavalry, in 1816, on the property of Thos. Eyre Powell, Esq. It is situated on the river Liffey, over which there is a handsome stone bridge of five arches, but so narrow that two carriages cannot drive abreast on it, from which it derives its name, and on the mail coach road from Dublin to Limerick. The town at present consists only of one street, on the western bank of the river; but it is yet in its infancy, and there is every prospect of its increase.

So the town grew and prospered until 1922, when the Free State government decided to close the barracks. Help came, remarkably, in the 1930s when two

Swans sail on the Liffey at Newbridge Park on a sunny day in March. The houses in the distance mark a former U-bend, cut off when the river took a shortcut and adopted its present-day course.

factories, Irish Ropes and Newbridge Silverware, were set up in the grounds of the old barracks property. The town also became a major depot for Bord na Móna's operations on the nearby Bog of Allen. Substantial remnants of the barracks survive, in red brick with yellow stone in a simple, classical style, hidden behind the shops and houses of the main street. On the left bank of the Liffey, upstream of the bridge, are the stone-built approaches to a watering place for the cavalry horses.

A very pleasing stretch of riverbank and former water meadow has been developed to form the Liffey Linear Park and is maintained by the Newbridge Tidy Towns Association (www.newbridgetidytowns.com). The greater part of the park is contained within a right-handed bend on the Liffey to the east and the Athgarvan Road to the west. From that point northwards the park is a narrow strip between road and river, going under the bridge to the boundaries of the Dominican College.

The bend is a greatly reduced replacement of a meander shown on Taylor's map of 1783. In the course of the 50 years between that publication and the first by the Ordnance Survey, the river had cut itself a straight path across the top of the U-curve of this meander and the 1838 map shows it as an ox-bow, naming the bend 'Old course'. But since then the Liffey has been trying to return to its former track. The 1937 map shows the straight section as a renewed curve, embracing a half-moon-shaped piece of land 'liable to floods'. Houses have been built along the outer side of the old course.

The parish of Carragh

There is so little agreement on the spelling of this name that the parish is very well concealed in indexed works of reference. Lewis gives it only one 'r', with an alternative of 'Carogh' and a third spelling, 'Kerogh'. I follow the example of the Ordnance Survey. The village scarcely existed in Lewis's time and the greater part of his entry dwells largely on land holdings and parish arrangements, but the following extracts are of wider interest.

> This parish, of which the name is sometimes written Kerogh, is situated on the river Liffey, and on the turnpike-road from Naas to Edenderry. The soil is fertile, the land is chiefly in the occupation of private gentlemen, and is in a state of excellent cultivation. Clover, turnips and other green crops are raised with success, and the potatoes are all drilled; there is neither waste land nor bog in the parish, but fuel is obtained in abundance from bogs in the immediate vicinity … On the river Liffey are the Yeomanstown mills, capable of manufacturing from 6000 to 7000 barrels of flour annually … In the R. C. divisions this parish is the head of a union or district … the chapel is a neat modern

edifice, near the site of the old parish church ... A school-house has been built by subscription, on a site presented by A. Mansfield, Esq., for a school in connection with the National Board, in which are about 120 boys and 90 girls.

The chapel, school and the beautiful old bridge formed the nucleus of the modern village of Carragh, now a prosperous dormitory settlement for workers in Dublin. The appearance and structure of Carragh Bridge strongly support its claim to be the oldest unaltered one on the Liffey. Con Costello, in his *Guide to Kildare and West Wicklow*, dates it to between 1450 and 1550. Supported by six stone piers with round-headed arches, it squeezes the commuter traffic to a single lane.

John Molloy, an international authority on herring and mackerel, was a long-time resident of the village. He spearheaded and edited *The Great Book of Caragh*, published by the Caragh Local History Group. In its 370 pages its many contributors provide a wealth of detail on the lands and people of the parish. Growth of its population led to the replacement of the 'chapel' mentioned by Lewis with a beautiful modern building in 1960.

The splendid mill in the townland of Yeomanstown is the first on the river downstream of the long-gone works at Greatconnell, and the Liffey meanders for very nearly 10 km between the two. The water level falls in this distance from 90 to 71 metres or 1 in 555, one of the gentlest descents in the entire length of the river. The mill, also known by the name of the adjoining demesne of Morristown Lattin, is powered from a weir on the upstream side of an island in

The mill of Morristown Lattin or Yeomanstown.

Carragh Bridge, certainly repointed and probably rebuilt from time to time. The original structure may date to the fifteenth century.

the river. The weir directs water through a mill race running through Shenagh Bridge to the most splendid waterwheel to survive on the Liffey. Shenagh Bridge has a single low segmental stone arch, curtained with a luxuriant growth of ivy. The four-storey mill building has been restored as a dwelling and new wooden panels have been attached to the iron skeleton of the waterwheel.

Sallins and the Leinster Aqueduct

Three substantial villages, Sallins, Clane and Straffan, all lie well within the valley of the Liffey but, unlike their upstream and downstream neighbours Newbridge and Celbridge, stand aloof from the river. Past inundations over the wide natural floodplain kept them away from the riverbanks.

Besides mentioning that it is the third stage for the canal packets plying from Dublin, Lewis had very little to say about Sallins. Since his time the village developed as the home of Odlums' mills which, in their early days, used water power from the Grand Canal. The same canal demanded the building of the nearby Leinster Aqueduct to carry road and waterway across the Liffey.

The most impressive of all the eighteenth-century works on the Liffey, the Leinster Aqueduct crosses the river 4 km downstream of Carragh Bridge. Its position was chosen by the Engineer in Ordinary in Ireland, General Charles Vallancey, a polymath of the highest order. He advised building the bridge above an existing ford, requiring the canal to take a U-bend to the south of the line it would otherwise have followed. The Canal Company's engineer Thomas

Omer had favoured the straight course, which would have made the canal descend into the valley by a series of locks. The eventual decision in favour of the aqueduct led to its design and implementation by Richard Evans, assistant engineer to the company.

The Leinster Aqueduct, built in 1780, carrying road, towpath and canal across the Liffey near Sallins.

A truly splendid structure, if designed for strength rather than beauty, the aqueduct of limestone ashlar has a solid appearance with five low segmental arches supported by pyramidal piers. Charles Taylor was so impressed by it that he included a beautiful engraving of plan and elevation in his map of County Kildare. The plan shows lock gates at each end of the stretch of the canal above the arches. These, if they ever existed, have long gone. The elevation shows a

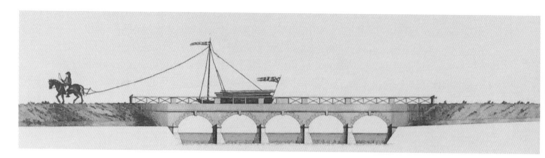

Part of Charles Taylor's engraving of the Leinster Aqueduct.

barge hauled by a horse and rider. The towing rope is attached to the top of a tall mast on the barge, which seems an unusual arrangement. A possible reason is that in places the canal flowed in a cutting with the towpath at a higher level. Snagging of the towrope on the bank could have been avoided by the raised attachment point.

On the left bank of the Liffey, a lane leads down to the riverside and allows crossing to the other side of the canal by a usually muddy track through a brick-lined tunnel. On the right bank of the river, downstream of the canal, three pipes descend to a concrete pump house. Now redundant, since the peat-fired power station at Allenwood closed in 1994, they served to bring water from the Liffey to the canal. This was needed in dry spells to supplement the water from the canal which supplied the heat-exchange system of the power station.

The half-buried nameplate of the Leinster Aqueduct.

Taylor's engraving shows an open lattice fence on the sides of the bridge deck. This was replaced by a solid stone wall with gently curved limestone coping. A plaque on this wall bears the words LEINSTER *AQUEDUCT* immediately above the path. Undoubtedly the legend contained more information than that, but the plaque is now partly buried under the footpath. The hidden information may include the date 1780, when construction began. The plaque has a luxuriant growth of orange lichens. Downstream of the aqueduct the Liffey flows placidly through an almost Dutch-like expanse of flat pasture with the mills, factories and houses of the canal village of Sallins on the horizon.

Bodenstown and Millicent

The road north from Sallins passes the ancient ruined church and the burial ground of Bodenstown. Perhaps associated with the St Boden whose well lies hidden from view beneath the waters of Lackan Lake, the burial ground has become a shrine to the memory of the Republican leader Wolfe Tone. His godfather Charles Wolfe, a clergyman and landowner, owned the nearby Blackhall House.

Opposite the cemetery, a small road led westwards to the river where it is crossed by the six-arched Millicent Bridge. Taylor marks the bridge crossing the river in a northwesterly direction, as it does to this day. Beside the bridge, on the right bank, two enormous beech trees grow, which may very well be as old as the bridge itself. They stand by the wall of a pleasant green pasture that slopes down to the riverbank.

Clane

Lewis gives Clane a great deal more attention than Sallins. He includes an enthusiastic paragraph on the glories, architectural and educational, of Clongowes Wood College which, founded in 1814, was an exciting innovation in his time. Sadly, it was built some miles from the banks of the Liffey and therefore merits only passing mention in this book – in spite of its poignant memories of James Joyce's experiences as a pupil.

The name of the townland on the left bank at Clane is Abbeylands, which commemorates a good 1,600 years of monastic attachment. The ruins of the Franciscan friary, founded in 1272, mark the spot celebrated in the townland name and may very well stand where St Ailbhe founded his monastery 700 years earlier. Between those dates a major synod was held at Clane in 1162 when, Lewis tells us, Gelasius, Archbishop of Armagh, assisted by 26 bishops and a great number of abbots, passed a decree assuring his see of a secure place in the control of the Christians of Ireland. No person, it said, should be admitted Professor of Divinity in any college in Ireland unless he had studied at Armagh.

Not long after the synod was held, the Anglo-Normans arrived on the scene, extending their holdings over the fertile plains of Anna Liffey. They built the motte which stands just to the west of the river where it changes its northerly course to meander gently eastwards for a while. The islands on the bend would have made it a fording spot and that would also account for the choice of the opposite bank for a monastery many years earlier. Mills on both sides of the river subsequently provided employment and the need for housing. A mill race is shown on the 1838 Ordnance Survey map and may have powered the 'woollen manufacture' that Lewis mentions. He also refers to quarries of good limestone and to the presence of a bridge of six arches.

A path on the left bank goes to the riverside, downstream of an abandoned weir beside a beautiful old willow tree. A small circular flat-topped mound overlooks the river on the left bank, upstream of the bridge. Tradition claims it as the burial place of Mesgegra, King of Leinster, who died in AD 33. It may well be, but the mound looks suspiciously like the nearby motte and its strategic position by the ford supports this. Of course, the invaders might very well have built their fort on top of the king's grave.

Alexandra Bridge

Taylor shows a bridge a little way to the south of Clane and it is also marked on the first Ordnance Survey map in 1838, crossing a broad stretch of the river where there are several islands. The bridge leads from the village to a mill complex. Described by Lewis as having six arches, it was replaced in 1864 by the present structure, named in honour of Princess Alexandra who, the year before, had married the future King Edward VII.

Built entirely of limestone, it has three wide segmental arches and a pair of smaller ones at each side, perhaps built to cope with floods or possibly simply to allow cattle to pass beneath the road above. If they had a flood-alleviation function, this has been made redundant by the building of earthen banks that confine the river to the three main arches. The stonework is stylish, with rusticated voussoirs and walls, string courses at the level of the decking and at the springing of the arches. The coping is gently curved. Semicircular cutwaters are capped by domes.

The carriageway was, no doubt, wide enough for the carts and carriages that used the bridge when it was built. But times have changed and pedestrians nowadays cross the Liffey with some trepidation. Traffic is heavy in both directions and there is barely room to walk on either side. On the south side a large but simple plaque with a plain border bears, boldly carved, the words 'ALEXANDRA AD 1864'.

On the right bank a cypress hedge by the roadside effectively blocks any view of the upstream face of the bridge. A downstream view may be had by climbing a post-and-rail fence and walking through cattle pasture to the water's edge. The left bank approach is easier, with access through housing estates both upstream and downstream.

Straffan

Wikipedia provides a detailed account of the ancient and modern status of Straffan. Lewis has relatively little to say about it, other than giving a list of landowners and their property. He mentions its proximity to both Grand and Royal canals, but says nothing about the Liffey which flows close by and forms a boundary to Straffan Lodge. The name is said to derive from St Srafán who, presumably, presided over a monastery there. The village is centred on a crossroads, nearly a kilometre north of the point where the river takes a sharp turn from its west–east course and flows northwards for a while. The bridge nearby is shown by Taylor in 1763 and his map also indicates a well-established demesne with a large house and extensive pathways. This house was accidentally burned, to be replaced in the 1820s by the ornate building that stands there today – although reduced in size by an impoverished member of the Barton family, who owned it in the 1930s.

The estate passed through the hands of several owners in the twentieth century, until purchased in 1988 by the Jefferson Smurfit Company. They transformed house and grounds into a country club with two superb golf courses. Catering for international tournaments, its fame culminated in the holding of the 2006 Ryder Cup there by the banks of Anna Liffey. Access to the river is confined to the elite who join the K Club. From the bridge there is a view upstream, along the manicured lawns, to the house. A concrete weir, which provides a head of water for a turbine, allows passage for ascending salmon by a series of pools on the left bank.

The trout and salmon of the Liffey at Straffan earned immortality in the scientific literature in the 1930s and 1940s research by Rowland Southern, Winifred Frost and Arthur Went. It was published by the Royal Irish Academy in six major papers, the final one by Frost in 1945 bringing the whole survey together. They showed that the trout in the lime-rich lower reaches of the Liffey were bigger and better than those in the acidic water upstream.

Downstream of Straffan, our river continues her leisurely way for 8 km, meandering through affluent farmsteads with large fields and few buildings. Public roads keep a respectful distance. Then, quite abruptly, the scene changes from rural to something close to suburban. Even though much of County Kildare has yet to be traversed, there is an element of Greater Dublin for the remainder of the journey of Anna Liffey.

6 | The parklands

The long redundant Magazine Fort of 1710 is one of the few restricted entities in the Phoenix Park, which slopes steeply down to the Liffeyside. Swift celebrated its construction with these lines: 'Now here's a proof of Irish sense / Here Irish wit is seen / When nothing's left that's worth defence / We build a Magazine.'

Somewhere downstream of Straffan the landscape of the valley changes from rural to suburban – and also industrial. This results in part from another of Anna Livia's perversities. Normal, healthy rivers proceed in an orderly manner in a fairly constant direction from source to sea. Headwaters are rapid and the lower reaches leisurely. But, besides following a circular course, the Liffey has more than one floodplain. The first, as we have seen, is upstream of Pollaphuca. The second extends to the vicinity of Straffan, where another series of plunges begins. This has much to do with the extreme youth of our river – very much less than 100,000 years a-growing in contrast to the millions enjoyed by rivers in regions that were not covered with ice in geologically recent times.

Although a number of the great landowners had developed pleasure grounds in their demesnes in the eighteenth century and earlier, most of their land was devoted to agriculture – the prime industry of the nation at that time. Close to the city, the villages of Celbridge, Leixlip, Palmerstown and Lucan were within reach of members of parliament and other wealthy people. Their country seats still had extensive farmland and numerous tenants to add to their incomes, but the great majority of the owners adapted these properties for comfort and leisure.

The eighteenth century also saw the beginning of substantial industries based on water power – in contrast to the many earlier mills, which were relatively small. It happened that the topography of the Liffey valley aided and abetted this development. Between Ballymore Eustace and Celbridge the river flows for 118 km and descends from the 150-metre contour to 60 metres, a gradient of one in 1,311. In the 38 km reach from Celbridge to Islandbridge the descent is 20 metres and the fall is one in 1,900. This, together with the increased flow from the tributaries, provides a much greater head of water and consequently more power. The 1838 survey shows twelve mills or riverside 'works' in the leisurely upper portion and twenty in the short, swift lower. These provided jobs for thousands of villagers and an explosion of riverside accommodation, mostly in the form of neat, if small, cottages.

A swollen Liffey rushes past the great mill built in Celbridge in 1805. Fronted by a new garden, it is now occupied by office premises.

The nineteenth and twentieth centuries saw a growing population of city workers, greater wealth and relatively rapid transport. The consequent creation of dormitory suburbs, as well as local employment, led to the expansion of the villages. The commuting population encroached on the farmland but, at the same time, demanded open spaces. As long ago as the seventeenth century the government had provided the incomparable playground of the Phoenix Park. From the late nineteenth century local authorities responded to the need for public space and, as far as funds permitted, created public parks on a truly splendid scale. Fragments of farmland have survived close to the city boundary, but the lower valley of the Liffey is essentially a place for humanity: homes, work and recreation rather than cash crops and edible beasts.

In the course of the twentieth century most of the mills ceased to operate: a few of them continued to accommodate factories, but many crumbled to form more or less picturesque ruins. Landowners sold a lot of their property to speculative builders and a little to the local authorities to become public parks. In the 1940s the Abercrombie Plan for Greater Dublin recommended serious consideration of the value of the Liffey as an axis for park development.

Over-encroachment in the case of the right bank at Celbridge led to the creation of a formidable conservation body, the Liffey Valley Park Alliance, which eventually succeeded in preserving some vital open spaces and in drawing public attention to the importance of the riverside as an entity.

Celbridge

In contrast to the crossing at Straffan Demesne and its slightly distant settlement, Celbridge is intimately connected with the river and the bridge is an integral part of the village. The 1838 map marks a bridge and a weir 500 metres upstream of the present-day structures. Both had been shown to be present by Taylor in 1783. Another weir, 400 metres upstream of that, supplied a mill race that served Temple Mills on the right bank. This is also shown by Taylor, but under the name of Terrils Ca. & Mills.

Lewis writes of Celbridge with justifiable enthusiasm:

This town, pleasantly situated on the left bank of the river Liffey, over which is a handsome stone bridge, and on the turnpike road from Dublin to Prosperous, is indebted for its origin to the Limerick family, from whom it was purchased by the Rt. Hon. W. Conolly, speaker of the Irish House of Commons, whose representative, Col. E. M. Conolly, is the present proprietor. It consists principally of one street; the houses, about 270 in number, are in general well built; the inhabitants are amply supplied with water. The woollen manufacture was carried on to a considerable extent, and a very large range of building was erected in 1805, comprising all the requisite machinery for that manufacture in its various branches; the works were put in motion by a water wheel of 200 horse power, and when in full operation afforded employment to 600 persons; but they are not at present in work. Adjoining the town, though in the parish of Donocomper, is a cotton-spinning and power-loom weaving factory, employing, when in full work, about 100 persons …

Celbridge Abbey, built by the late Dr. Marley, Bishop of Clonfert, and now the residence of J. Ashworth, Esq., proprietor of the woollen manufactory in the town. The house is associated with the memory of Dean Swift, who is said to have spent much of his time here in the society of the lady whom he has celebrated under the name of Vanessa; and a rustic seat on the bank of the Liffey, which passes through the demesne, and over which is a spacious bridge of stone, is said to have been planned by him.

The riverside in Celbridge is dominated by the splendid mill building of 1805, four storeys high, sixteen bays wide, with fresh-looking stonework and yellow-painted window frames. On the opposite bank a footpath extends from the bridge to the former school, converted to an office block. Just upstream of the old stone bridge, which carries the busy main road across the river, an iron footbridge has been added. It gives a good view of the great mill building and a pleasant garden. Access to the river south of the bridge is restricted by an impressive range of uncompromising high stone walls.

One set belongs to the old mill buildings, which are accessible and have been transformed to a complex of offices and leisure and community facilities. The design is attractive – with the amazing flaw that this development completely hides the river from view, except through the windows of the various offices.

One set belongs to the old mill buildings which are accessible and have been transformed to a complex of offices and leisure and community facilities. The design is attractive – with the amazing flaw that this development completely hides the river from view, except through the windows of the various offices. Seldom has an opportunity for the creation of a riverside amenity been so effectively neglected.

The second set of walls screens the grounds of Celbridge Abbey from view. It is relieved for a space by a car park, backed by an almost impenetrable hedge which has grown up along a chain-link fence. A small and unintentional breach in the latter allows a view of an old mill race and across this to the carefully tended grounds of Celbridge Abbey.

The great house of the name was redesigned towards the end of the eighteenth century by Dr Richard Marley, uncle of Henry Grattan, who wrote of his love for this same riverside walk. The main house had fallen into decay by the 1960s and was restored with great devotion by the present owners, the St John of God Brothers.

A narrow stone footbridge joins the two parts of the demesne. Upstream of the bridge an outcrop of limestone forms a small cliff. Above it the roots of beech trees intertwine and wander in all directions, trying to find a little soil for anchorage. Between the beeches and the weir a summer house with a stone seat occupies the 'quiet romantic spot overlooking the weir' where Vanessa made her bower. Vanessa, Esther Vanhomrigh, had come to live in Celbridge Abbey after the death of her father and there she pursued her passionate and tragic romance with Jonathan Swift. The original bower was destroyed when the bridge was built some time after Vanessa's death. The lack of originality in the newer bower matters little. The Liffey still runs over the weir, shaded by old trees and the spot remains quiet and romantic.

The appearance of Celbridge improves greatly downstream of the bridge, where the village street runs in a straight line to the main gate of Castletown. Affluent houses line the left bank of the Liffey on the east side of the road, with their gardens running down to the river. The first of these to be built, Kildrought House, takes its name from *Cill Droighid*, the Irish name which would be anglicised to Celbridge. Set back from the street, Kildrought predates Castletown itself by a few years. It was built for Robert Baillie in 1719 to the design of Thomas Burgh, the Surveyor General, whose other Liffeyside buildings include Dr Steeven's Hospital and the Royal, now Collins, Barracks. Refurbished many times and once left nearly to decay in the course of 250 years, the present owners restored Kildrought to its original beauty in the 1980s. It is open to visitors for some weeks every year.

Not inappropriately, the place where Arthur Guinness was born in 1725 has long been occupied by a licensed premises. The broad, straight main street of Celbridge with its neat houses was developed later in the eighteenth century. This picture was taken in 2016, shortly before the establishment, now The Duck, was refurbished.

The houses on the west side of the road through Celbridge, away from the river, are mostly smaller dwellings, but all imply a degree of comfort and space. In one of them, now long gone, the original bearer of one of the Liffey's best-known names was born in 1725. Arthur Guinness lived there for 30 years. The site is now – appropriately enough – occupied by two pubs, the Duck and the Village Inn.

Castletown

Seething with history and romance, Castletown can be described only in superlatives of grandeur and beauty. The great house is approached from its gate in Celbridge by half a mile of avenue, shaded by ancient lime trees. The front lawns are sheltered by a yew hedge, itself protected by a line of sentinel Florencecourt yews. The view from the lawn is of an enormous expanse of parkland, studded with elderly, but still splendid, oaks and other trees.

A generously endowed female creature guards the main gate to Castletown.

Not only is Castletown one of the first and finest of the great houses of Ireland, but its founder and his successors are well known from contemporary publications and from the correspondence of Lady Louisa Conolly and others. Nonetheless, discovering details of the planning and construction of the house required a considerable element of detective work on the part of art and architectural historians. This process was delightfully described in the magazine *Country Life* in 1969, in a series of articles by Maurice Craig and others. They were reprinted as a single booklet and published by the Irish Georgian Society.

The originator of Castletown House was William Conolly, a native of Ballyshannon, who made a fortune by buying and selling some of the many forfeited properties that were available following the turbulent times of William III. Elected Speaker of the Irish House of Commons, he clearly wanted to make a statement of his personal wealth and power. Happily, this piece of self-aggrandisement was equalled by a patriotic view that his home should be a shining example of the resources and skills of the people of Ireland. The designers had to be among the best architects in the world and the house was to be a model to Irish landlords of how their dwellings should appear. Many of them followed his example and Palladian mansions, most of them smaller than Castletown, abound in all parts of the country.

The glorious symmetry of Castletown, inspiration for many of the noblest dwellings of Ireland.

In 1719 the Florentine architect Alessandro Galilei was employed to design the general outline. Building began soon afterwards, perhaps in 1720, but Galilei had returned to Florence by that time and did not visit Ireland again. There is evidence that the work was in progress in 1722, under the control of Edward Lovett Pearce. Although closely involved in the planning he, too, was in Italy for most of the time the house was under construction. The entrance hall, the colonnades, the wings and, perhaps, much of the detail of the interior were his contribution.

The nineteenth-century Christ Church stands within the gates of Castletown at the head of the main street of Celbridge.

Tragedy surrounded the progenitors of Castletown. William Conolly died in 1729 in his town house in Dublin and it seems that he did not enjoy very much time in his country seat. Pearce died just three years later, in his early 30s, after an amazing professional career that had been crammed into six or seven years. After the Speaker's death, his widow, Katherine, retired to Castletown where, besides leading a dazzling social life, she showed her enthusiasm for ebullient architecture. Her most notable work was the 'Conolly Folly', the magnificent obelisk and summer house, which stands between Castletown and its stately neighbour Carton and was visible from both.

A second phase in the construction of Castletown began when the Speaker's grand-nephew, Tom Conolly, and his wife, Lady Louisa, moved there in 1759. The cantilevered staircase was completed the year after they took up residence and the magnificent plasterwork of the hall was added at about the same time. Lady Louisa was responsible for much of the interior design, in particular the gallery, which was finished in 1775.

Many of the great eighteenth-century houses were substantially altered by their owners in the nineteenth century. One of the joys of Castletown is that the interior remains very much the same as it was in 1821 when Lady Louisa died peacefully at the age of 78. Many of the rooms contain the furniture of her time.

While the great front rooms downstairs have an air of formality and were used on state occasions, those in the rear and upstairs are much more homely. One of the most unusual is the Print Room. Its walls are decorated with pictures cut out from magazines that were then embellished with specially printed borders. Many ladies in the eighteenth century papered rooms with their favourite pictures in this way, but the example at Castletown is the only one of its kind to have survived in Ireland. The charm of the collection is that it shows what appealed personally to the creator, rather than what a design consultant thought was right.

In 1965, Castletown was put on the market, and the future of the great house stood in jeopardy. Much of the land was sold for building and, for some time, nobody wanted the mansion. It was rescued by the Hon. Desmond Guinness who, in 1967, bought the house and 120 acres of parkland for £93,000. The purchase included the entrance gates and the avenue from the village, together with the fields that slope down to Anna Liffey and also some delightful pockets of woodland. In 1979, the property was acquired by the Castletown Foundation, which initiated major restoration work. Five years later, house and grounds became the inheritance of the people of Ireland and the restoration is being pursued under the guidance of the talented architects of the Office of Public Works. The Castletown Foundation continues to be involved as an adviser and is still the legal owner of the greater part of the contents of the house.

Besides being open for guided tours, the house today is a venue for concerts and other cultural events and offers food in a daytime restaurant in the former kitchen. The east wing is being refurbished to serve as a conference centre. The grounds along the Liffey are open to all and allow for riverside walks by adults, children and dogs.

Widely scattered trees are a feature of eighteenth-century parkland, providing shelter for horses and cattle as well as being fine ornaments. Planting for future generations continues at Castletown.

The backdrop is of woodland in all directions. The fact that some of it is a narrow fringe takes nothing from the general effect of a stately home safely screened from the busy outside world. Taylor's map of 1783 shows the two great avenues of lime trees, which converge to this day on the house. One leads to Celbridge, where its line continues along the street. The other points to the Wonderful Barn, built by John Glin in 1743 to the order of Katherine Conolly. Details of this and other contributions to the landscape are given by James Howley in *The Follies and Garden Buildings of Ireland*. Taylor shows extensive woods to the west and north of the house, evidently meant for pleasure, being traversed by many paths. The eighteenth-century plan of the demesne preserved in the house shows extensive lakes at the rear. The wood to the northwest was divided in two by an avenue pointing to the Conolly Folly and Carton. Taylor also shows the parkland to south and east of the house, a pond to the south and a fringe of trees along the riverbank.

The riverside at Castletown

The Doric temple on a ridge downstream of an abandoned weir commanded a view of the river when it was built, but trees have since grown up to spoil that effect. On the floodplain, upstream of the temple, stand remnants of a collection of conifers planted in the nineteenth century. A splendid Wellingtonia dominates the scene, but a very unusual tree in Irish collections is a Cembran pine, distinguished by long, long needles and salami-shaped cones. Fine old oaks abound in the demesne – a not uncommon feature. But young trees are plentiful, too, and they are unusual and more than welcome since oaks are not immortal.

Across the river, Donacomper House can be glimpsed beyond the trees. Its present-day appearance is the result of an extension in the 1830s in Gothic style designed by William Kirkpatrick. In 2010 Bord Pleanála refused permission for a housing scheme on the riverside property of Donaghcomper on the grounds that it would destroy the ambience of the parkland.

To the east of the temple, beyond the parkland and separated from it by a haha, the Liffey flows over a low weir and around an island, succeeded by a long, calm pool, created in 1949 by the building of the Leixlip hydro dam, 3 km further downstream. Beech and ash line the right bank and mallard dabble peacefully. The left bank is bordered with alder and willow, young trees for the most part. Both of these species thrive in damp soil and therefore can live close to rivers. But from time to time the river washes away the bank so that the trees collapse and are replaced naturally by a line on the new margin. The fallen trees for a while regenerate when their side-branches grow upright and form new trunks.

Downstream of the temple, a little way back from the riverbank, a strip of beech woodland extends nearly all the way to the east gate to the demesne.

The trees are relatively young, most of them less than 50 years old. There may have been extensive felling of the wood during the twentieth century, with replacement by trees grown from the seeds of the previous generation.

Self-sown beech trees on the left bank at Castletown.

On the right bank stands St Wolstan's House, overlooking the river and the ruins of the priory that gave that demesne its name. Founded at the beginning of the thirteenth century by the Anglo-Normans, it was dedicated to St Wulfstan, Bishop of Worcester, then newly canonised by Pope Innocent III. Not only did the invaders bring their living men of religion with them, they also installed their private saints. The big house that eventually replaced the monastery was built in the seventeenth century but greatly enlarged in the eighteenth so that the earlier work is well hidden.

On the left bank of the river, the stonework and sluice gear of a former weir survive. Together with a corn mill, it is marked on the 1837 map. The mill race it controlled became redundant when the ESB dam was built further downstream at Leixlip.

The east gate to Castletown and the Gothic gate lodge stand close to the river. The house bears the name of Batty Langley, the English landscape architect and garden planner whose book of designs was very widely used in Ireland. The lodge was completed in 1785 and faced inwards towards the big house rather than fronting to the gateway and its rather narrow approach road. Clearly the avenue of limes, which points down the main street of the village of Celbridge, was the entrance designed to receive visitors of rank. The lodge and the grounds were separated from the demesne when it was sold in 1967, but they were acquired by the state in 2006 and restoration work began shortly afterwards.

The Batty Langley Lodge (1785) and the east gate to the Castletown Demesne.

Riverside trees at Castletown.

Leixlip dam and the Salmon Leap

Lax, the word for salmon used by the Vikings and unchanged in modern Scandinavian languages, survives in Leixlip, the 'salmon leap'. This refers to the waterfall where the Liffey rushed over exposed bedrock a little way upstream of the promontory now occupied by Leixlip Castle. There the Vikings – and many generations before them – watched the salmon as they leaped out of the water to gain the upper reaches of the river and its tributaries where their spawning beds lie. Between Celbridge and Leixlip, the river has a fall of 18 metres. After the Second World War, in 1949, a dam was built just downstream of the Salmon Leap, to take advantage of the head of 18 metres between this point and the weir at Celbridge. The dam created a narrow reservoir about 3 km in length at a height of 45 metres above sea level, 142 metres lower than the surface of the Blessington Lakes. The head of water is almost exactly the same as at Golden Falls and the equipment is a single Kaplan turbine with the same rating, 4,000 kilowatts, as the main generator there.

Leixlip Reservoir, created by the building of the hydro dam in 1949, is a popular venue for canoeing and fishing for roach.

The power now supplied to the nation by the ESB had been used locally long before the 1940s. Now submerged beneath the reservoir, a mill race left the river on the right bank, apparently without a weir, and flowed for 1.2 km to supply a 'Flour Mill' at the Salmon Leap. Lewis describes this considerable undertaking:

The flour-mills erected by Messrs. Reid and Co. are capable of producing from 700 to 800 barrels weekly; the water wheel is 28 feet in diameter, and in turning 5 pair of stones acts with a power equivalent to that of 60 or 70 horses.

New Bridge

A little more than 2 km downstream of Celbridge, both Taylor and the latest Ordnance Survey maps mark the third 'New Bridge' on the Liffey. Which it was in 1308 when it was first built and when it presumably carried the great Slighe Mor along the Eiscir Riada that followed the esker across the bogs to the west. Rebuilt more than once, until the mid-twentieth century it had four arches. The creation of the Leixlip dam by the ESB necessitated replacement in 1949. Although the surviving structure probably contains stones hewn by mediaeval quarrymen, its design was radically changed and the new New Bridge has only three arches.

The rebuilt 'New Bridge' upstream of Leixlip hydro dam. The building on the right is the Salmon Leap Canoe Club.

Leixlip village

Lewis is mildly enthusiastic about the village, but, surprisingly, he had nothing to say about its name and the Vikings. He describes the salmon leap in his essay on Lucan because it lay within that parish. The village of Leixlip seems to have been going through a depressed state in his time:

This place was included in the grant originally made to Adam Fitz Hereford, one of the earliest of the English adventurers, who is said to have built the castle, which is situated on an eminence overlooking the river Liffey, and according to tradition was the occasional residence of John, Earl of Morton, while governor of Ireland in the reign of his father, Henry II. It was afterwards granted to the abbey of St. Thomas' court, Dublin; and by an inquisition in 1604 it appears that Thomas Cottrel, the last abbot of that house, was seized of the manor of Leixlip and the right of a flagon of ale out of every brewing in the town. The castle and manor were subsequently purchased by the Rt. Hon. Thomas Conolly, Speaker of the Irish House of Commons, and are now the property of Col. Conolly, of Castletown. This venerable mansion was the favourite retreat of several of the viceroys, of whom Lord Townsend usually spent the summer here; it is at present the residence of the Hon. George Cavendish, by whom it has been modernised and greatly improved.

The town is situated near the confluence of the Rye Water with the river Liffey, over which is an ancient stone bridge of three arches, and on the mail coach road from Dublin to Galway. It consists only of one street; the houses are irregularly built, and with the exception of a few of handsome appearance, have generally an aspect of negligence and decay; the inhabitants are amply supplied with water from springs.

Lewis was more enthusiastic about the surrounding countryside:

The parish comprises 7974 statute acres, as applotted under the tithe act; a considerable portion of the land is in pasture for fattening stock for the Dublin, Liverpool, and Bristol markets, and the remainder is under tillage. The soil is good, and the system of agriculture lowly but progressively improving; there is neither waste land nor bog, and, from the consequent scarcity of fuel, the peasantry are dependent on such precarious supplies as they can find in the roads and hedges. Limestone is very abundant, and is quarried to a considerable extent, for building, and also for burning into lime for manure. The country around, though deficient in those striking features of romantic grandeur which distinguish the neighbouring county of Wicklow, concentrates much that is pleasing and picturesque in landscape. The surface is finely undulating and richly diversified with wood and water, and the view embraces the town with its ancient bridge, numerous elegant seats with highly cultivated demesnes, ancient and picturesque ruins, distant mountains, and a variety of other interesting features of rural scenery ... The church, an ancient structure with a massive square tower, has been recently repaired by a grant of £291 from the Ecclesiastical Commissioners.

The 1838 map shows Leixlip as a small rural village, but with a considerable level of industrial development. There is woodland on both banks in the region of the Salmon Leap where, on the right bank, a woollen mill is marked, fed by a mill race from 500 metres upstream. The Salmon Leap waterfall, the wood, the mill race and the mill have all disappeared beneath the waters of the reservoir. On the bank opposite Leixlip Castle the map marks 'Remains of an intended canal'. It may have been conceived in the hope of allowing cargo vessels to pass the rapids. A canal in the grounds of Castletown was also mooted. In the village itself, a distillery is shown on the map, close to the church, and there is a mill dam in the river, upstream of the bridge. Downstream, on the left bank, are the corn mill and the ironworks mentioned by Lewis.

Two late twentieth-century developments changed considerably the fortunes and comforts of Leixlip. First, the establishment of the Intel factory provided well-paid work for a large labour force and a consequent explosion of the population. Second, the completion of the M4 motorway restored the village to the enjoyment of its own inhabitants in place of the unending stream of transport when the narrow street catered for all the traffic between the cities of Dublin and Galway.

The gazebo in the grounds of Leixlip Castle where the Rye Water meets the Liffey.

Leixlip Castle continued to change ownership a number of times after Lewis described it. The incumbent in 2016 was the Hon. Desmond Guinness, who had lived there for nearly sixty years after buying it in 1958. It is open to visitors on specified days throughout the year. The castle combines a great many rare and distinguished features with an atmosphere of a welcoming family home. Central rooms with massively thick walls preserve the fabric of the twelfth-century castle. The greater part of the building is eighteenth century, when the fanciful archaisms of a tower and battlements were recreated but combined with contemporary large windows and opulent rooms. Decorations on the walls in the house include great continental tapestries, prints, paintings and drawings ancient and modern and a feast of furniture of many centuries.

In the village the riverbank is accessible from the car park near the old church. A footpath gives access upstream to the confluence with the Rye Water which flows here at the bottom of the cliff on which Leixlip Castle was built. Across the Rye a gazebo overlooks the Liffey and further upstream the ESB dam towers above the river. Downstream the footpath leads past the church mentioned by Lewis and recently restored once more. The path becomes less friendly as it follows the riverbank but does go far enough to allow a glimpse of the sturdy old bridge which, thanks to the completion of the M4, has been relieved of its heavy burden.

A long island lies opposite the car park, but it is hard to distinguish from the slope of the valley since both are richly wooded. This woodland hides the steep bank which rises to a plateau occupied by the extensive buildings of a major water treatment plant. The access road to this is a turn to the north of the old bridge and it leads to a pleasant picnic place and fishing stand on the banks of the reservoir, immediately upstream of the dam.

In the village, across the road from the river, an alley leads up to a disused quarry. The greater part of the rock is massive limestone, sadly deficient in fossils. It was deposited in calm, deep seawater, not far from a shore formed by the Wicklow Mountains. It took many thousands of years to build up the thickness of rock exposed there and, not surprisingly, the sequence of events was interrupted from time to time. This is shown by the presence of black shaley bands in the limestone. The shale is derived from clay particles, carried out into the sea beyond the edge of a delta, in much the same way as the lake muds would be deposited 300 million years later in Glacial Lake Blessington. By only a small stretch of the imagination, you might say that the shales represent the deposits of an ancestral Liffey, but it was a Liffey without birds or flowers or people.

Leixlip spa and Louisa Bridge

In the eighteenth century, Leixlip had some importance as a spa resort. The Rye Water, which flows through the nearby Carton Demesne and joins the river upstream of the bridge in Leixlip, cut a deep valley to the north of the village. A great earthen aqueduct was built towards the end of the eighteenth century to carry first the Royal Canal and, later, the railway. The Galway road crosses canal and railway at Louisa Bridge and, on the slopes below the bridge, are remnants of the spa. Slightly warm water, highly charged with iron and lime, still flows from a spring there and there is swampy ground, bright in summer with orchids and other wild flowers.

Parks between Leixlip and Lucan

Immediately downstream of Leixlip lie housing estates and a sewage treatment works on the left bank with private demesnes and a golf course on the right. Then follows a marvellous expanse of public park, administered respectively by Fingal and South Dublin councils, whose jurisdictions have been separated from each other by the river since 1994. St Catherine's is on the left bank and Lucan Demesne on the right. They are joined at the top by an iron footbridge and a pair of aqueducts. The respective councils have plans to build another footbridge at the bottom, downstream, end so that a circular walk through the twin parks will be a possibility.

St Catherine's

A priory dedicated to St Catherine was founded early in the thirteenth century by Warisius de Pech. One of its benefactors was Adam de Hereford, who had been a co-founder of St Wolstan's, upstream of Leixlip and across the river from Castletown. The priory buildings of St Catherine's were ultimately replaced by an affluent dwelling and its farmyard. The big house is long gone, but parts of the eighteenth-century farm buildings remain and serve as a machinery store for the park maintenance.

St Catherine's Park today contains one of the very best areas of old demesne woodland on the Liffeyside. Curving to the right, 2 km downstream from the Salmon Leap, the river cut a steep bank, 10 metres high, below a large area of level ground 40 metres above sea level. The level ground above it provided the private owners of St Catherine's with pasture – and their public successors with playing fields. Too steep for grazing, the high bank was gentle enough to allow beech trees to grow. So a beautiful strip of beech wood grew up. While it is marked as woodland on the 1838 map, the trees today are relatively young, few, if any, being more than 100 years old. As in the case of the woodland at Castletown, it seems that there may have been extensive felling, perhaps during the Second World War. Although lacking ancient giants, the woodland is mature and totally delightful, shaded and almost mysteriously dark in summer, with a ground cover of ferns and ivy, an understorey of holly and hazel and

The water meadow of St Catherine's Park, bordered by beech woodland.

White clover and a common blue butterfly in the water meadow.

Naturally regenerated beech woodland in St Catherine's Park.

a border of hawthorn, blackthorn, elder and some ash trees, with occasional young elms.

A 'Woodland Walk' is signposted, running steeply downhill from the car park to the level of the river, then following the water meadow and returning by a steep climb to the upper parts, where the trail runs within the wood itself. The lower path is separated from the river upstream by the water meadow, downstream by scrub woodland which contains occasional conifers that testify to the presence long ago of an arboretum. The trail leads to the water's edge at the weir which, viewed from the opposite bank, features in a number of Thomas Roberts's paintings. The weir was centred on a pre-existing island and the water flows swiftly on the left bank. The mill race was on this side and, although dry for the most part, survives as a deep cutting beside the path. Its construction was a considerable feat of manpower in days long before any mechanical diggers had been conceived. The 1838 survey shows a mill race on the left bank which splits in two, the pair of streams running parallel for 500 metres. This map shows a quarry where they meet again, but no mill. A single mill stream then runs beside the Liffey for another 500 metres and rejoins the river a little way upstream of the splendid weir in the village of Lucan. The only construction noted on the nineteenth-century map at this point is 'Piers of old br.'

Lucan Demesne

A path, leading upstream from the bottom of the hill of the woodland walk, leads to the farmyard of St Catherine's. Further upstream, a dense hedge shields a large sewage works from the public gaze. The eastern boundary of the plant is bordered by a path which leads down to the river and so to a footbridge that continues the walk into the Lucan Demesne on the right bank. The footbridge is a good place for spotting the trout, or occasionally salmon, which are invisible from the riverbank.

A large portion of the property, developed by the Sarsfield family in the seventeenth century, is in public hands under the care of the South Dublin County Council. The entrance to this park is at the top of a steep bank to the west of the village of Lucan, where the former main road goes beneath the bypass. A steep track leads past a little wood of mature beech trees, down to the path by the riverside and the weir, immortalised in the paintings of Thomas Roberts in the 1760s.

Four of his views of the weir and the surrounding landscape were displayed in the National Gallery until it began to undergo major refurbishment in 2011, and more are reproduced in the study of the artist by William Laffan and Brendan Rooney. Their splendid and scholarly book, which provides the background to Roberts' work, incidentally has much to say on the history and

The Weir in Lucan House Demesne (120.3 x 70 cm) in the 1760s by Thomas Roberts (1748–1777). Photo © National Gallery of Ireland.

The calm waters of the Liffey break as they pass over the rapids between Lucan Demesne weir on the left and an ivy-clad retaining wall at the base of the beech woodland on the right.

development of Lucan Demesne. Five of the pictures reproduced include the weir, which remains a central feature of the landscape. Two of these, one in the National Gallery and one in a private collection, look across the weir from the right bank with a venerable ash tree slanting across the water. Both show an angler; one has two men relaxing on the riverbank; the other has a courting couple, the man playing on a flute. The tree is perilously close to the water's edge and is not shown in another view. It had probably fallen by the time the latter was painted.

A third painting, from higher up on the right bank, shows sheep grazing and a couple enjoying the scenery from a four-wheeled carriage drawn by a single horse. A fourth, in more sombre colours than the others, looks upstream at the weir and includes a herdsman with two cattle drinking in the river. The fifth, from a little further upstream, includes an elegant couple, identified as Roberts' landlord and patron, Agmondesham Vesey, with his lady.

The valley is narrow and steep-sided below the car park, but widens upstream on the right bank. Footpaths have been provided both beside the river and at a higher level. The land between the river and the park boundary, formerly pasture dotted with trees, is now maintained as a hay meadow, mown late in the summer so that the wild flowers among the grasses have time to bloom. The grass on the margins of the footpaths is kept mown. Part of the reason for doing this is to make sure that the park looks cared-for because the delightfully unkempt appearance of hay meadow would otherwise look suspiciously like neglect on the part of the park authorities.

Downstream of the weir stands a great multi-stemmed sycamore. The remarkable hole in its trunk was left where two once-separated stems grew together again. Close upstream are four fine oaks evenly spaced with many more remaining by the bank. They might be 100 years old. A small number of much older oaks grow beside the river and in the parkland and these may very well date to the eighteenth century.

Lucan

Lewis was very impressed by the beauties of Lucan and its environs. The parish in his day extended upstream as far as the Salmon Leap – which explains why he described the vanished waterfall in this section rather than under Leixlip. He was particularly taken by the rock formations near the bridge in Lucan and also has some observations on James Gandon's discovery of a cave in the grounds of his residence on Fort Hill.

The town is beautifully situated in a fertile vale on the eastern bank of the river Liffey, over which is a handsome stone bridge of one arch, built in 1794, and ornamented with balustrades of cast iron from the Phoenix iron-works, near Dublin. At the other side of the bridge, on the eastern bank of the river, is the picturesque glebe of the incumbent, the Rev. H. E. Prior. The total number of houses is 187, most of which are well built, and many of them are fitted up as lodging-houses for the reception of visiters, who, during the summer season, resort to this place to drink the waters, which are found efficacious in scorbutic, bilious, and rheumatic affections. A handsome Spa-house has been erected, consisting of a centre and two wings, in one of which is an assembly-room, 62 feet long and 22 feet wide, in which concerts and balls are given; the house affords excellent accommodation for families. The mineral spring, from its having a higher temperature than others in the neighbourhood, is called the "Boiling Spring;" the water, on an analysis made in 1822, was found to contain, in two gallons, 70 grains of crystallised carbonate of soda, 20 of carbonate of lime, 1 of carbonate of magnesia, 2 of silex, 6 of muriate of soda, and 14 of sulphur. The scenery of the neighbourhood is beautifully diversified, and its short distance from the metropolis renders the town a place of fashionable resort and of pleasant occasional residence. A chief constabulary police force is stationed in it, and petty sessions are held on Tuesdays. The parish, through a portion of which the Royal Canal passes, is in a high state of cultivation; the soil is fertile and the crops are abundant. Lucan, the interesting residence of Mrs. Vesey, is a spacious mansion, situated in a highly embellished demesne, comprising nearly

500 statute acres extending along the banks of the Liffey; within the grounds is a monument to one of the Sarsfield family, near which are an ancient oratory dedicated to St. John, and thickly covered with ivy, and a holy well.

Having given details of the ownership of the land and of the parish clergy, Lewis continues with an interesting picture of village worship and education and of help for the poor in 1837:

A neat church with a tower and spire was erected in the town in 1822, towards which the late Board of First Fruits advanced £1100 on loan … In the R. C. division … the chapel, a very small edifice, is about to be rebuilt. There is a place of worship for Wesleyan Methodists, erected in 1832. About 250 children are taught in two public schools, of which the parochial school, with an infants' school attached, was built and is supported by subscription. The other is a national school. There are three private schools, in which are about 70 children. A poor-shop, with a lending library, and a loan fund have been established; and a dispensary is open to the poor of the neighbourhood.

He goes on to matters geological and archaeological:

The vicinity affords some highly interesting specimens of irregular stratification of limestone, which occurs in parallel layers separated by seams of decomposed calpe, dipping uniformly at a small angle to the E. N. E. In a bank on the left side of the Liffey, a few yards only above the bridge, the strata become sinuous, forming curvatures of nearly two-thirds of their respective circumferences; and single slabs taken from the disturbed beds have an arched outline, conforming to the general curvature of the strata. At Canon Brook, for many years the residence of the late Mr. Gandon, architect, is a singular cave, discovered by that gentleman; it consists of one principal apartment and two side cells of smaller dimensions, curiously secured all round with stone, to prevent the walls from falling in; many curious relics of antiquity were found, consisting of celts, pieces of bone curiously inscribed and sculptured, military weapons of copper or bronze, and various others of more recent date. The hill in which these apartments are excavated is about 300 feet above the level of the vale, and is called the Fort Hill, from its being crowned with a fortification, the works of which are still in good preservation. The monastery of St. Catherine, founded by Waryn de Peche in 1220, though its endowment was augmented by subsequent benefactors, was, on account of its poverty, assigned, in 1323, to the

abbey St. Thomas, Dublin; there are no remains. Opposite the gate of
Col. Vesey's demesne was a very ancient, and splendid cross, round
the site of which it was the custom at R. C. funerals to bear the corpse
previous to interment. Above the modern bridge are some fragments
of an older structure, said to have been built in the reign of John. Lucan
gives the titles of baron and earl to the family of Bingham.

The combination of the spa with a series of rapids and, hence, watermills
made Lucan into the most substantial village on the river in the early
nineteenth century. The spa turned it into something of a resort, with plentiful
accommodation, and the mills provided work for a large labour force. While the
village has expanded almost beyond recognition to become a major dormitory
suburb, substantial traces remain of its industrial past. Weir and bridge still
dominate the waterside, as they did in the nineteenth century. However, the
watermills and riverside industry have departed, leaving no trace besides the
redundant mill race and sluice gates upstream of the bridge and a new retail
complex downstream. A red-brick chimney has been preserved in the latter
and there is a fine terrace of workers' houses nearby.

Locally quarried limestone forming the crest of the Lucan Demesne weir.

Vying with Sarah Bridge downstream as the most graceful of the crossings of the Liffey, the bridge at Lucan replaces a succession of older bridges upstream that were from time to time destroyed by floods. Half an arch of the last of them leans out over the right bank at the wall of Lucan Demesne.

Social and historical aspects of Lucan have recently been chronicled in the book *Aspects of Lucan*, edited by Patricia O'Donohue and containing four essays on its history, together with very comprehensive bibliographies. Although no trace has yet been found of a Viking settlement, there is a record of their ships sailing up the Liffey in 917 to establish a base upstream at Cooldrinagh. The Manor of Lucan was created in 1169 when Henry II made a grant of the land to Alard FitzWilliam. The first of many bridges was built in the reign of King John.

The Liffey of Lucan today flows from the privacy of the residence of the Italian Ambassador – the former Sarsfield House – to a little waterfront park in the village which runs on the right bank from the ruins of the old bridge, past the weir to the present crossing. Across the water from the original village, the river in times gone by excavated a cliff in the glacial till. A more recent strip of floodplain below this provides space for the road with the curious name of Barnhill Crossroads that runs beside the river. A terrace of two-storey houses for the employees of the former ironworks is squeezed in between road and cliff. The contorted rock strata described by Lewis stand behind the houses at the west end of the town.

The folding in the limestone on the left bank at the upstream end of Weirview on Barnhill Crossroads, described by Lewis.

The right bank pier of a former bridge at Lucan has been adapted to extend the garden of a modern house on the edge of the village.

A new road was cut into the cliff opposite the bridge in the twentieth century, bringing traffic through housing estates and on towards Coolmine. Deposits of sand and gravel are being quarried to the north of the cutting. Downstream of the bridge, on the right bank, a small park has been created on the edge of the Village Court housing development. Beyond it the bank rises steeply above the river to the woodland that hides the St Edmundsbury complex.

Turner's ironworks

Lucan weir, which diverted the river to provide a head for Turner's ironworks on the left bank. A salmon ladder in the centre allows the fish to leap to their spawning grounds upstream. The contorted rock strata outcrop is behind the row of houses.

The beginning of the mill race that led to Turner's ironworks on the left bank of the Liffey at Lucan.

Upstream of the bridge in the village, the dominant feature of the river today is the weir slanting from the right bank to the left. A portion of it appears in Roberts' view of Lucan House in or about 1770. The weir is shown in the 1837 map and the mill race runs, as it still does, underneath the bridge. In those days it bordered a long, narrow island, now occupied by a retail park. This provided a head of water close to the bridge which gave motive power for an industry of international fame, described by Lewis in these words:

> Also of interest are the gates, which were designed by Richard Turner, and made at his Iron Works in Lucan. This business was on the site of Hills Mill, during the 18th and 19th centuries. Turner was a famous ironmonger of his day being credited with many great works including greenhouses at Kew.

The Sarsfield legacy

A history of the demesne and its owners is the subject of a study by Suzanne Pegley, published in 2008 as one of four essays in Patricia O'Donohue's *Aspects of Lucan*. According to her research, early in the seventeenth century the lands around Lucan came into the hands of Sir William Sarsfield, whose descendants would continue to own it for many generations. The seventeenth century witnessed extremely complicated changes of ownership and also the failure of any male Sarsfields to survive for long enough to establish themselves on the demesne. The hero general Patrick died in 1693 at the Battle of Landen in Flanders, fighting for King James. The inheritance passed through Charlotte, a sister of Patrick's, on her marriage to the Vesey family. Agmondesham Vesey was the eighteenth-century owner who was largely responsible for the design of the present manor house and the landscaping of the demesne. Suzanne Pegley quotes Arthur Young's enthusiastic description of it in the 1770s:

> The house is rebuilding, but the wood on the river, with walks through it, is exceedingly beautiful. The character of the place is that of a sequestered shade. Distant views are every where shut out, and the objects all correspond perfectly with the impression they were designed to raise: it is a walk on the banks of the river, chiefly under a variety of fine wood, which rises on varied slopes, in some parts gentle, in others steep; spreading here and there into cool meadows, on the opposite shore, rich banks of wood or shrubby ground. The walk is perfectly sequestered, and has that melancholy gloom which should ever dwell in such a place. The river is of a character perfectly suited to the rest of the scenery, in some places breaking over rocks; in others silent, under the shade of spreading wood.

The classical house is still hidden by trees and has been the residence of the Italian ambassador since 1947.

Lucan to Chapelizod

Until 1990, when the West Link toll bridge was completed, no permanent crossings of the Liffey existed between these two villages, though a number of ferries are marked on the old maps. The shape of the valley may explain why very few people wanted to cross this stretch until late in the twentieth century. With only two exceptions, where the river swerves to the right, the left bank between Lucan and Chapelizod is high and steep with a narrow strip of level ground, just wide enough to fit the long-established road which barely accommodates two traffic lanes. The greater part of the steep bank is densely wooded. A few houses have been tucked into it and there are back entrances to Luttrelstown and other demesnes that occupy the high ground above and are invisible from the riverside. The big houses on this side look across the river and effectively stand aloof from it. Knockmaroon was an exception: it occupied land on both banks and its owners built a lattice girder bridge to give access to their fields to the south.

The situation on the right bank is very different: the land slopes gently down to the river and the great houses were set in parkland in which the water plays a major role. Except where it comes close to the banks at the two villages, the main road stays about a kilometre away from the river.

There is a little green space between road and river on the left bank – crying out for the authorities to acquire it and open a wonderful park and footpath. Until this happens the points of interest, though few, compensate to some degree for the lack of public access on the other side. A narrow footpath leads from Lucan as far as the entrance to Anna Liffey Mill. Further downstream occasional car parks give access to the Liffey which, in places, is separated from the road only by a stone wall.

Mills diabolical and otherwise

Downstream of the bridge at Lucan, Rocque's 1762 map of the County of Dublin shows a mill on the right bank where the river turns to flow westwards for a little. Folklore gave it an alternative name of 'The Devil's Mill' and this name, though lacking an apostrophe, is given on the 1838 map. While the name is clearly marked, there is no trace of a mill on that side.

The involvement of His Satanic Majesty came about in the seventeenth century. Henry Luttrell, having wasted his inheritance in various ways and having no other source of income, offered his soul to the devil. Part of the pact was that Henry would be permitted to continue his present life until he gave the devil an impossible task. The building of a mill on the snipe grass in this bend of the Liffey was one of the attempted impossibilities. The devil accomplished this overnight but was ultimately outwitted when Luttrell took to Bible study and a quiet life.

Marked as 'Flour Mills' in 1837 and given a very substantial ground plan, the present-day Anna Liffey Mill, built in 1820 by William Delaney, is supplied from a weir built directly opposite it. The original waterwheel powered four millstones. Ownership passed through several hands before it was leased to the Quaker George Shackleton and his son Abraham in 1859. This was the beginning of family ownership, which lasted for three more generations until the retirement of Richard Shackleton in 1978. Outstanding leaders of their profession, the Shackletons were in the forefront of innovations. They introduced roller mills in 1884, replacing the traditional stone wheels, and also substituted horizontal turbines for the old mill wheel. In 1936 they converted the turbines from providing direct power to generating electricity.

After Richard Shackleton left, Roma Foods took over the operation and used the mills to produce semolina rather than flour. In 2002 Fingal County Council acquired the great nineteenth-century seven-storey stone building, which stands by the side of the road that runs by the Strawberry Beds. The purchase included the milling machinery and the fine classical house that was the owner's residence. Cutbacks a few years later led to the postponement of ambitious plans for conservation of the mill and its transformation to a theme park.

The Wren's Nest

The 1838 map marks the 'Wrens Nest' (again without an apostrophe) 3 km downstream of the Devil's Mill, placing it to the north of the road and evidently giving the name to the ancient inn. The V-shaped weir, which has acquired the Wren's name since then, is shown beside extensive buildings of the New Holland Iron & Starch works on the left bank. The mill buildings have disappeared, almost without a trace but water still rushes through the remains of a headrace and under stone arches before it returns to the river.

Steel bars sprout from the ground and scattered chunks of masonry serve as memorials to half-forgotten industry. On the right bank at the Wren's Nest an impressive mill race begins a journey that brought the water a distance of 3 km to provide power for the great industrial complex of Palmerstown.

A car park at the charming old Wrens Nest pub is the best place to stop for a visit to the weir, a busy place in summer where the deep water above and below allows for swimming. And negotiating the weir is one of the most hazardous and popular challenges for canoeists. Downstream, woodland and hedges close in again and keep all but boating folk away from the left bank for most of the

The mill race from the Wren's Nest provides a very important habitat for kingfishers, dragonflies and many other creatures.

The V-weir at the Wren's Nest. The sluice controlled water entering the 3 km mill race that powered machinery at Palmerstown.

way to Chapelizod. Traffic, even though relatively light, effectively excludes pedestrians from these parts. It was very different until early in the twentieth century.

The Strawberry Beds

The *Discovery* map places the Strawberry Beds upstream of the West Link toll bridge and opposite Fonthill and Hermitage. The steep south-facing bank has good, well-draining soil, which produced heavy crops of strawberries. Within easy reach of the Dublin fruit market and of Dubs taking a Sunday walk, this stretch of the Liffey became famous. The Strawberry Hall pub was a permanent centre, but there were also roadside stalls. The fruits were served, with cream, on cabbage leaves at a price of one penny. Single-storey thatched cabins shown in old photographs survive, reroofed and rebuilt in places, tucked into the hillside. They include the recently refurbished Lower Road National School, established in 1900.

Nessa O'Connor, in *Palmerstown: An Ancient Place*, mentions that there were ferries at the Strawberry Beds in 1816, and two ferry points are marked in that region on the 1837 map. Her book has photographs of one of the boats with passengers in the 1920s and of the ferryman Michael Treacy in 1930. The craft was a clinker-built rowing boat.

Le Fanu describes the misfortunes of two drunk military officers who tried to cross the river in the region of Knockmaroon by a borrowed ferry without the assistance of the ferryman. The chapter 'Swans in the Water' in *The House by the Churchyard* describes a ferry boat operated by heaving on a rope across the river.

Knockmaroon Hill

Downstream of the Strawberry Beds, Knockmaroon Hill rises steeply, its southern slopes undercut by the Liffey – but with just enough level ground to allow a road and occasional houses to be tucked in. Precipitous in places, with the yellowish glacial till exposed, it was elsewhere too steep for grazing and therefore allowed to develop as woodland. Hawthorn scrub dominates the upstream, western part, which lacks trees of any size. The slope to the east is gentler and is clothed by a beautiful stand of mature woodland. On the level ground above the valley on the left bank, Scots pines dominate the scene, as viewed from the more accessible Waterstown Park across the river. Above these trees stands the splendid clock tower. Built in 1880 as a water tower to fill the baths and supply the farm of the Guinness owners of Farmleigh, the family took the opportunity to create a thing of beauty and of service to the wider public.

Out of sight of the river, the more or less level and very fertile ground dominated by the clock tower is occupied by stately homes and their demesnes. Several were developed by the magnates of the brewery just down the road. Some remain Guinness family property; others have acquired different owners, among them Farmleigh, which is run by the Office of Public Works on behalf of the people of Ireland. Details of the legends, history and buildings of Knockmaroon Hill and other Liffeyside holdings were published in 1977 by James O'Driscoll in *Cnucha: A History of Castleknock*.

The clock tower of Farmleigh demesne stands above the steep, wooded left bank.

Waterstown Park

The lands on the right bank where the ferries of old deposited their passengers have been transformed from private demesne to public space. Opened in May 2009, Waterstown Park was created from a number of estates between the toll bridge and Palmerstown. Its green fields slope quite steeply down to the riverside, but the park has no less than 5 km of tarmac footpaths and 2 km of cycle track. Across the river lie the Strawberry Beds and, near the toll bridge, the cliffs of yellow glacial till. Above these and out of sight from the right bank the ground is fairly level land occupied by private demesnes and housing developments.

Waterstown Park extends from the West Link Bridge to Palmerstown. It concentrates on space for walkers and cyclists and gives views of the steep and rather inaccessible left bank, where yellowish glacial till is exposed in places.

West Link Bridge, opened in 1990 and duplicated in 2003 to cope with increased traffic, crosses the Liffey upstream of the Strawberry Beds and Waterstown Park. It stands 42 metres above the river.

Waterstown is dominated to the west by the West Link Bridge, a hugely successful utilitarian structure whose size and pure lines make it a pleasure to contemplate from the Liffeyside. Over the greater part of the valley within the park, the grass along the borders of the tarmac paths is kept short by mowing. Beyond this it is allowed to grow tall, restoring the hay meadows of long ago and their wealth of wild flowers. A strip of wasteland extends along the steep slope below the housing estate on the southern boundary of the park. Hawthorn and other shrubs grow out from a tangle of brambles: inaccessible to humans, it provides a safe haven for wildlife. Small stands of planted birch trees punctuate the green.

The eastern part of Waterstown is less open and more taken over by scrub, which grew up over the years before the park was improved and when the land was more or less abandoned. 'Scrub' might sound somewhat pejorative – and it is certainly at odds with the carefully tended rose beds or shrubberies that one might associate with well-kept suburban amenities – but, apart from the beauty of the flowers and berries of the hawthorn, blackthorn and other species, it offers a secure home for foxes, badgers and various thrush and finch species. Scrub in fertile land, like that of the lower Liffey valley, is a transitory life form. It develops when grazing animals are too few to keep the bushes down but, ultimately, destroys itself by providing a shelter for oak and other trees that will shade it out and live for centuries. The bushes do, however, survive on the edges of the woodland – and it was on the edges of the primeval woods of Europe and Asia that many of our most familiar and best-loved garden birds, such as robins, blackbirds and chaffinches, evolved.

The usual view of the kingfisher is of its brilliant colour as it flies above the water from one perch to another. When it sits still on a leafy branch, waiting to spot a fish, its colours keep it remarkably well hidden. *Photo: Michael Finn.*

Access from the park to the riverbank is impeded by the old mill race which runs for 3 km from the Wren's Nest weir down to the riverside factory complex of Palmerstown. With its slow-flowing water, overhung by bushes, it is a perfect habitat for kingfishers which greatly prefer such small streams to more open waters. Two bridges, one an ancient stone arch, the other a concrete pipe, cross the mill race and lead to the riverside. Easy walking through the park towards the east comes to an end at the currently ruined and boarded-up Waterstown House. A little way downstream of it is the bramble-encased abutment of the lattice girder bridge which provided a walkway to the grounds of Knockmaroon house. It is possible, but not especially comfortable, to walk along the mill race to the nineteenth-century cottages and houses of Palmerstown. There the water's edge is occupied by the factory, which occupies the rebuilt eighteenth-century mill buildings. The easier approach to this complex is by car from the N4 highway, following the directions for Stewart's Hospital.

Palmerstown

Named Palmerstown on the old maps but, following a twentieth-century plebiscite of the residents, spelt Palmerston, this medieval leper colony developed into a major industrial centre in the eighteenth century. The mill race from the Wren's Nest provided much of the power, the remainder coming from the weir below the village.

In Lewis's day the parish extended over 1,465 acres and there were 1,533 inhabitants.

> Near the village, which is irregularly built, and in which the dwellings are of a humble character, there was an hospital for lepers, previously to the Reformation. At the commencement of the present century here were extensive printing works, large iron works, oil and dye stuff mills, and wash mills; lead and copper works have been established for 16 years; there are large cotton-mills, employing about 120 persons, and a flour mill on the Liffey which bounds the parish to the north.

The village, originally confined to the steep bank between the river and the main road to the west, spread out of the valley and across the road. As the twentieth century progressed, it became more and more divided, with the two sides of the main street separated by ceaseless traffic. The opening of the N4 bypass restored it to its former peaceful bustle.

Not long before her tragic death at the age of 42, Nessa O'Connor, a member of a long-established Palmerstown family, completed a study of the village and its surroundings. Published in 2003 as *Palmerstown: An Ancient Place*, her researches give a wealth of detail about the rise and fall of industry there. Burials unearthed in the nineteenth century testify to the existence of a Bronze Age community. The name has been established at least since the twelfth century and may refer to 'palmers', those who had made a pilgrimage to the Holy Land. Until the dissolution of the monasteries under Henry VIII in 1539, the settlement was part of the property of the Knights Hospitallers of Thomas Street in Dublin who maintained a leper hospital in the townland of Saintlawrence, a little to the east of the present village.

Ruins of a medieval church still stand above the right bank and there is an ancient burial ground and traces of a fair green. These were instituted by the landlords who controlled the rich farmland, but the community would have been a small one before the eighteenth century. Great days came to Palmerstown then, when the mill race from the Wren's Nest weir provided power for an increasing number of factories. For reasons not fully understood, the industry powered by the various turbines almost ceased around 1837 and never recovered to the same degree.

While there is no reason to doubt that the Liffeyside monasteries operated mills in early Christian times, the earliest historical record of such undertakings comes from 1306. And that is a sadly negative one, telling how the Sheriff commanded that a new mill be pulled down as it was affecting the flow of the river. Over 200 years later a corn mill at Palmerstown is noted at the time of the dissolution of the monasteries in 1539. And then there appears to be no further mention until 1713, when John Twigge leased a plating mill to two ironmongers.

It seems possible that by this time the very remarkable mill race that follows the right bank from the Wren's Nest weir all the way to Palmerstown had been built. A weir, though unnamed, is clearly marked at the spot by Rocque in 1762. From this the race runs for 3 km, sometimes close to the river, sometimes as much as 100 metres away. Excavated in the hillside in places, retained by an embankment in others, in former times it broadened into a number of mill ponds at the bottom of Mill Lane, where the great complex of mill buildings stands. The water power was used as recently as the 1960s and, happily, the mill race remains in reasonable condition, awaiting true salvation when funds permit Fingal County Council to complete their ambitious transformation of the old riverside demesnes to a public park. In addition to the Wren's Nest supply, the Palmerstown mills were powered from a V-shaped weir on the spot: it is difficult to approach but visible from the car park of the Anglers' Rest on the left bank.

William Petty in 1683 marks no mills at 'Palmerstown' – or anywhere else. Rocque shows 'Mardyke Mill' and so does Taylor, who also names a 'Red Mill' downstream and an 'Old Mill' upstream of the Mardyke. The 1838 Ordnance Survey map marks 'Lead and Copper Mill' upstream of Mill Lane on the right bank at a weir and then, proceeding downstream, an 'Iron Mill' and, further on,

'Palmerstown Mills', including an 'Oil Mill' and a 'Cotton Mill'; and there are more on the left bank, immediately downstream of the weir.

Nessa O'Connor gives details of the development of the mills, beginning with 'slitting mills' in 1712, through a long period of expansion with the number of installations still increasing in the first three decades of the nineteenth century. Quite suddenly, it seems, the industries collapsed, and by 1837 only the oil and copper mill was still in production. Most of the eighteenth- and nineteenth-century buildings are dilapidated – a few of them very imposing ruins commemorating their former glory – but riverside industry still thrives in the steelworks and other operations.

Stewart's Hospital

The nineteenth century saw the creation of Stewart's Hospital, immediately downstream of Palmerstown village. The hospital is now an integral part of the community and its library and sports facilities are shared with the public. The complex is centred on the former stately home of John Hely Hutchinson, Provost of Trinity College, MP and holder of many other high offices. He purchased a property on the right bank of the Liffey in 1763 and enlarged and embellished the old house that had stood above the bend of the river. The estate remained in the family into the nineteenth century, but by 1837 was beginning to show signs of neglect. In 1869 the house was acquired by a relation of Hely Hutchinson, Dr Henry Hutchinson Stewart. Nearby in Lucan he had established an institution

Stewart's Hospital grew from a stately home overlooking the secluded riverside downstream of Palmerstown.

for children with severe mental problems and he moved this to the property at Palmerstown. Later in the century the old house was swallowed up by the colossal Victorian building that is still the centre of Stewart's Institution.

A secluded little park, encircled by a footpath, occupies a former water meadow on the outer side of a sharp bend of the Liffey, overlooked by the great grey pile of the hospital. Access is by an unobtrusive gateway in the wall of Mill Lane and the park extends northwestwards as far as the ivy-covered walls of the former oil mill. Below the hospital building a steep, wooded slope rises, which would once have been the riverbank and curves around to form a natural amphitheatre.

The level ground probably once lay within an ox-bow, a U-shaped curve whose bend was cut off when the river jumped across the opening during a flood and proceeded on a shorter course. Whatever happened in the distant past, Anna Liffey still makes a U-turn at this point. Her overall trend is from west to east, but she flows southeast for a few hundred metres, then takes a broad turn southwest, followed by a sharp bend to resume her eastward journey to Dublin.

From the stagnant tail-race of the old mill, a footpath follows the curve of the river, separated from it by a fringe of willows. A little stone bridge crosses a small side-stream at the point of the U-bend and carries the path into an old beech wood on the steep slope. Within the U is a wonderful jungle, bright with wood anemones in early spring. A little later, both there and in the wood, marvellous sheets of wild garlic show their white flowers and scent the air.

Wild garlic blooming at Palmerstown in April.

Concrete steps lead up the slope to a path high above the river on the left bank. It passes a limestone cliff, which may have been quarried long ago. Massive beds of pure limestone are separated from each other by layers of black shale, showing changes hundreds of millions of years ago from deposition in a clear deep sea to a muddy estuary and back again. There is – or was – a lower path close to the river, with a post-and-rail fence. But this part of the park became overgrown and blocked in places by fallen trees. Young beech and sycamore cover the hillside, growing up among a few giants. Laurel and snowberry abound, evidence that the woodland was once carefully landscaped as part of the old demesne. Other remnants of the demesne planting include the fine row of pine trees that line the path leading down from Mill Lane to the tail-race.

Chapelizod

Although administratively within the City of Dublin, Chapelizod retains its integrity as a separate village, thanks to the presence downstream of the war memorial park, with Con Colbert Road on the right bank, both of which preclude an infill of suburban or urban dwellings. Long before either of these was conceived, the royal deerpark of Phoenix Park ensured that the left bank of the valley remained virtually free from building. William Petty, apparently ignorant of the legendary importance of the village, named it Chapell Lizard, but everyone knows that this was the site of the chapel of the fair princess Isolde.

Lewis's account of the parish gives it a very respectable antiquity, with details of the ownership of the land going back to the twelfth century. This is far from surprising, considering its proximity to the port of Dublin, the value of the rich pastureland on all sides and its control over a substantial salmon fishery:

> CHAPELIZOD, a parish, in the barony of CASTLEKNOCK, county of DUBLIN, and province of LEINSTER, 3 miles (w.) from Dublin; containing 2181 inhabitants, of which number 1632 are in the village. This place is supposed to have derived its name from La Belle Isolde a daughter of one of the ancient Irish kings, who had a chapel here. The lands belonging to it were granted by Hugh de Lacy, in 1173, to Hugh Tyrrell, which grant was afterwards confirmed by Hen. II. In 1176, they were given by the Tyrrells to the hospital or the Knights Templars of Kilmainham, and after the suppression of that order remained in possession of their successors, the Knights of St. John of Jerusalem, till the dissolution of the monasteries, in the reign of Hen. VIII. They subsequently passed through various hands till 1665, when the Duke of Ormonde, by command of the king, purchased the entire manor, with the mansion, from Sir Maurice Eustace, for the purpose

of enclosing the Phoenix park, and the old mansion-house became the occasional residence of the Lord-Lieutenant … In 1690, Gen. Douglas, on his march to Athlone, encamped for one night at this place; and soon after, King William himself, subsequently to his expedition to the south, passed several days here in issuing various orders and redressing grievances. In 1696, Lord Capel, Lord-Deputy of Ireland, died at the vice-regal residence here after a long illness, during which several important meetings of the council took place; and though the house was repaired by Primate Boulter, when Lord-Justice of Ireland, in 1726, it has never since been occupied by the lord-lieutenants: a house near the village, called the King's, is said to be that occasionally used as the vice-regal lodge. The village, which is of considerable size, and extends into the parish of Palmerstown, in the barony of Newcastle, is situated on the south-western verge of the Phoenix park, and contains 200 houses, of which 103 are in that part of it which is in the parish of Palmerstown. It is within the delivery of the Dublin twopenny post, and is chiefly remarkable for the beautiful scenery in its vicinity, especially along the banks of the Liffey, towards Lucan, and for the extensive strawberry beds which are spread over the northern side of the vale; the woollen manufacture was formerly carried on very extensively, and continued to flourish till the commencement of the present century, when there was a large factory, two fulling-mills, and an extensive corn and wash mill, which have been succeeded by a flax-mill on a very large scale, erected by Messrs. Crosthwaite, the present proprietors, and affording constant employment to more than 600 persons. There are also a bleach-green and several mills.

The village has been immortalised by one of its most distinguished inhabitants, Sheridan Le Fanu, who conjures up a vision of its eighteenth-century glories on the first page of *The House by the Churchyard*:

In those days Chapelizod was about the gayest and prettiest of the outpost villages in which old Dublin took a complacent pride. The poplars which stood, in military rows, here and there, just showed a glimpse of formality among the orchards and old timber that lined the banks of the river and the valley of the Liffey, with a lively sort of richness. The broad old street looked hospitable and merry, with steep roofs and many coloured hall-doors …

Chapelizod was one of the areas that the planners of Dublin City Council identified as a special place meriting a detailed survey and development plan. In 2003 the firm of Colin Buchanan and Partners published a beautiful document detailing the history of the village, its present state and a scheme for its future. Buchanan and Partners did not mince their words: 'Due to the wealth and range of associative, cultural, aesthetic and economic values that the village possesses, it is considered to be of immense local, regional and national significance.' Their report and plans can be seen on the council's website (www. dublincity.ie).

The Buchanan report extends the long history of milling at Chapelizod by showing the position of a 'Pre-Norman mill-race' which makes a fair claim to be the oldest definitely known use of water power on the Liffey. In 1292 the royal mill at Chapelizod was destroyed by a flood and the exchequer allowed the keeper £6 for his loss. A new mill was built the following year at a cost of £18 5s 7d and three farthings. This sum covered materials, labour and millstones. Lewis continues the story from the seventeenth century:

> In 1671, Col. Lawrence obtained a grant of several houses and about 15 acres of land adjacent to the village for 41 years, at an annual rent of £42, for the purpose of establishing the linen manufacture, under the auspices of the Duke of Ormonde who, with a view to promote its success, invited over numerous families from Brabant, Rochelle, the Isle of Rhé, and other places, who were skilled in the art of manufacturing linens, diapers, tickens, sail-cloth, and cordage, and established those manufactures here in the greatest perfection.

The eighteenth-century works extend from about a kilometre downstream of the mills at Palmerstown where a weir crosses the river, slanting from west to east. The 1837 map shows it as serving an extensive woollen mills on the left bank and a smaller corn mill on the right. Both received their power directly from the weir, without any mill race. No trace of these is shown on more recent maps. A further kilometre downstream is the great weir of Chapelizod, which directed nearly half the stream through a mill race and created the substantial island upstream of the old bridge in the village. Starting out from a point on the right bank the weir measures about 400 metres and joined together a row of small islands.

The woollen industry survived through the greater part of the nineteenth century and Crosthwaite's linen mill flourished until it was eclipsed by the rise of linen production in Ulster. The entrepreneur William Dargan, between bouts of railway engineering and founding the National Gallery, encouraged the local people to grow flax and established a mill for spinning linen thread. In the 1850s he had the houses of New Row built for his workers.

The weir at Chapelizod.

In 1878 the Distillers Co. Ltd of Edinburgh acquired Dargan's thread factory and converted it into the Phoenix Park Distillery, the only source of Scotch whisky in Ireland. James Joyce's father was secretary to the distillery for some time and this explains in part the central position enjoyed by Chapelizod in *Finnegans Wake*. Le Fanu's *The House by the Churchyard* was another influence on Joyce's work. The Mullingar Inn, close to the bridge, bears a plaque announcing that it was 'the home of all characters and elements' in *Finnegans Wake*. The old bridge was renamed in Joyce's honour in 1982.

Archaeological studies indicate the establishment of a settlement well before the arrival of the Anglo-Normans that may have been of considerably greater size and importance than the pre-Viking Dublin further down the river. But, while the seaport had ample space for expansion, the village was hemmed in by steep banks on three sides and a stretch of land liable to frequent flooding downstream. After the industrial boom of the nineteenth century, Chapelizod gradually became more a dormitory suburb than a place of local employment.

Central Chapelizod retains the street plan which developed in its industrial days. Perhaps 'plan' is too grand a word for the random scattering of great mill buildings and small homes for those who worked in them. It made for the numerous narrow streets which persist to this day, with consequent traffic congestion. The old mills were for the most part situated on the island that extends from the four-arched bridge upstream to the slanting weir. Their walls were finally demolished in the second half of the twentieth century and replaced with attractive apartment blocks built of yellow brick. Upstream of these a triangle of green space has been left between the river and the mill race.

The bridge at Chapelizod, renamed in 1982 to commemorate the centenary of the birth of James Joyce, whose father worked nearby.

Sluice gates by the Liffey in Chapelizod survive as memorials to the village's industrial past.

Sluice gates remain in place together with some traces of the limestone fabric of the industrial buildings.

Small streets of renovated and restored mill workers' houses abound on the left bank and are separated by the main road from larger dwellings on the steep hillside. A grey four-storey block of a building is the original house by the churchyard. Above it is the Church of Ireland church, with its ancient square bell tower and nineteenth-century nave. Perhaps it occupies the site of the chapel of the legendary princess. The exclusiveness of the riverbank properties in the nineteenth century is sadly emphasised by the walls of the numerous dwellings that completely conceal Anna Liffey from public view.

Phoenix Park

The magnificent seven square kilometres of Phoenix Park are considerably less than the extent of the original royal estate, created in the twelfth century. In 1174 Strongbow granted to the Knights Templars the property that he had usurped. When that order was suppressed in 1312 the land passed to the Knights Hospitallers and was ultimately seized by Henry VIII in 1542. His park embraced both banks of the river and included the area on which the Royal Hospital Kilmainham would be built in the 1680s with its gardens going down to the riverside.

Much has been written about this wonderful park. Maurice Craig, in *Dublin 1660–1860*, gives a delightful account of the essentials of the history of the park's early development and ownership. Two excellent books were published in the 1990s on behalf of the park's present owners, the people of Ireland, by their agent, the Office of Public Works. Both concentrate on the natural history of the park, but give a great deal more than that: Paddy Reilly and John McCullen described the wild plants; and Frank Kirk wrote a wide-ranging introduction to the wildlife.

These were followed by a sumptuous work by John McCullen, *An Illustrated History of the Phoenix Park: Landscape and Management to 1880*, a highly readable scholarly text, lavishly illustrated with contemporary drawings and paintings. The author crowned a career as a superintendent of public parks when he was appointed to the post of Chief Park Superintendent with the Office of Public Works. In 1984 he and his family moved to a residence in the park, a privilege enjoyed by few citizens. His book concentrates on the period 1800 to 1880 when, as he says, 'most of the infrastructural development of the Park took place'.

The seven square kilometres of the park could comfortably hold the entire human population of Ireland. In September 1979 about half the people of Ireland came together here to greet the pope. On normal days, the park accommodates Áras an Uachtaráin the president's palace, the zoo, a polo ground and many playing fields for more popular sports, hospitals, the offices of the Ordnance Survey, the residence of the US Ambassador, the beautiful formal People's Gardens and a wide open space hundreds of acres in extent known as the Fifteen Acres. John McCullen quotes that devoted Dubliner and master of the macabre Sheridan Le Fanu as explaining that, within the level ground, was an artillery butt in an enclosure of 15 acres. In *The House by the Churchyard* Le Fanu describes a fatuous duel there between two officers.

The soil of the park is derived from a sandy deposit from the Ice Age and makes first-class pasture. That, and its proximity to a source of salmon for food in winter, drew Neolithic cattle barons to the region. They buried their dead there and, during the 1830s, two of their tombs were discovered at Knockmaree, near the Chapelizod gate. Dated to between 3300 and 3500 BC, they were constructed some centuries before Newgrange. In the form of chambers built of large uprights, each was roofed with a massive capstone. A thousand years later, Bronze Age people used the same site to bury the cremated remains of their dead. A long gap in current knowledge of the people of Phoenix Park followed.

Traces of ring forts and other earthworks on the Fifteen Acres were revealed by aerial photography and date to the first 500 years of Christianity in Ireland. Somewhat later, Vikings buried their dead near here, but mostly on the right bank of the Liffey, beyond the present park boundaries.

The left bank of the Liffey was excluded from the park in 1682 when Sir John Temple built a new wall from Parkgate Street to Chapelizod. A little under 2.5 metres high, it ran for nearly 2 km more or less parallel to the riverbank, but separated from it by a strip of floodplain or river terrace. As part of his fee for building the wall, Temple acquired this strip of land. Some of it has been developed for housing, part has become the property of boat clubs and other sporting bodies, and a substantial portion, immediately to the east of Chapelizod, is maintained as an informal public park.

Liffey Valley Park

This refers specifically to a delightful property that runs along the right bank from St Laurence Road in Chapelizod to the west boundary of the War Memorial gardens. The contrast between the two is remarkable: the latter is an immaculate manicured garden, the former something of a wilderness – except for the provision of a well-maintained path for pedestrians and cyclists. Wilderness is rare enough within city boundaries and this makes the park very special.

The greater part of the park is a narrow strip of level ground at the bottom of a steep part of the valley. This runs for about a kilometre downstream from the entrance from St Laurence Road. Above it to the south is the busy and noisy Chapelizod bypass, but the traffic is kept out of sight because the bank has been planted with a variety of trees, now well grown. Birch and rowan take up much of the space and the rowan berries provide bright splodges of colour and abundant food for birds in autumn. The trees include a number of oak saplings and are mostly native species. But there are a few exotics, including horse chestnut and Turkey oak, and the inevitable self-sown sycamore. Further downstream mature beech are remnants of times before the park was established.

The bypass road, which confines the park to a narrow strip bounded by the river to the north, turns slightly to the south about halfway to the Memorial Garden and the Liffey flows northeastwards so that the park widens, still with its steep bank by the river, but with a nearly level triangle south of the path.

Because the ground is free from livestock and is not mown, vegetation is free to develop unhindered. A jungle of grasses and many species of wild flowers and shrubs covers the slopes. In places blackthorn is beginning to take over the strip of land that runs between the path and the river, and trees including ash and sycamore are beginning to establish themselves. The growth of native plants is so luxuriant that it is actually inhibiting the growth of the notorious invaders Indian balsam and Japanese knotweed. The positive side of this relative neglect of the park is that it will give generations of botanists and schoolchildren an opportunity to see how woodland establishes itself and changes its character over a long period. It underscores the fact that the typical Irish landscape of green fields, hedges and riverbanks, with lawn-like grass, is a human creation, not a natural one.

A mute swan at Islandbridge. This species was introduced to Ireland as a domestic fowl by the Anglo-Normans and has never quite given up its association with people.

Even the Liffey itself at this point is an artificial creation. The exquisite silence and depth of this 2-km stretch of winding river downstream of Chapelizod owes its form to the barrier of Islandbridge Weir.

Across the Liffey from the park the strip of almost level ground between the wall of Phoenix Park and the riverbank is occupied by boat clubs and some green space, accessible to the public, with sports grounds and a number of fishing stands. The upper part of the valley is overlooked by the mid-nineteenth-century Church of the Nativity of the Blessed Virgin Mary, while downstream the river seems to disappear temporarily into an area of woodland.

The Irish National War Memorial

As originally conceived, the First World War memorial park at Islandbridge would have embraced both sides of the Liffey, with a central avenue running from the entrance gate on Colbert Road, down past the cross to the temple and across the river by a three-arched bridge. But the bridge was never built and the formal part of the gardens effectively ends at the temple, while the riverbank is flanked less formally by a wide lawn, backed by a footpath. Clumps of reeds and yellow flag grow in the shallows and give shelter for swans, moorhen and mallard, while the lawn is a place of joy for dogs, children and their carers.

Formal and informal parts together constitute a very beautiful and, appropriately, peaceful place today. But their history was turbulent – as might befit a memorial to such a savage war. A meeting of more than a hundred representatives from all parts of Ireland, held in Dublin in July 1919, led to the appointment of a Memorial Committee to raise funds for a permanent monument to the Irish men and women who had lost their lives in the war. It took ten years of meetings to decide where it would be built. The site finally chosen was public property, being at the time part of Phoenix Park. The Free State government agreed to fund work on the park, while the money raised by the committee would pay for the actual garden.

Sir Edwin Lutyens, who had already designed gardens in Ireland and was regarded as the very best architect of war memorials, was engaged, and work began in 1931. The labour force comprised equal numbers of men who had served in the British Army and the National Army and the work was completed just in time for the next war. A long period of limited tending of the gardens ended in the 1980s, since when they have been given the careful attention they so richly deserve.

The stone cross that is the centrepiece of the memorial stands out on the hill slope above the floodplain of the Liffey, but the pavilions and exquisite rose gardens which flank it are hidden from the river. The lower part, more park than garden, comprises five tree-lined avenues radiating from the Doric temple in which lines by poet Rupert Brooke are carved on the floor. Some of the trees are mature specimens, more than seventy years old, dating to the time when the garden was created. Others are younger and include flowering cherries and almonds, giving colour and a wonderful fragrance in spring.

Islandbridge

The ancient weir at the four islands, where the tidal part of Anna Liffey begins, was first mentioned in existing records in the twelfth century. It runs from west to east, parallel to the right bank of the Liffey where the river turns sharply towards the north for a short distance before resuming its easterly course. The

The Doric temple in the Garden of Remembrance.

The rose garden of the War Memorial at its most brilliant in August.

weir is 250 metres long and leads to a mill race which was excavated to serve factories between it and the Liffey on the new island that it created. The mill race runs for a further 250 metres and ends just upstream of the bridge. The industries shown on the 1837 map were a calico printing factory and flour mills, while Lewis describes various structures, industries and activities:

> A beautiful bridge crosses the Liffey at this place: it consists of one elliptical arch, 104 feet 10 inches in span, the key-stone of which is 24 feet above high water mark. The first stone was laid, in 1791, by Sarah Countess of Westmorland, after whom it is named Sarah bridge. Here are very extensive artillery barracks, with an hospital, but it is intended to remove the artillery to the buildings of the Foundling Hospital, when the institution shall have been closed after the children now maintaining in it are provided for elsewhere. Print works were established in 1786, which had been greatly enlarged by the present proprietor, W. Henry, Esq., who has a handsome residence near them: they are on the banks of the Liffey, and furnish employment for between 500 and 600 persons. Here is also an extensive flour-mill belonging to Messrs. Manders and Co. Near the village is a spring, called St John's well, at which a kind of festival of considerable antiquity is held on St John's eve. It is much frequented by the working classes from the metropolis, for whom tents are pitched and the usual entertainments of patron days provided.

Some of the mill buildings have been converted to residential use and a number of apartment blocks were built on the old industrial property towards the end of the twentieth century.

The islands, even before the weir was constructed, provided a crossing place and a succession of bridges in due course replaced the ancient ford. John de Courcy provides a detailed study of the succession of bridges. An account of a dispute over fishing rights in the *White Book of the City of Dublin* in 1261 mentions a bridge over the Avenelif at Kilmaynan, but its exact location is not clear and it might have crossed the river upstream at the islands. A 'narrow bridge' in the vicinity is mentioned as the scene of an unfriendly encounter between Sir William Skeffington and Silken Thomas in 1535.

A very different story begins in 1577 when an eight-arched stone bridge was built on the orders of the lord deputy Sir Henry Sidney. In addition to its human load this bridge carried an aqueduct bringing water, probably from upstream of the weir, to the nearby city. It lasted for more than 200 years until its destruction by an exceptional flood in 1787.

Planning of a new bridge began immediately and a three-arched structure was proposed. Arches and piers inevitably obstruct the flow of a river, with consequent risk of flooding. So the plan was abandoned in favour of the beautiful single elliptical arch, described by Lewis, which continues to serve and carries unthinkably heavy traffic compared to the horses and carts for which it was created. Designed by the Scottish engineer Alexander Stevens the elder, and completed in two years, its original name was changed to Island Bridge by order of the Corporation in 1922.

Three hundred metres downstream a lattice girder railway bridge crosses the river, and leads the line to the tunnel that runs beneath Conyngham Road and then under Phoenix Park. The North Wall extension line that it carries, completed in 1877, branches off from the main line to Heuston Station at Islandbridge Junction, to the northeast of the deep railway cutting at Kilmainham. This branch line, emerging from the tunnel just to the north of Infirmary Road, effectively encircles the north side of the city and returns to the Liffeyside at the North Wall.

Between these two bridges the riverbanks on both sides have seen radical changes to their occupancy. On the left bank a former garage and industrial site was transformed into a remarkable conurbation of classical-style apartment blocks in yellow brick. Named Bridgewater Quay, it is one of the most attractively designed housing developments in greater Dublin. The right bank is lined by the northernmost buildings of Clancy Barracks. East of the railway bridge Conyngham Road runs between the wall of Phoenix Park and a variety of riverside dwellings. Few of the spacious nineteenth-century homes with ample gardens leading to the riverside remain. I have happy memories of lunch with the Quaker Wigham family in one of them in the 1950s, followed by an exploration of the river in their rowing boat.

Mallard nest, rear their families and accept breadcrumbs by the Liffey at Islandbridge and a great many other spots where the river runs slowly and there are bankside bushes and reeds for cover. *Photo: Michael Finn.*

The Royal Hospital Kilmainham

Maurice Craig, in *Dublin 1680–1860*, gives an account of the history of the Royal Hospital from its conception in 1679 up to and including its rather unhappy state in 1949. More recent developments, together with a sketch of life in the institution, are described by Catherine Marshall in her excellent contribution to the hospital's website (www.rhk.ie). Designed by the Surveyor General William Robinson, who was clearly influenced by the architecture of Les Invalides in Paris, the first stone was laid in 1680 by the Viceroy, the Duke of Ormonde.

Occupation by the old soldiers for whom it was built began in 1684 and the building was completed in all its glory with the addition of the tower in 1701. Restoration work began in the 1960s, and in 1991 the former pensioners' hospital was reborn as the Irish Museum of Modern Art. The only major seventeenth-century secular public building in Ireland, it remains one of the most beautiful.

Christine Casey, in her volume on Dublin in *The Buildings of Ireland* series gives an account of the twentieth- and twenty-first-century developments as well as detailed descriptions of the architecture of the hospital and its associated buildings. These include commodious classical dwellings to the east for the Deputy Master and the Adjutant General. The Deputy Master's was redesigned in 2000 as an additional art gallery.

The commanding site chosen, on the edge of the ridge separating the Liffey from its tributary the Cammock, was part of the original Phoenix Park. The boundaries of the property shown by Rocque in 1756 include, to the west, the walled gardens and the parkland extending on either side of a tree-lined avenue to the pedestrian entrance on the South Circular Road. They coincide approximately with the present-day extent. But Rocque shows an orchard to the east of the hospital. Another tree-lined avenue runs through this orchard towards the northeast, where the entrance to the grounds was on the south quays. The original vista from the hospital ran across the water meadows down to the Liffeyside and over to the Magazine Fort. These open spaces survived until the building of the railway in the 1830s.

Narrow roads on the steep side of the Liffey valley make for a rather miserable entry from the east to this delightful institution. Its triumphal western approach from the South Circular Road is reserved for pedestrians. Once inside the property, visitors are rewarded with an unusual variety of attractions within a relatively small urban space: history ancient and modern, architecture, art, good food, an informal park and a very formal garden, with more distant prospects of mountains, parkland and riverside.

The spectacular west entrance gate has a remarkable history. In 1804 a 'Military Road' was made as an approach to the hospital from the south quays and in 1820 the turreted Richmond Gate was built there to the design of Francis

Johnston. The new railway encroached on the Military Road and the now redundant gate was rebuilt in its present position in 1846.

The Royal Hospital on the right bank and Phoenix Park on the left bring marvellous expanses of parkland and wide open spaces to the built-up margins of the urban Liffey, which will be the subject of the next chapter.

7 | The city:
Islandbridge to East Link

Two great events in Anna Liffey's life begin at Islandbridge Weir. She makes her first encounter with the tide and she gradually exchanges the freedom of her passage through moorland, fields and parks for the constrictions imposed by generations of entrepreneurs and engineers in Dublin's fair city. The western city boundary crosses the Liffey some 3.5 km upstream of Islandbridge, a little way below the mills at Palmerstown. Although traces of the river's unconstrained existence survive, the reach between Islandbridge Weir and Palmerstown is more suburban than urban. Happily, it enjoys an abundance of public open spaces. Downstream of the weir and the islands that give the spot its name, Anna Liffey flows within secure boundaries, a human encroachment that began with the Vikings.

Islandbridge Weir took advantage of a string of islands to provide a head of water to drive turbines where the bridge of the same name now spans the Liffey. The weir made an artificial barrier to the reach of the tide, which had formerly travelled further upstream. It also created the marvellous 2-km stretch of calm water beloved by boat clubs.

This chapter owes a great debt to four outstanding books whose authors will be quoted frequently. The late John de Courcy was a civil engineering professor at University College Dublin and contributed the text to the delightful book and poster published by the O'Brien Press at the same time as Wolfhound Press produced *The Book of the Liffey*. In 1996 de Courcy's *The Liffey in Dublin* was published by Gill & Macmillan. This encyclopaedia of the urban river combines scholarship with eminent readability. In particular, it has brought together extensive material from the original sources of Dublin's history.

The third book, covering the whole of the inner city between the canals and from Islandbridge to the Grand Canal Docks, had a wider scope. *Dublin* by Christine Casey is one of the series on the Buildings of Ireland published by Yale University Press. The author is an art and architectural historian, lecturing in University College Dublin, and her book gives a meticulous account of the buildings of the Liffeyside and further afield.

The fourth work, by Michael Corcoran, entitled *Our Good Health: A History of Dublin's Water and Drainage*, was published by the City Council in 2005. It provides a wealth of detail on what went on beneath the roads and buildings of the Liffeyside in the more or less distant past and what continues to proceed down there unobtrusively and efficiently. This invisible undertaking, devised mainly by civil engineers – to supply clean water and remove foul – is as important as the roads, parks and buildings in making comfortable city life a reality.

A conglomeration of history: (centre) Christ Church Cathedral, begun in 1030 but thoroughly remodelled and rebuilt in the 1870s; (left) a portion of Scott Tallon Walker's Civic Building of 1994 on the site of the Viking settlement of Wood Quay; (right) the corner of the Franciscan friary which envelops the church of Eve and Adam; (front) O'Donovan Rossa Bridge of 1816 by James Savage.

The first part of this chapter is devoted to the thousand years in the course of which the lower parts of the river were progressively confined and urbanised. The second part describes some, but not all, of the most notable features of the quaysides and crossing places in the twenty-first century.

A thousand years of constrictions

The establishment of a busy port required in the first place the building of wharfage, and this began with wooden structures at Wood Quay. At the same time, houses for the families of the seafarers, and the people who served them or depended on them, developed. The high ground and steep sides of the valley below High Street provided plenty of space for dwellings, secure from flooding. But the desirability of having houses and harbour facilities as close to the river as possible led before long to the building of earthen banks and the earliest constriction of the tidal river. As the population of the city grew and the businesses associated with the seaport increased, riverside land became more and more valuable and, a few centuries later, reclamation on a grand scale began.

This process continued from the ninth century for more than a thousand years. Earthen banks persisted until late in the twentieth century between Islandbridge and Heuston Station, but they came to be encased in concrete at the time when the apartment blocks on both banks were built. Downstream of the level ground, where the railway terminus would ultimately grow, the construction of quay walls of stone had begun in the seventeenth century.

The Ford of the Hurdles

The Four Masters, in their record of the accession of Conn of the Hundred Battles in AD 123, tell the tale of the miraculous road-building that occurred on the occasion of his birth:

> The night of Conn's birth were discovered five principal roads to Teahmhair, which were never observed till then. These are their names: Slighe-Asail, Slighe-Midluachra, Slighe-Cualann, Slighe-Mor, Slighe-Dala. Slighe-Mor is Eiscir-Riada, i.e. the division-line of Ireland into two parts, between Conn and Eoghan Mor

O'Donovan's voluminous footnotes to the *Annals* indicate that Slighe Cualann extended from Tara to Dublin and Bray; 'its position was, perhaps, not very different from the present mail-coach road'. The Eiscir Riada runs westwards from Dublin, south of the Liffey. Howard Clarke, in the *Irish Historic Towns Atlas*, provides a map of these great roads, which shows how all of them, except Slighe Asail, converge close to Áth Cliath. Evidently the river crossing was an

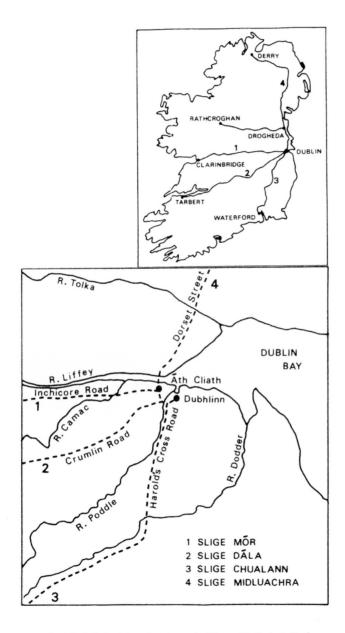

The ancient roads of Gaelic Ireland, based on the work of Howard B. Clarke in Noel Kissane's *Historic Dublin Maps*. Courtesy National Library of Ireland.

important one and its time undoubtedly extended back long before the second century AD and the days of Conn of the Hundred Battles. Áth Cliath was the most easterly point where a road heading from north to south close to the coast could cross the Liffey. Further downstream, until the building works of the seventeenth and eighteenth centuries, the river broadened and became one with Dublin Bay, much too wide for a passage on foot or horseback from north to south.

The line of gravel hills that compose Eiscir Riada made for the most convenient route across the mainly boggy midlands to the west. This provides a logical explanation of why it meets with Slighe Midluachra, Slighe Cualann and Slighe Dala. The reason for Slighe Dala's origin close to Áth Cliath is less clear but could be associated with the existence of the other three. This point on the tidal Liffey evidently had been one of major importance long before the Vikings developed their trading post at Duibh Linn, the dark pool.

The ancient riverside to 1610

John Speed's map of 1610 is the earliest meaningful plan of the city. It shows a small walled town with dense housing on the right bank of the Liffey and an area roughly equal in size, but with far fewer buildings, on the left. Along the riverbank, the walls extend from just upstream of 'The Bridge' for 400 metres

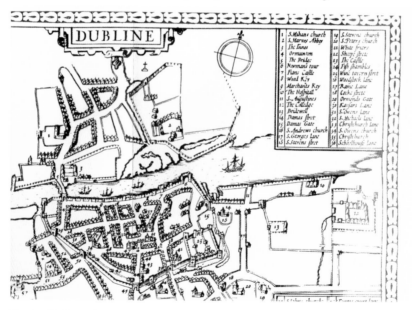

The city of Dublin and the Liffeyside in 1610 as shown by John Speed. Quays on the right bank extend as far as 'Newman's tour' – Isolde's Tower on Essex Street – and the dark pool of the Poddle, still open to the main river. To the east the estuary widens, showing the extent of the tidal land that would be reclaimed in the latter half of the seventeenth century. The sole bridge, now Father Mathew's, lies a little downstream of the site of the Ford of the Hurdles.

downstream to the estuary of the River Poddle at 'Newman's Tower': in today's terms from Father Mathew Bridge to Capel Street Bridge, along Merchant's, Wood and Essex Quays. The foundations of Newman's Tower were revealed in the course of excavation in 1992, on Exchange Street. At this point the river widens towards both north and south, but a quay wall or sea wall is shown by Speed on the right bank extending from the Poddle estuary as far as the western boundary of 'The Colledge'. The shoreline is shown less than 20 metres from the boundary wall of this, the new university. Three ships lie at anchor off the quays.

Information on the buildings of Dublin, before the establishment of the Viking port, is largely conjectural. Domestic dwellings, even the palatial ones, in those days were made of clay and wattle or other biodegradable materials and leave few traces in the archaeological record. Churches of stone were certainly being built before Viking times, but it seems that none of them survived in Dublin in their original forms. They may well have been rebuilt on the same sites in later centuries.

Clarke provides in the *Atlas* a map which shows the Ford of the Hurdles at the present day St Augustine Street, believed to follow the line of the ancient Slighe Midluachra. This is a little way upstream of Father Mathew Bridge and Church Street. On the assumption that the contours of the valley have not changed significantly, the river in the past would have had a breadth of 300 metres at this point. On the right bank, the ground rises steeply from the

Pugin's 1874 Church of St Augustine and St John stands near the site of the ancient church of St Molua, overlooking the Ford of the Hurdles.

shore to the summit of the ridge on which the city would be built. Clarke gives positions for two churches, one dedicated to St Molua, the other to St Columba. St Molua's church is at the crossroads where Slighe Midluachra from north to south meets the east–west Slighe Mor. This is where St Augustine Street now crosses Cornmarket and meets Francis Street. High Street, Cornmarket and Thomas Street follow the path of Slighe Mor.

Upstream of the ford is the long sandbank which came to be known as Usher's Island and extended some 500 metres upstream as far as Watling Street. The earliest record of the name of the island dates to 1557 when John Usher sought a lease for it. The ground would remain in the possession of his family until the early nineteenth century. Speed shows the island as a water meadow, bounded to the east by a short tidal estuary and a small stream. A little way downstream of the island is 'The Bridge'. The same point marks the western boundary of the walled city. Further downstream Speed shows the defensive wall following the riverbank eastwards as far as the Poddle.

The inlet or pool of Duibh Linn is not marked by name on any of the old maps and the authorities differ as to precisely where it was. The Poddle estuary is a likely candidate, although there is a view that the pool was on the Liffey itself, perhaps downstream of the Ford of the Hurdles. But it is hard to conceive of the broad, intemperate river being described as a 'linn' and easier to imagine it as referring to the backwater made by the Poddle. In summer when the stream ran low, and the estuary was free from strong currents, this is likely to have formed a dark pool.

On the left bank of the Liffey the buildings of 'The Innes', with their adjoining fenced field, extend for 150 metres by the riverside. A little way downstream of the fence a river, the Bradogue, joins with the Liffey and beyond it three tidal inlets encroach on much of the land that now lies beneath the area bounded by the Four Courts and Capel Street. To the east of them, a long, narrow inlet runs parallel to the shore, separated from the Liffey estuary by a spit of land. This lies within the octagonal fence marking the property of St Mary's Abbey.

Upstream of 'The Bridge', the fields of Usher's Island are unnamed and on the left bank there is a small development bounded by present-day Church Street, Hammond Lane and Lincoln Lane, where there was a small inlet. Beyond that lies open country. In effect, apart from the quayside development on the right bank, the Liffey at this time followed its natural course. It would remain that way through the turbulent years of the seventeenth century and until the dramatic changes which began following the demise of Cromwell and the Restoration of the monarchy.

Downstream of the Ford and Merchant's Quay, Wood Quay had begun centuries earlier, having first been developed by the Vikings, with evidence of the beginnings of Dublin port in 841. An earthen bank below the escarpment, where Christ Church Cathedral stands, was identified in the course of the

Wood Quay excavations of the 1970s and dated to 900. Over a period of 400 years, quays of earth, wood and stone were built further and further out into the river. Land reclamation behind these structures had begun there by the late twelfth century and around 1260 a stone quay wall was built to replace the structure of wood. It follows the line that exists to this day.

Developments from the Restoration

The return to Dublin of James, Duke of Ormonde as Lord Lieutenant, following the Restoration of King Charles II in 1660 and the end of the Cromwellian nightmare, had a special significance for the city of Dublin and for its river. Maurice Craig tells of Ormonde's years of exile in Paris and his exposure to its architecture. When he returned to Ireland, entrepreneurs in Dublin were embarking on massive building and development projects. Among them was Sir Humphrey Jervis. He had planned to build houses, as in other Irish cities, on the riverside, facing away from the water – a practical, if unpleasing, approach since it allowed the inhabitants to consign their domestic waste to the tide.

Inspired by the beauties of Paris and the Seine, Ormonde, through the City Council, persuaded Jervis to introduce the broad, paved quay and move the line of houses back from the river. Jervis named his development Ormond Quay and established a precedent that was followed by other entrepreneurs. Prior to 1662, the city of Dublin was small and its riverside restricted to the frontage of 600 metres from Merchant's Quay to the old Custom House on the right bank and less than 200 metres of Inns Quay on the left. In the course of the next 50 years, the quays would be extended upstream to Watling Street and downstream to the River Dodder, attaining a length of 4.2 km.

About 1680, Jervis was engaged in developing a market to the north of the present Ormond Quays and in reclaiming the waterfront. His vision would radically change the appearance of the riverside and mark a major departure from the medieval layout. In effect, his undertakings transformed Anna Liffey to her proud place as the central axis of the city, rather than its northern boundary.

The National Library's collection *Historic Dublin Maps*, edited by Noel Kissane, reproduces the works of John Speed, Bernard de Gomme, Charles Brooking and John Rocque, who published at intervals from 1610 to 1756. These provide a literally graphic illustration of the constriction of the Liffey in the course of the century or so of its most dramatic changes.

The later seventeenth century: de Gomme

Compared with the other three, de Gomme's map is lacking in detail, but it does give an impression of the developments midway between the times of Speed and Brooking. The scene in 1673, as sketched by de Gomme, was of a city still bordered to the north by the Liffey, although with much the same suburban layout that Speed showed beyond 'The Kings Inns'. There is one bridge, which meets the right bank at the eastern tip of 'Sir William Usher's Island' and leads to the 'Bridge Gate' of the intact city wall. Downstream of 'The Bridge', 'Merchant's Key', 'Wood Key' and 'Blind Key' are marked, the last-named curving from the riverside to the south until it meets 'Dammas Street'. In 1780 this riverside part of Blind Quay was renamed Lower Exchange Street.

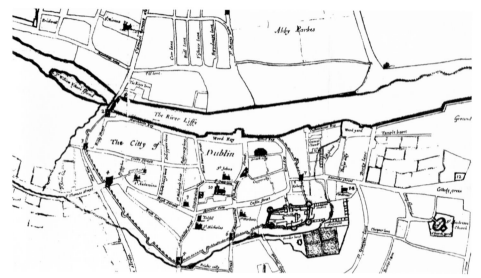

Part of de Gomme's map of 1673, from present-day Parliament Street to the future O'Connell Bridge. It shows the beginning of reclamation in the region of Wellington and Aston's Quays. *National Maritime Museum, Greenwich, London.*

Speed had shown, in 1610, the mouth of the Poddle as an open inlet to the east of 'Newman's Tower', with one long and one short spit of land. The Poddle estuary was divided into three parts by two sandbanks prior to the reclamation which had taken place by 1673, when de Gomme shows a wall running from Wood Quay that cuts off the Poddle estuary from the river and then takes the name 'Customhouse Key'. Beyond this is a 'Wood yard' extending to where 'Dirty Lane' – subsequently dignified as Temple Lane – meets the river. From there a wall begins parallel to Temple Bar and runs slightly north of east for 800 metres as far as present-day Moss Street. De Gomme marks the space between this wall and 'Lazy Hill' – now Pearse Street – as 'Ground taken in from the Sea'.

On the left bank, which runs roughly parallel to the right, de Gomme shows a quay wall extending from 'The King's Innes' eastwards to a point opposite to his 'Wood yard', after which the shoreline downstream is irregular and apparently unenclosed.

The eighteenth century: Brooking and Rocque

Fifty-five years after de Gomme, Charles Brooking shows a very different city in 1728. The defensive walls have gone and five bridges cross the river. Usher's Island has been built over and is fronted by the quay that bears the same family name and which extends as far upstream as Watling Street. Houses and gardens occupy the land to its west.

Across the river the building of quays and extensive housing has progressed and quays extend in an almost unbroken line from Queen Street to 'Great Marleborough Street'. The one interruption is at Church Street, where there are buildings on the riverbank upstream and downstream of 'Old Bridge'. From west to east, the quays are Arran, The Inns, Ormond and Bachelors Walk, which goes

A portion of Brooking's map of 1728, inverted to give the conventional north–south orientation. The Royal Hospital at Kilmainham and Dr Steeven's Hospital are shown on opposite sides of the River Cammock, which flows through open fields and gardens, to be occupied later by railway station and brewery. The Liffey curves to the north as it did until its relocation in the 1820s. Bloody Bridge (now Rory O'More's) is the furthest upstream.

further east than it does today, ending at a building opposite Hawkins Street. The construction of Arran Quay and the reclamation of land behind it was the work of William Ellis, who in 1682 was granted a lease of the riverside land from Parkgate down to the buildings to the west of Church Street.

On the right bank Brooking shows houses, separated by laneways, going all the way to the riverside from Temple Bar so that they interrupt the line of the quays between Aston's and the old Custom House. From White's Lane, now Cornmarket Place, on the right bank and 'Great Marle borough Street' on the left, quays run nearly parallel for 1.6 km, as far as the Dodder and the Tolka respectively. The East Wall has already been built. The right bank quays are 'St. George's' and 'Sr John Rogersons'. Buildings on this side go downstream to a little way past Lime Street. A particularly interesting feature of Brooking's map is its panoramic view of the city, showing water still present to north and south of the new sea walls. Ringsend, in this scene, is an isolated seaside village, backed by open fields.

In 1728 Bachelors Walk extended to the east of Sackville Street, and the North Wall Quay began a little way downstream of this at an inlet marked on the map as North Wall Slip. Between the inlet and the end of Bachelors Walk, two merchants' yards ran down to the waterside, causing a break in the line of the quay. On the opposite side of the river, Aston Quay ran from Anglesea Street to Hawkins Street and met George's Quay. Burgh Quay would be named later.

Speed and de Gomme show one bridge in the city. Brooking has five, two upstream and two downstream of the crossing at Church Street, which he names 'Old Bridge'. Brooking's are, from upstream, Bloody Bridge, Arran Bridge, Old Bridge, Ormond Bridge and Essex Bridge, the last at Capel Street, immediately upstream of the old Custom House Quay.

The cartographer John Rocque established himself in Dublin from 1754 to 1760 and published two maps of the city in 1756. The first, entitled 'A plan of the city of Dublin and the environs', is reproduced in Noel Kissane's collection. The second, 'An exact survey of the city and suburbs of Dublin', is on a larger scale and was published with a commentary by Colm Lennon and John Montague in 2010. The 'plan' shows the Liffey from Islandbridge to a point about halfway along the South Wall. The 'exact survey' is more detailed but goes no further east than 'Rogersons Quay'. Some changes in street and bridge names have been made in the course of 28 years after Brooking, but otherwise the picture is much the same. Arran Bridge has been renamed Bridewell Bridge and Arran Quay extended upstream to a point midway between Church Street and Queen Street. This extension is named Back Quay and ends at John's Street. Upstream of this very small street Rocque shows a garden and then a rectangular bay which he names Gravel Walk Slip. Later maps mark it as a 'watering place' and its maintenance as such was a requirement in a lease granted by the city authorities to Richard Tighe.

A field or garden lies to the west of this, fronting on to the river as far as Bloody Bridge, and beyond it is Pembroke Quay, measuring about 100 metres. On the right bank, between Merchant's Quay at Winetavern Street and Aston Quay at Anglesea Street, the Liffey has been contained by a wall, but there is still no indication of a broad quay downstream of the old Custom House. Further to the east, Aston Quay ends at Hawkins Street and Bachelors Quay continues to go as far as Great Marlborough Street. On both banks, therefore, riverside properties go to the water's edge and the unbroken line of quays has yet to be completed. An important development shown by Rocque is a triangle of reclaimed land marked as 'Amory's Ground'. It would be the site of Gandon's Custom House. Beyond it, Rocque shows the successful drainage and infill of the North Lotts and the layout of the new road system.

An eighteenth-century interlude

In her *Irish Quakers* Isabel Grubb quotes from a contemporary fragment describing a rare, maybe unique, occurrence in the river of the city:

> In the winter of the year 1739, an intense frost covered the River Liffey with such thick ice that tents were erected upon it, where various things were sold and fires kindled to dress victuals, people attracted by the novelty of the sight crowded upon the river especially to see a ship of war which lay blocked up there.

Completion of the quays

De Courcy notes that in 1811 the Watering Place was filled in and the quay extended upstream to Arran Bridge to be named first Ellis's and subsequently Ellis Quay. The next break on the left bank going downstream was at the end of Bachelors Quay, near Marlborough Street where there were yards and buildings owned by the city. Around the time of the building of Carlisle Bridge and Gandon's Custom House, these were demolished and the quay was extended to join the original North Wall. William Eden, Chief Secretary to Carlisle, the Lord Lieutenant, had in 1782 written to John Beresford to request that his name be given to the proposed new quay and somehow his plea was remembered and granted 32 years later. Completed in 1814, the quay had been named in 1795. The name was its sole connection with the earthly paradise.

The Liffeyside in the twenty-first century

The eastern city boundary of Dublin and the influence of the Liffey reach far beyond the Poolbeg Lighthouse and includes no less an entity than the North Bull Island. Until the later decades of the twentieth century Butt Bridge marked the boundary between city and docklands. But the city, as an abode of the land-based, resumed its march downstream and effectively now reaches the East Link Bridge, while displaying pleasant memorials to its former domain of shipping.

Bridgewater Quay on the left bank at Islandbridge with high-rise apartments on the right bank replacing the former barracks.

Although de Courcy's *The Liffey in Dublin* is the only work which concentrates on the river of the city, many books include details of the architecture of the quaysides and its history. A comprehensive account of the buildings would demand a substantial book in its own right; fitting the topic into a single chapter demands ruthless editing. What follows attempts to give an outline of the present-day buildings and their history – but it has to be highly selective. This is a personal account of what I like best.

Conyngham Road

William Conyngham was a Wide Streets Commissioner. The straightening and widening of an ancient road to the west was undertaken according to a recommendation of the Commissioners towards the end of the eighteenth century. Conyngham Road begins at the graceful single span of Island Bridge and runs past the Wellington Testimonial as far as the main entrance to the Phoenix Park. Access to a riverside walk at Islandbridge is possible by way of the ramp that leads down to the houses of Bridgewater Terrace, the most pleasing of the post-1950s buildings that line the road. Replacing a former garage, it is a collection of pastiche classical terraces of three storeys, entered by steps leading to hall doors on the first floor. The grounds are beautifully maintained and the riverside walkway extends the full length of the estate, ending at the Liffey Viaduct downstream. This space, together with a parallel path on the right bank, is under the care of the City's Parks Department.

The Wellington Testimonial and the arch on the north side of Conyngham Road, which marks the position of the railway tunnel. The wall is of random rubble with scotch coping, made from locally quarried limestone. It is 7 feet 9 inches (2.36 metres) in height. Building began in 1836 and ended in 1849.

The roadside above the river to the east of Bridgwater Terrace is occupied largely by offices and apartment blocks, built since the 1950s. They replace, for the most part, homes of the mildly affluent in the nineteenth century. Their gardens sloped down to the riverside and some of the families – including the Wighams, whom I visited in the 1950s – had landing places and small boats.

Only two of the old-world houses remain, one with a single storey and an entrance on the street. The other has two storeys above a garden and is entered from the side. Both are whitewashed and have slate roofs with red ridge tiles. They make a pleasant break in the mostly massive apartment blocks. A more recent building that relieves the monotony is the red-brick office of the Local Government Computer Services Board – not just a new office but an entire concept undreamed of by the Wide Streets Commissioners or the residents of the demolished houses. Nearby, medium-sized apartments do better than the large ones in having not only appropriate names – River Park, Chesterfield, Wellington and Phoenix – but pleasant arches and stairways to their entrances.

The side of Conyngham Road away from the river is bordered by the boundary wall of Phoenix Park, interrupted close to Islandbridge by a pedestrian entrance to the park and a little further to the east by a blind archway. The latter marks the railway tunnel that runs under the park as far as the grounds of the Garda headquarters. The boundary wall ends at the main entrance to the park. Originally built in 1682 along the outer edge of the higher river terrace, the wall needed frequent repairs throughout its life. John McCullen gives details of major rebuilding works in the nineteenth century, to the design of Decimus Burton.

The view along the railway line from Conyngham Road to the Dublin Mountains, Kilmashogue, Tibradden, Cruagh and Killakee and the Liffey headwaters.

Tunnelling beneath the street and the park, the railway line that crosses the Liffey heads due south for 250 metres before turning south-west to join the main line by a point. Unremarkable as a piece of railway engineering, it demanded a break in the roadside buildings that gives a surprising view far away to the mountains.

The Liffey Railway Bridge of 1877 that carries the line from Heuston Station, in a tunnel underneath Phoenix Park, to join the northern network.

Parkgate Street

The handsome main entrance to Phoenix Park, which gives the street its name, has had a chequered existence. The four stone piers, with scalloped, domed tops, and the two gate lodges were built to the design of Francis Johnston and completed by 1813. The piers supported gates fashioned in the ironworks of Robert Mallet. Piers and gates were removed in 1932 to accommodate the crowds that gathered for the Eucharistic Congress. The entrance for the following 50 years was left wide open until the piers, without the gates, were replaced in the 1980s.

The south side of the road, opposite the park gates, is lined by an assortment of three-storey nineteenth-century terraced houses, most of them fitted with twentieth-century shopfronts. A pathetic remnant of former affluence remains in the form of the façades of four residences, bricked up and with an abundant growth of buddleia and other interesting plants. Once-handsome iron railings enclose their basement areas and the doorways, which might well have had good fanlights, are hidden by billboards.

Between the lower part of Parkgate Street and the river, the triangular patch that extends westwards from Seán Heuston Bridge has long been a factory site. It is enclosed by a singularly drab high wall of limestone, relieved by an attractive stone entrance arch with a gate lodge on its left. Too narrow for modern transport, the arch has been made redundant by a featureless breach in the wall. Within the factory grounds a manager's residence in classical style still stands and, on the riverbank, there is a small cluster of nineteenth-century buildings in limestone with red brick details. Marked as a 'Printing Works' on the 1962 map, the premises are now occupied by Hickey Fabrics. The apex of the triangle, where the high walls meet the bridge, is ornamented by a neat little round turret.

The turret on Parkgate Street, upstream of Seán Heuston Bridge, marks the beginning of the north quay wall that borders the Liffey for 2.4 km as far as Butt Bridge and the unwalled quay for a further 1.8 km to The Point, where the North Wall meets the East Wall.

The interceptor

Beneath the surface of Parkgate Street lies the beginning of one of the least obtrusive but most important of all the works of the urban riverside – the decisive answer to an appalling nineteenth-century proposal that the malodorous Anna Liffey be roofed over and transformed from an unofficial open sewer to a hygienically closed one. Happily, the vision and skills of city engineers saved Dublin's noble river from such ignominy. Following the proposal of his predecessor, Parke Neville, who had died in office, the City Engineer Spencer Harty put in train the building beneath the quays of a pair of 'interceptor sewers'. These intercept the contents of the system of sewers branching all over – or under – the city, which had formerly been discharged directly into the river. The interceptors direct the sewage to the treatment plant at Ringsend. Begun in 1896, the project took ten years to complete. The south quays interceptor begins a little way downstream of Islandbridge, within the Clancy Barracks grounds at Hospital Lane. Opposite Marlborough Street the north interceptor passes beneath the Liffey by a siphon and joins its southern companion under Burgh Quay.

Heuston Station: from water meadow to rail terminus

Upstream of the bridge, on the left bank, the nineteenth-century factory walls and a bright new apartment block go down to the quayside. John Taylor's map of 1816, drawn before any of these were built, shows the area between the river and Park Gate Street as an open space, named 'Long Meadows'. The larger space on the right bank has no name on his map, but the riverside, and also the banks of the River Cammock, are shown as being lined with trees. The fields were probably used for grazing horses or for hay meadows, as implied by the name of the fields on the opposite side.

The level ground here and the higher plateau on which the Royal Hospital stands are marked by the Geological Survey as 'River-gravel Terraces'. This implies that the valley, in the course of the last glaciation, had been filled with gravel carried down by the moving ice. Since the ice melted, the river had been carrying the gravel away again, as it searched for its ancient, pre-glacial bed. The terraces were formed at different stages of this progress. Most important from a historical rather than prehistorical point of view, the lowest of the terraces, not yet built over by the expanding city, was a water meadow. In 1845 it provided the Great Southern and Western Railway Company with a highly desirable area of level ground, close to the city centre, on which goods yards and sidings could conveniently be developed. The palatial railway station, built between 1845 and 1846, was designed by the English architect Sancton Wood. The railway property on the left bank reaches upstream as far as the Liffey Railway Bridge that leads to the Phoenix Park tunnel.

Seán Heuston Bridge

Twice renamed, the former King's Bridge was built in response to a personally expressed wish of George IV who was asked what form of monument he would like to have erected to commemorate his visit to Dublin in 1821. A ferry had operated at this point for some time and, from 1733, was of considerable importance in carrying visitors across the water to Dr Steevens' Hospital on the right bank. The king himself chose the design for the bridge from a number of plans submitted for royal approval. The architect was George Papworth and the material was cast iron, something of an innovation. The contractor was the ironmaster Richard Robinson, proprietor of the Phoenix Iron Works, situated close by on the left bank.

Seán Heuston Bridge, originally King's Bridge (1827), from the footpath upstream. Trees beyond the bridge surround the Croppies Memorial Park. To the right of the bridge stands the chimney of the former John Jameson distillery, with its twentieth-century lift and viewing chamber. The quay wall, with its luxuriant growth of ivy and other plants, is pierced by the tunnel that admits the Cammock River to the Liffey. Furthest right is a corner of Sancton Wood's railway station building.

In the words of Maurice Craig 'an agreeably vulgar affair', the bridge is interesting as an early specimen of a cast-iron structure. This material resists corrosion and therefore enjoys a long life but it is weak in tension, though strong in compression. This demands a particular design so that the forces of its weight and load press outwards from the centre. So the single graceful span of King's Bridge is shallow in the centre and has deep cantilevered ends, butted against massive granite pillars. Probably to make the structure stronger, the actual bridge does not extend from quay to quay, but spans a river narrowed by side abutments.

Conceived for nothing heavier than horse-drawn vehicles, there were fears for the safety of the bridge as road vehicles increased immeasurably in weight. In 1980 the City Council restricted access to the bridge to vehicles of less than two tons. In the following decades it was strengthened to accommodate the Luas trams and refurbished so that the attractions of crowns and leafy decorations on the spandrels are once again clearly visible.

In 1922 the bridge was renamed in honour of Patrick Sarsfield and the stone crowns that had formed the centrepieces of the parapet on both sides were removed. The celebration of the twenty-fifth anniversary of the Easter Rising led to the final name change to commemorate Seán Heuston. He had commanded a detachment of the Volunteers in the Mendicity Institution, a little way downstream of the bridge, in Easter Week and was executed not far away at Kilmainham on 8 May 1916.

Frank Sherwin Bridge

Opened in 1982, this three-span structure of reinforced concrete was built immediately downstream of Seán Heuston Bridge to accommodate the greatly increased flow of traffic. Incorporation of the bridge was accompanied by a reversal in the traffic flow on the quays, from anticlockwise, with eastbound traffic on the south side, to clockwise. The design of the bridge was an in-house project of the City Council under the leadership of Richard Fowler and it was constructed on site by Irishenco Limited. The piers are founded on bedrock and were built within coffer dams. For this the Council and its agents won an Irish Concrete Society Award.

Frank Sherwin, who had died the previous year, was a true Dubliner, born in Dorset Street in 1905. He had fought as a youth in the War of Independence and in the Civil War, in due course becoming a member of Fianna Fáil, which he left after failing to secure a nomination to a Dáil election. A colourful politician, he served as an Independent TD from 1957 to 1965.

Reconstruction of the river: Wolfe Tone and Victoria Quays

While the building of the quays and their walls in the course of recent centuries was a very considerable feat of planning and engineering, they are unremarkable when compared to a prodigious undertaking of the 1820s, when one of Anna Liffey's curves was forcibly straightened, just downstream of the King's Bridge. The following paragraphs are based on John de Courcy's description of the essentials of this spectacular work.

In the early 1820s a consortium of about a hundred citizens signed a memorial to the Lord Lieutenant seeking his support for major works. The quayside would be extended upstream from Pembroke Quay to the point where the ferry to Steevens' Hospital operated. Then a bridge would be built to replace the ferry. In the event, the first result of the memorial was the building of the bridge, to be opened in 1828.

The new quay was completed in the 1840s – but not along the existing left bank. It takes a gentle northward curve from Pembroke (now Sarsfield) Quay, between Ellis Street and Liffey Street West, and this meant that the river had to be completely realigned so that part of its left bank was actually moved to lie to the right of the line of the former right bank.

It is not easy to understand why such a major excavation was undertaken. The reason given by the consortium was the unsavoury nature of Barrack Street. The site of five fairs a week, it witnessed the dissolute behaviour of certain inhabitants who ministered to the various recreational needs of the thousands of soldiers who occupied the nearby barracks. But the worthy aim of sanitising the neighbourhood might have been accomplished by something less than moving the entire river. Records of the names of the Croppy Boys have not survived, but one of the leaders and heroes of their cause, Wolfe Tone, was honoured in the 1940s when the quay's name was changed from Prince Albert Quay to honour the great republican thinker and leader.

Today the Croppies Acre has been transformed from playing fields to a large, open park, tree-lined on its south side, with a memorial erected in 1985. Just upstream of this is the Croppies Memorial Park. It occupies the original north bend of the Liffey before the river was pushed to the south.

A south quay was built parallel to the new north quay. Queen Victoria drove along it in 1861 on her way from the new King's Bridge Station to Westland Row and it was later named in her honour. The least said about the wall of the brewery the better. Relieved only by an attractive but redundant gatehouse, it presents visitors and travellers with 400 metres of brick wall and, in spite of some brave efforts to compete by apartment blocks on quays downstream, takes a high place in the search for an award for the drabbest vista in Dublin's mostly fair city.

The bright side of Victoria Quay lies in the abundance of wild flowers and even trees that grow on the wall itself above the water. Certain species of flowers and ferns in the course of their evolution found ways of rooting in crevices on cliff faces, their essential requirements being lime and sufficient crumbly soil to hold a little rainwater. The granite blocks of the quay walls provide no such comforts, but the lime mortar is quite another matter. Victoria Quay faces north, which means that its wall receives relatively little heat from the sun and therefore less evaporation of the water. That explains why there is more vegetation there than on the opposite Wolfe Tone Quay. But something more subtle is needed to account for the richness of Victoria's flora compared with that of the north-facing quays further downstream.

The Guinness barges

By 1873, the Guinness cooperage and racking sheds had been established on the hill slope between St James's Street and the river, to the north of the original brewery. In that year the firm built a wooden jetty on Victoria Quay and an internal railroad system to bring the casks from the racking sheds to the waterside. They purchased the *Lagan,* built in Belfast by Harland and Wolff, and she became the first of a fleet of 'steam lighters' which would ply between Victoria Quay and City Quay or Custom House Quay for the next 88 years.

Not too many living Dubs remember the vessels of the original fleet, as they were all replaced in the 1930s by ten true native Dublin-made vessels. They were known as the 'Farmleigh' class, this being the name of the first of them and of the nearby Guinness family home. Designed by engineers employed in the

The Guinness brewery began in 1759 on a site on St James's Gate, up the hill and across the road from the Liffey. A neighbour on Thomas Street was Roe's distillery, whose main source of power was the windmill of 1760, the tower of which is preserved within what has since become Guinness property. The brewery expanded down the slope of the valley to the riverside. The pair of red-brick chimneys belong to the electric powerhouse built in 1948.

brewery and built by Vickers in Liffey Dockyard between 1927 and 1931, they served lovers of stout until the last voyage of the last of them, the *Castleknock* on Midsummer Day 1961. All ten found good homes and enjoyed long lives, some having sailed to Lough Neagh to transport sand dredged from the lake bed. The barges were replaced by less picturesque but more flexible and efficient road haulage to supply the seagoing Guinness ships, which continued to operate.

The Farmleigh class lighters measured 24.4 by 5.4 metres, carried a cargo of 90 to 100 tonnes and travelled at up to 7.5 knots. Powered by steam, they had specially designed superstructures. The smokestack was hinged at the base and lowered by a crewman just before the barge passed beneath each of the low bridges.

In their first decades, the barges were by far the most cost-effective means of bringing the product downstream, being considerably faster and having much greater capacity than the horse-drawn drays. But they operated under the same constraints that made them the sole commercial craft on the Liffey upstream of Butt Bridge. Sailing was possible only between two hours before and two hours after high tide. The whole fleet therefore had to move in convoy over a relatively short period and this meant much time spent idly as they waited to be loaded or unloaded, rather than allowing for each to move as soon as it was filled.

Rory O'More Bridge

The old name, Bloody Bridge, commemorated trouble instigated by the seventeenth-century ferrymen who understandably feared for their livelihoods when the structure was first built. The ferrymen encouraged a band of apprentices to tear down the new wooden bridge. Twenty of them were apprehended by the authorities, and a rescue attempt was made, in the course of which four of the apprentices were killed.

The fracas took place over the first of three wooden bridges at the site, built in 1670, joining Watling Street to Ellis Street. The third was replaced in 1704 by a four-arched stone bridge, which lasted for just over a hundred years before showing serious signs of disintegration. Thereafter it survived for nearly fifty more years, in spite of complaints about its narrowness and unsightly appearance, besides the frequent repair work it needed.

The second cast-iron bridge was made in England and placed on the Liffey in 1861, in time for Queen Victoria to cross it later that year. It is named in honour of Rory O'More, a hero of Cromwellian times.

The replacement, commissioned by John Halpin Junior, the Port Engineer, is a graceful single span of cast iron measuring 28.5 metres. Cast in Lancashire, it was assembled by John Killen of Malahide and completed in 1861. Queen Victoria crossed it in August of that year and it subsequently bore her name and that of Albert, the Prince Consort. It was renamed in 1939 in memory of a hero of the 1641 rebellion, Rory O'More, who had on one occasion escaped from his pursuers on a boat on the Liffey which brought him to waiting horses nearby.

An inscription in Latin commemorates the Benediction held at an altar on the bridge by the Archbishop of Dublin after the celebration of High Mass in Phoenix Park on 23 June 1929, the centenary of Catholic emancipation. The congregation had numbered half a million.

James Joyce House and Bridge

The quay on the right bank, downstream of Rory O'More Bridge, entered world literature in 1914 thanks to James Joyce's short story 'The Dead' in his collection *Dubliners*. Named Usher's Island in commemoration of the former sandbank, the quay was developed as a stately residential area in the eighteenth century. One of the very few survivors of the old houses that lined the quayside is 'the dark gaunt house' No. 15, where two of Joyce's great aunts lived. The story is far from being entirely fiction and has inspired film makers and playwrights, above all the exquisite film of the same name made by John Huston towards the end of his life. The house has a pleasing doorway with Ionic pilasters but its fanlight pales to insignificance when compared with that of its neighbour, which sadly has little more than the splendid entrance to show. After enduring varying degrees of neglect and, ultimately, sensitive care, restoration of No. 15 began in earnest in 2004 when Brendan Kilty acquired the building and set to work on making a worthy memorial to Joyce and those he inspired.

The door of 15 Usher's Island.

The fanlight and portico of the neighbouring doorway on Usher's Island survived the demolition of the rest of the house.

James Joyce Bridge by Santiago Calatrava, opened in 2003, connects Usher's Island to Blackhall Place. The skyline is broken by St Paul's Church, the Four Courts and the Central Bank.

Across the road from the house, the bridge named in the writer's honour was opened on Bloomsday (16 June) 2003. One of the two Liffey bridges designed by the Spanish architect Santiago Calatrava, it depends, like the older crossings, on arches. But this was the first in which the arches stand above rather than beneath the roadway. They are inclined outwards and the bridge deck, measuring 41 metres in length, is suspended from these tubular steel bows by cables. The bridge was constructed beside the River Lagan in Belfast by Harland and Wolff and installed by Irishenco. Far from simply providing access from the south quays to Ellis Quay and Blackhall Place, this crossing was designed for leisure, comfort and beauty by night and day. The walkway on each side has seats and an elaborate lighting system that spotlights the steel structure.

From Mellows to Father Mathew

The north quay, named in honour of Richard Butler, Earl of Arran and second son of the Duke of Ormonde, is dominated by Patrick Byrne's beautiful church of St Paul. Dedicated in 1837, it was the successor to an early eighteenth-century chapel. Beside the church is the rather stark white presbytery built in 1922, when the garden space between it and the road was also created. Red brick and a classical format predominate over the greater part of Arran Quay, the result of numerous rebuildings from the late nineteenth century to the end of the twentieth.

Liam Mellows Bridge. Built in 1768 and named Queen's Bridge in honour of Queen Charlotte, consort of King George III, it is truly a part of Georgian Dublin.

A bridge built between Bridgefoot Street and Queen's Street in 1683 collapsed 80 years later. Rebuilt in 1768, it has survived, making it the oldest bridge in the city. The original name was Arran, though it was also called Bridewell and Ellis's. The man responsible for the successful structure was the polymath General Charles Vallency. His work, with its three arches and gentle curve, is widely held to be the most beautiful of the old bridges. Named Queen's in 1768 in honour of Charlotte, wife of King George III, the bridge was rededicated to Queen Maeve in 1922 and received its present title in 1942.

The Four Courts and its surroundings

Some or all of the four courts of Chancery, King's Bench, Common Pleas and Exchequer first sat by the Liffeyside in 1796, while building work continued around them. Gandon's masterpiece, completed in 1802, was gutted by fire following shelling by government forces 120 years later. Re-establishment, under the care of the Office of Public Works architect T. J. Byrne, concluded with the replacement of the dome in 1931. The courts were built on a tongue of firm ground which lay close to the left bank of the river, with tidal flats on either side. Long before these were reclaimed, St Saviour's Priory stood on this plot, but in 1541 its Black Friars were expelled. Shortly afterwards, the property was made over to the Society of King's Inns.

Truly magnificent from a distance, the Four Courts façade has many good small details and deserves a close inspection, from both an architectural and an

The Four Courts. The gently curved quay wall has a balustrade in place of the solid granite walls that line the quays as far downstream as Butt Bridge.

VIEW OF THE LAW COURTS, LOOKING UP THE LIFFEY, DUBLIN.

Malton's picture of the Four Courts in the 1790s shows the eighteenth-century predecessor of James Savage's bridge, now named for Father Mathew. The waterside building on the left was demolished to make way for Merchant's Quay. A balustrade safety wall was added to Inns Quay after the building of a new bridge downstream at Winetavern Street ended the days of merchant shipping on this reach of the river.

institutional viewpoint. The pediment statues are of Moses, Justice and Mercy; the corners are occupied by Authority and Wisdom – all the work of Edward Smyth. The Four Courts building occupies the greater part of Inns Quay, whose name goes back to the sixteenth-century occupation by the legal profession. The quay runs between the sites of the oldest bridges in the city and owes its present appearance to work which began in 1816 when cast-iron balustrades with granite bases and coping were added to the redundant wharf and the adjacent bridges to complement the classical appearance of the scene.

Across the river from the Four Courts, the dominant building on Merchant's Quay is the Franciscan friary whose community in 1989 established the Merchant's Quay Project to serve people affected by drug use and HIV. In 2012 the project moved into the adjacent Riverbank Open Access Centre, where it provides practical and spiritual support and three free meals a day to people in need.

The austere stone façade of the friary is broken by the Italianate portico and entrance to the Church of the Immaculate Conception – better known for centuries as Adam and Eve's and immortalised in literature in the very first phrase of *Finnegans Wake*: 'riverrun, past Eve and Adam's, by swerve of shore to bend of bay ...'

Historians differ on whether worship in Penal times took place in an inn of the name or in a Mass house approached through or past the hostelry. The

The Franciscan friary that envelops Adam and Eve's Church, whose 1930s dome is a feature of the city skyline.

nineteenth-century church is a spacious building with a south entrance on Cook Street, which runs parallel to Merchant's Quay and is bordered by the much rebuilt thirteenth-century city wall. The position of this wall implies a need to protect the citizens from waterborne attackers. However, peaceful developments on the quayside between river and wall began less than a century later. The various buildings were replaced over and over and the oldest to survive are four Georgian houses. The greater part of Merchant's Quay is occupied by the 1992 office development Marshalsea Court.

Father Mathew and O'Donovan Rossa Bridges

Marked as 'The Bridge' on Speed's map of 1610, the crossing that now honours Father Mathew joins Bridge Street and Church Street upstream of the courts. Standing on the site of Dublin's earliest bridge, built in or about AD 1000, the original provided a more satisfactory route than had the tidal Ford of the Hurdles nearby. Rebuilt only three times in the course of its first 800 years of existence, this crossing exceeds all the others in its multiplicity of names. De Courcy lists fifteen. Among others, the Danes, King John and the Lord Lieutenant Earl Whitworth were so honoured. The bridge had been rebuilt early in the nineteenth century by James Savage to the same design and for the same price as one he had built downstream at Winetavern Street a few years earlier. Whitworth's name gave way to that of Father Mathew in 1938 to mark the centenary of Mathew's temperance crusade.

The early nineteenth-century bridges designed by James Savage. Father Mathew's (left), is the successor of the earliest crossings of the Liffey in the city. O'Donovan Rossa's (right) joins Winetavern Street to Chancery Place.

The crossing marked by Speed in 1610 would remain the only one in or near the city until later in the seventeenth century when a wooden bridge was built downstream by Humphrey Jervis. It was replaced shortly afterwards in 1684 by a five-arched stone structure that was swept away by a flood in 1802. Its successor was designed by James Savage and the contractor was George Knowles. The foundation stone was laid in August 1813 by the Duchess of Richmond and the bridge, named in her honour, opened to traffic on St Patrick's Day 1816. The keystones are decorated with heads carved by John Smyth. The lady represented on the central arch on the downstream side is Anna Liffey herself, flanked by Plenty and Industry. Upstream are Commerce, Hibernia and Peace. No plaque exists to commemorate builders or duchess or even the Fenian leader Jeremiah O'Donovan Rossa who came to be remembered there by order of the Municipal Council in January 1922.

Wood Quay

Much dust has settled on Wood Quay since the last quarter of the twentieth century. The riverside Civic Offices, designed by the legendary firm of architects Scott Tallon Walker and completed in 1994, are a worthy complement to Gandon's works and have an additional feature in the form of an outdoor green hillside to the south and a bright and beautiful space indoors. Stone steps and seats in the outdoor amphitheatre are packed on summer days for outdoor performances of opera. The green looks up the hill to Christ Church Cathedral – much rebuilt, but a spiritual focus for the city for more than a thousand years.

Before the building work began on Wood Quay a major archaeological excavation was conducted by Pat Wallace of the National Museum from 1969 to 1981, which revealed a wealth of detail about the lives and commerce of the Norse founders of the city and their descendants. On an autumn day in 1979 I brought my two young sons with me to join 15,000 citizens in a plea to have the offices built somewhere else and transform the remnants of the Viking city to an open park. It would have been beautiful and, given the cathedral, an even more noble setting. While it didn't happen that way, the excavation did take place and is commemorated, besides technical and popular reports, with a wonderful exhibition not far away in the National Museum in Kildare Street.

In a later excavation between 1990 and 1993, the base of the thirteenth-century circular Isolde's Tower was revealed and remained in full quayside view for some years. Once a corner bastion of the city walls, the tower was subsequently engulfed in a good office block, but the princess was left with no more than an oblique view of the sky. Still, her situation has been improved from her former burial and she can now be seen by passers-by on Lower Exchange Street.

Fishamble Street separates Wood Quay from Essex Quay and once upon a time led to a slipway where fishing boats discharged their catch to be sold at the adjoining shambles or market. Enjoying a secure place in musical history since 1742, when Handel conducted the first performance of his *Messiah* in a theatre a little way up the hill, there is reason to believe that the street itself is more than 1,100 years old.

Essex and Upper Ormond Quays
Early in the eighteenth century Essex Quay was completed, finally closing off the confluence of the Poddle with the Liffey and reducing the connection from the sea to the Duibh Linn to an arched culvert. The man commemorated in the name of the quay was Arthur Capel, Earl of Essex, a late seventeenth-century viceroy of uncommon integrity and commitment to the welfare of the people of his vice-realm.

The quayside buildings were replaced again and again, with the last eighteenth-century work being demolished in the 1990s. The oldest and by far the most distinguished survivor is the Sunlight Chambers block on the corner of Parliament Street. Described by Christine Casey as 'Quattrocento-cum-Victorian-Mercantile', it was begun in 1889 to the design of Edward Ould of Liverpool for the soap manufacturers and, later, industrial giant Lever Brothers. The ornate decoration includes a brightly coloured frieze illustrating methods of soap-making at the time of the Renaissance.

On the left bank the Duke of Ormonde's inspiration for the Dublin riverside (above, page 193) is honoured in the names of two adjacent quays. Upper Ormond Quay runs from O'Donovan Rossa Bridge to Grattan Bridge, and is faced with office blocks of varying ages and degrees of repair or replacement. It does retain something of the eighteenth-century style of red brick and four

Sunlight Chambers, built in 1789, with a frieze celebrating the manufacture of soap ancient and modern.

Lower Ormond Quay, a fashionable residential quarter in its earlier days, retains much of the outline of an eighteenth-century street, with a number of original doorways and other details.

storeys, but the majority of the ground-floor windows and doors have been updated. Just upstream of Capel Street, No. 33 has the distinction of the transfer from God to Mammon in the rebuilding of the mid-nineteenth-century Presbyterian church to serve as a bank branch office. The old ecclesiastical stonework survives at ground level.

Grattan Bridge to the Halfpenny Bridge

The earliest ancestor of Grattan Bridge, better known as Capel Street Bridge, was begun in 1676 by Humphrey Jervis. The work had the blessing of the Earl of Essex but faced strong opposition from merchants in the old city, who were acutely aware of the probable effects on their livelihoods of the development of a left-bank market. Until 1685 a wooden opening span in the new bridge allowed shipping to continue to reach Wood Quay, but its replacement by a stone arch marked the beginning of 300 years of moving the port further and further down the river.

Grattan Bridge, joining Capel Street to Parliament Street, is the nineteenth-century successor of constructions begun 200 years earlier in 1675. The brown algae on the quay wall visible at low tides show the presence of salt seawater.

By the 1750s the bridge was undergoing its second phase of serious destruction, the seventeenth-century foundations being far from equal to the caprices of Anna Liffey. George Semple was invited to plan a replacement. He believed that a bridge should be founded on the bedrock and, using coffer dams to keep the water out, excavated down to the limestone that lies beneath the city. His foundations withstood the forces both of the river and of a succession of flattenings and widenings of the bridge deck imposed first by the Ballast Board and later by the City Council.

The superstructure of Semple's bridge was similar to that of James Savage's two that were built upstream 50 years later, but it was replaced between 1873 and 1875 by Bindon Blood Stoney, Chief Engineer to the Dublin Port and Docks Board. He changed the form of the bridge from arched to flat, at a slight incline from south to north, retaining Semple's foundations but introducing elliptical arches. The carriageway was widened and new footpaths were placed on cantilevered wrought-iron beams. Zinc-topped iron parapets replaced the former stone, and the wonderful seahorses with their tasselled fins were added.

Lower Ormond Quay extends downstream from Capel Street to the Halfpenny Bridge and Bachelors Walk. While the upper portion of the quay was associated with the left-bank markets area, the lower was more fashionable. A number of good buildings have survived from the eighteenth century. The Morrison Hotel, on the corner of Swift's Row, was rebuilt in 1999 to the design of Douglas Wallace.

Malton's picture of the Four Courts (above, page 212) also shows the right bank with a glimpse of Thomas Burgh's 1707 Custom House and busy with the shipping that was finally banished when Carlisle Bridge was built in 1792. A slipway entered the river at the modern Temple Lane and another at Lower Fownes Street. The space between them, occupied by houses reaching to the water's edge, was the last part of the city quay alignment to be filled in, giving the Liffeyside its present-day appearance. This work was competed in 1813 and the new quays commemorate one giant and one lesser mortal: Wellington and Crampton.

The well-known Meathman was at the time engaged in the final battles of the Napoleonic Wars. The Iron Duke, incidentally, was a descendant of the Usher family of the island upstream and had been educated not far away, at White's Academy in Grafton Street, where Bewley's Café would be built later in the nineteenth century. The most distinguished building of Wellington Quay is Merchant's Arch, introduced in 1821 as part of a guildhall. Its arched passageway joins the Halfpenny Bridge to Temple Bar.

Crampton Quay, terminated towards the west by Asdill's Row, has been in existence since 1758. But the position of its eastern junction with Aston Quay has endured a considerable amount of to-ing and fro-ing. Today Crampton's is the shortest of the city quays, its buildings comprising a single development of three-storey, red-brick nineteenth-century business premises. The frontage is divided into six sections, separated by vertical floral friezes. Each section has a pair of windows on the upper two storeys. It ends at Bedford Row, a narrow street which, together with Asdill's Row, connects the quayside to Temple Bar. The individual commemorated is Philip Crampton, a bookseller who turned to property development and was Lord Mayor in 1758.

The Liffey's two footbridges join Lower Ormond Quay to the right bank. The graceful Millennium Bridge by Howley Harrington, supported by a tubular steel structure, was opened in 1999. The City Council's excellent website www. bridgesofdublin.ie describes it as 'a simple symphony of water, light, movement and form, perfect in its unobtrusiveness'. The bridge was made in Carlow, brought to Dublin by road and lifted into position by a single crane.

The plaque of the Millennium Bridge occupies an unusual place – level with the nearby pavement rather than on the bridge parapet. It serves a dual purpose, being also a manhole cover.

The Halfpenny Bridge, opened in May 1816, in its time was also a pioneering construction and the earliest cast-iron bridge in Ireland. The gracefully curving ribs were made in six sections in Coalbrookedale in Shropshire by the Quaker firm of Darby, which would later supply 'famine pots', the iron soup boilers used by relief workers. The three arches bearing lamps were added late in the nineteenth century. It has had many names, including Wellington Bridge (briefly) and Metal Bridge, and nobody uses its official designation of 'Liffey Bridge'. The Ordnance Survey currently gives it both its official title and 'Ha'penny Bridge' – the latter reflecting the long-established pronunciation of the small sum of money imposed as a toll charge until 1916.

For generations an icon of Dublin's scenery, the appearance of the bridge has received very mixed opinions from Dubliners. Hugh Lane considered it 'hideous' and engaged Lutyens to design a beautiful stone bridge on the site to house his paintings. But history intervened. The metal bridge survived and the pictures eventually found lodgings a little way up the left bank of the Liffey on Parnell Square.

The graceful Ha'penny Bridge of 1816 contrasts with the uncompromising block of Desmond Fitzgerald's O'Connell Bridge House of 1965. To the right, in the shade, is Merchant's Arch of 1821 by Frederick Darley and, on the left, the delightful innovation of the Boardwalk. Conceived by the City Council architects in 1997, it combined the utilitarian purpose of relieving congestion on the footpaths with an opportunity for citizens and visitors to enjoy the charms of Anna Liffey. It won an Irish architecture Regional Award for the arch0itrects McGarry Ní Éanaigh in 2001. In the distance, Gandon's Custom House cupola and dome are visible above the Loopline Bridge with the Financial Services Centre to the right.

Aston Quay

Bearing the name of the seventeenth-century developer Major Henry Aston, the quay is dominated by the noble Ballast Office, standing at the junction with

The tympanum of the former McBirney's department store on Aston Quay.

Westmoreland Street and towering above O'Connell Bridge. The quay wall opposite was built in 1704 to the design of Francis Tunstall, and de Courcy considers that this was the prototype for all the riverside walls. They adhere to a pleasing uniform style: granite ashlar topped with a gently curved ridge at a perfect height to lean on and look at the water.

The Ballast Office was the title of an ancestor of the Port Company and occupied a premises of the same name built for it in 1801. Altered at

The Ballast Office clock, moved to Westmoreland Street from its original aspect over the river.

intervals in the nineteenth century, it was demolished in 1979, a few years after the Dublin Port and Docks Board had vacated the site to follow the docklands downriver. The exterior of the new building, designed by Scott Tallon Walker, is largely a replica of its predecessor. The blue clock with gilded details, by A. Booth & Son, Dublin, dates to 1870 and originally faced over Westmoreland Street.

Between Price's Lane and Aston Place, the nine-bay, four-storey Italianate building dates from later in the nineteenth century. Stucco work on the tympanum above the main doorway presents a cluster of shamrocks and the name Hibernian House. Below this a red granite fascia commemorates in letters of gold its long life as McBirney's department store.

Bachelors Walk

Predating O'Connell – originally Carlisle – Bridge by more than a hundred years, Bachelors Walk was created by John Amory, who reclaimed the tidal land to its north late in the seventeenth century. The quay of the name extended from Liffey Street downstream as far as Marlborough Street. Today the four properties immediately upstream of the bridge are five-storey buildings and rather drab, save for the bright colour wash of No. 33 and the brilliant floral decoration of No. 29. This block ends at Bachelors Way. The greater and very much more pleasing part of Bachelors Walk extends from there to the Halfpenny Bridge and Liffey Street.

Much redevelopment has taken place, but upstream from the Arlington Hotel two tolerably well-preserved eighteenth-century town houses survive, still with their red-brick frontage, classical doorways, stone steps and fanlights. No. 7 is a third. The twentieth-century redevelopment buildings were four-storey; the older ones were taller, with five storeys, and they begin at Litton Lane, an alley so narrow that it is not shown even on the large-scale map of the centre of Dublin. Externally unappealing, the Blessed Sacrament Chapel of 1995 has an exciting interior. Consecrated at a time of declining religious observance it did something to reverse a trend of riverside churches closing their doors to worshippers. The adjacent shopfronts present a notable collection of nineteenth-century decorations.

In 2005 shipping returned to Bachelors Walk. Many, perhaps most, of the great coastal cities of the world offer water-bus trips for their visitors. The Liffey

The spectators in *The Liffey Swim* (91 x 61 cm) by Jack B. Yeats (1871–1957) are assembled on Bachelors Walk. Painted in 1923, the picture includes cranes at work on rebuilding inner Dublin following seven troubled years. The annual event had been inaugurated three years earlier by Bernard Fagan, a Corporation engineer, who wanted to demonstrate the success of the diversion of sewage from the river, which had been completed in 1906. More than 500 swimmers took part in the 2017 event. *National Gallery of Ireland*.

languished long years without such a facility because the water was too shallow for a substantial vessel at ebb tide and the bridges were too low at high tide. This unhappy situation ended when the motor vessel *Spirit of Docklands* was officially named in Dublin at a special ceremony on 29 June 2005. Insofar as it was conceived and built in Sweden, it is a true descendant of the Viking ships that had helped to found the port of Dublin more than a thousand years earlier. Very appropriately, it was blessed by a City Quay priest, Father Paul St John. Those attending the ceremony included the boat's designer, Peter Lund-Nielsen of Ole Steen Knudsen, Denmark and its builder, Klas Westers.

The *Spirit* accommodates 52 passengers, measures 23 metres and is capable of travelling at 9.5 knots. The solution to the problems of height and depth lies in the provision of variable ballast tanks. These allow it to rise in the water at low tide so that it floats clear of the river bed and to sink (partially) at high tide and pass safely beneath the bridges. The voyage begins at Bachelors Walk and turns for home at the East Link Bridge.

O'Connell Bridge

Named in honour of the Liberator after it was rebuilt in 1880, the original crossing at this point was an elegant structure designed by Gandon and opened to carriages in 1795. First mooted around 1750, the proposal for a bridge downstream of Capel Street was greeted with the usual objections by the merchants of the south side. As it happened, they commanded a majority in the City Assembly and they succeeded in delaying the undertaking for nearly half a century. When it was finally built, the new bridge was named after the fifth Earl of Carlisle, who had been Lord Lieutenant in 1780 when the first positive steps in the planning were taken.

Gandon's first and very elaborate design was dismissed on the grounds of cost. His next was simpler, with three circular arches, the centre one higher than the others, giving the bridge an overall curve. The keystones were embellished with heads carved by Edward Smyth, representing the Liffey and other rivers of Ireland. These were removed when the bridge was rebuilt and they ended up gracing the red brick walls of the Tropical Fruit Company (now Poggenpohl) on Sir John Rogerson's Quay, where they may be seen to this day.

Possibly sufficient for eighteenth-century traffic, Gandon's creation had begun to deteriorate less than 50 years after it was built. There was no lack of agreement on the need to improve it and in 1864 Dublin Corporation announced a competition for a new design. It was actually won by the ironmaster Richard Turner's proposal for a single-span iron bridge. But this was turned down both on aesthetic grounds and because there were doubts about the strength of such a structure.

The bridge in use today was the concept of the Engineer to the Port and Docks Board, Bindon Blood Stoney, whose design of three elliptical arches and an almost level surface was adopted. Construction began in 1877 and the bridge was opened three years later. The point had been made that no fewer than seven roads converged on the bridge – the four quays together with Sackville, D'Olier and Westmoreland Streets. The decision was taken to build the bridge to the same width as Sackville – now O'Connell – Street and this resulted in the very unusual footprint of a bridge wider than its length.

The decoration of O'Connell Bridge changes from time to time. The name Carlisle Bridge was incised on the parapets but covered over before long by the existing plaque, which gives credit to designer and contractor as well as the civic dignitaries involved. The original lamp standards that lined the centre of the bridge were replaced in the 1950s by a concrete fountain, which acquired the name 'The tomb of the unknown gurrier'. Fortunately, the lamps had been preserved in some Corporation yard, the gurrier's grave was consigned to history and the standards were resurrected. The sea beasts which support the lamps on the parapets were removed later, but that was only for repair work and they returned in due course. The most recent addition to the décor was the assortment of Rachel Joynt's brass objects in the pavements on the right bank.

The buildings that overlook O'Connell Bridge include one totally delightful work, several of little interest and the Ballast Office, already mentioned. The apex of the angle where D'Olier and Westmoreland Streets meet is occupied by an office block described by Christine Casey as 'a Portland stone baronial exercise with Gothic and Ruskinian leanings'. Designed for an insurance company by J. J. O'Callaghan in 1898, it is lavishly decorated from turret to ground floor arcade. Senior citizens remember with pleasure the flashing coloured lights of the Bovril electric sign.

To the Loopline

The visual barrier imposed on the citizens of Dublin by the construction of the Loopline Bridge in 1888 finally and permanently banished all shipping, other than specially designed craft, from the reaches upstream of Butt Bridge. In spite of protests by the great and good – in contrast to earlier objections to new bridges made by merchants with vested interests – the decision to link the Dublin to Kingstown and Dublin to Drogheda railways was made. Although an impressive piece of nineteenth-century railway engineering, few people, if any, have ever considered the Loopline Bridge to be a thing of elegance and it effectively cut off from the city the long-established view of ships and Custom House.

Its companion, Butt Bridge, was designed by Stoney and opened to traffic in 1879. His bridge originally comprised a stone arch at each end with a cantilevered span between them which could swivel on a central pier, opening a pair of passages for shipping. But the berthage for sea-going ships upstream on Burgh Quay and Eden Quay came to an end less than ten years later with the Loopline. The present crossing at road level, designed by Joseph Mallagh and opened in 1932, was the first Liffey bridge in Dublin to be built of reinforced concrete rather than stone or iron.

Bachelors Walk and Aston Quay had extended eastwards to Marlborough Street and Hawkins Street respectively and were cut in two when O'Connell Bridge was built in 1795. The portion of Bachelors Walk downstream of the new bridge was named Eden Quay. Until 1814, the riverside between Marlborough Street and the Custom House and its docks had been occupied by buildings and yards. These were replaced by wharfage in 1814, thereby extending Eden Quay. Until the building of Butt Bridge, it was closest to the city and a busy centre for shipping and merchants – as was its companion Burgh Quay on the right bank.

Burgh Quay: above and below ground

The frontage of a riverside brewery between Hawkins Street and George's Quay was replaced in 1816 by a new wharf, thus completing the unbroken quayside from Usher's Island to the Grand Canal Dock and the River Dodder.

It was named Burgh Quay, perhaps in honour of the great eighteenth-century engineer and architect Thomas Burgh, but possibly owing much to the fact that a later Thomas Burgh was one of the Wide Streets Commissioners responsible for the development. The quayside buildings included the Corn Exchange, which survives only in the form of its classical façade.

An ornate memorial pillar in limestone and pink granite, topped by a small Celtic cross, stands at the junction of Burgh Quay and Hawkins Street and bears the words:

> This memorial was erected in memory of Patrick Sheehan a constable in the Dublin Metropolitan Police force who lost his life on the second day of May 1905 in a noble and self-sacrificing effort to rescue John Fleming who had in the discharge of his duties descended the main sewer close by this spot and was overcome by sewer gas. It was also intended to commemorate the bravery of a number of other citizens who also descended the sewer to assist in rescuing the aforementioned thereby risking their own lives to save those of their fellow men.

The text is written in Irish on the opposite side of the pillar and, on the face between these two the Lord Mayor and other dignitaries appended their names for posterity. The accident happened during the construction work of the north and south sewerage interceptors, which meet underneath Burgh Quay.

Rosie Hackett Bridge

Hawkins Street, with its memorial, came to be joined with Marlborough Street on the left bank on 20 May 2014 with the opening of Rosie Hackett Bridge. A simple but elegant structure designed by the architect Seán Harrington – already involved in Liffey crossings by the James Joyce Bridge upstream – it also has nearly as specialised a function as the Halfpenny Bridge. Private motorists are prohibited and it serves only pedestrians and public transport. Buses and taxis used it from the start but its principal function is to carry the North–South Luas connection. For pedestrians it shortened the walk for many by enabling them to cross downstream of O'Connell Bridge. And it provided seating for people to sit and admire the river.

By the addition of the Boardwalk, space and seats on bridges, and the tree-lined walks of the former quaysides downstream, the twenty-first century added a remarkable dimension of leisure to the transport and commerce of the environs of Anna Liffey.

8 | And so to the sea:
Docklands ancient and modern

Liffeyside transformations: campshire converted from crane track to pedestrian use; eighteenth-century Custom House; nineteenth-century Loopline Bridge; twentieth-century Liberty Hall and Matt Talbot Bridge.

Regeneration

Inspired thinking on the part of individuals in various authorities has brought about the removal of interesting but unlovely nineteenth-century riverside warehouses and the creation of the delightful, tree-shaded open spaces where they stood and where the great cranes used to trundle along the campshires.

Wikipedia defines the word *campshire* as the stretches of land between the quay and road on both the north and south quays in Dublin and refers its readers to the excellent website www.reflectingcity.com, where the recent developments and future vision for the docklands are described with an abundance of detail on past and present. The derivation of the term is surprisingly well concealed: it is absent from recent Oxford dictionaries, both etymological and architectural. A hint of meaning is given in the *New Shorter Oxford English Dictionary* of 1993, which defines a late fifteenth-century term *campshed* as 'a facing of piles and boarding along the bank of a river'. That sounds like a possible origin for the riverside stretches that were filled in behind the quay walls.

While these upper reaches of the docklands have been transformed into gleaming new office buildings and hotels, with abundant space for leisure-seeking citizens, the lower regions continue to expand to provide port facilities. Both developments are exciting – but not without conflict. Legal wrangles on the propriety of various actions by developers will make very interesting reading when they are resolved, and the results will have a visual effect on aspects of the developments. But that will take some time.

A notable battle took place from 2008 to 2010 between the Dublin Port Company, which wanted to continue the reclamation of tidal land towards the east, and a majority of members of the City Council, who considered that such a step would encroach upon the amenities of the inner parts of Dublin Bay. The Port Company's plan was to add 21 hectares to their property in the interests of extending the deep-sea cargo-handling facilities. An Bord Pleanála, in June 2010, ruled in favour of the City Council – but not for the reasons that the council had put forward. The planning application was refused because the development would have removed the 21 hectares from

The Linesman by Dony MacManus, 2000.

the wildfowl habitat, thereby infringing EU regulations concerning the status of the bay as an Area of Special Protection under the Birds Directive. The most remarkable outcome of this was the discovery by the Port Authority that they could find 21 hectares within their existing property by means of a major redevelopment scheme.

The birds – and birdwatchers – gained temporary respite, perhaps for some decades. But, unless the sea level rises spectacularly as a result of global warming, dry land will ultimately take over the present-day tidal flats, no matter what regulations are made. The tidal flats will be replaced by a similar landscape further out, but the area of sea within Dublin Bay will inevitably be reduced and the area of dry land increased. This encroachment of land has been in progress for some thousands of years, beginning when Hibernia, relieved of the weight of a great ice field, arose from the azure main to her present level. That was a relatively fast and very dramatic movement – but there were no people around to witness it.

Later developments have been more subtle. On the one hand, the silt carried down by Anna Liffey herself and by the Tolka and the Dodder, built up a delta. Its bounds are confined by rocky coasts to north and south so that the typical triangular shape of the Greek letter can no longer be fully formed. This siltation is a normal feature of the mouths of rivers, great and small. But Dublin Bay has an unusual second source of fine sand. The bed of the Irish Sea is still feeling

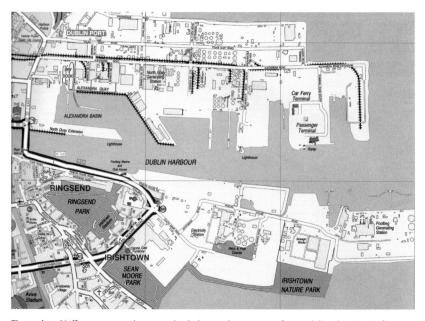

The enclosed Liffey estuary as shown on the Ordnance Survey map of 2011. Other than a strip from Ringsend southwards, the entire area shown in off-white, together with the parks, is reclaimed land.
© Ordnance Survey Ireland Permit No. 9166

the effects of the glaciation, and marine currents continue to bring sediments into the bay from outside.

The effect of the siltation is clearly visible in the extent of the wonderful area of tidal flats that constitute the twin Bulls – North and South. Since the end of the eighteenth century permanent dry land has been building up on the North Bull in the form of its long island. In addition to the rich hunting ground that the sand flats provide for myriads of wading birds, they have endowed generations of Dubliners with an incomparable privilege enjoyed by few of the residents of the world's capital cities. Dubliners, parked in their cars or walking along the strand, have a view, when the tide is out, over miles of land, uninterrupted by hills, trees or buildings and, on their very doorstep, a sense of unlimited space.

A wealth of detail of the history and development of the Port of Dublin is available in H. A. Gilligan's masterly *History of the Port of Dublin*, published in 1988. Gilligan began work as an official of the Dublin Port and Docks Board in the 1940s and retired in 1983, after seven years as Secretary to the Board. Few people, if any, had a greater knowledge of the workings of the docklands and he supplemented this with further research after his retirement. His book is the Old Testament of the Liffey's docklands. At the time of its publication, the East Link Toll Bridge was four years old and the great transformation of the quays upstream of it from cargo to leisure and to office-bound business was just beginning.

The New Testament era began in earnest with the establishment of the Dublin Docklands Development Authority in 1997. This phase has been ably chronicled by Turtle Bunbury in his *Dublin Docklands: An Urban Voyage*, published in 2009.

Surviving nineteenth-century buildings on Custom House Quay. Beside them the tower cranes build anew.

The Authority's Mission Statement embodies high ideals, many of which have been achieved:

> We will develop the Dublin Docklands into a world-class city quarter paragon of sustainable inner city regeneration – one in which the whole community enjoys the highest standards of access to education, employment, housing and social amenity and which delivers a major contribution to the social and economic prosperity of Dublin and the whole of Ireland.

The port proper had been pushed downstream by the building of Matt Talbot Bridge in 1978 and Gandon's Custom House had long before then abandoned its purpose as an office for levying cargo and shipping duties from the vessels actually at anchor in its adjoining docks. Visually, the black lattice of the Loopline viaduct separates the city of the nineteenth century from its late twentieth-century renewal.

The North and East Walls

Downstream of the point where Butt Bridge now stands, the untamed Liffey in former times spread over a great area. The right bank was 250 metres to the south, bordered by Lazar's Hill, now Townsend Street, and very much the end of the town in a west–east direction. To the north the tidal flats extended for 200 metres to a shoreline close to Beresford Place. From this relatively narrow neck, the estuary increased quickly in width and, where the East Link now crosses the river, the waters spread for more than 2 km, from Irishtown to North Strand Road.

The constriction of these nether parts of Anna Liffey had begun in 1708 when the Directors of the Ballast Office extended the south quay, on the right bank, by arranging with the leaseholders along the foreshore to build retaining walls on a line slightly south of east, beginning at George's Quay, which runs due east. George's Quay, labelled 'St. George's Key' by de Gomme in his map of 1728, was built early in that century. Probably named for King George I rather than the mythical saint, it was an important berthing place for cross-channel packet boats and for the ferries which transported passengers from Ringsend. It was the spot where George Frederick Handel set foot in Dublin in 1741, the year before the first performance of his *Messiah* a little way upstream.

George's Quay ran from a riverside building at its west end to Sir John Rogerson's Quay at a point between Moss Street and Lime Street. In 1715 extension eastwards of George's Quay on the right bank began with the construction of City Quay and Rogerson's. While Rogerson's name is deservedly commemorated for complying with a requirement to build the retaining wall on his property, John Mercer failed to complete a similar barrier upstream, between Rogerson's and George's. The City Council accordingly had the work done and named it City Quay to commemorate their worthy decision.

On the left bank, reclamation of the shore from Bachelors Walk downstream began in 1710, with the construction of new quays. These were originally faced with kishes, large baskets made from woven timber and filled with stones. The system is still used, but the kishes have been replaced with 'gabions' of steel mesh rather than timber.

Spoil from dredging the main channel of the river was spread behind the new quays to raise the level of the foreshore above that of the highest tides. This transformed the lower estuary of the river, in the course of the eighteenth century, from tidal flats to level dry land. It must have ended, too, the legendary right of Fellows of Trinity College to shoot snipe on the nearby university property.

As early as 1728, the north quays extended all the way downstream to the East Wall, a distance of nearly two kilometres from the Barracks. The planning and workmanship were not quite good enough and repairs were needed from time to time until a final rebuilding was carried out in 1869. This latter construction was a notable achievement. Warehouses have come and gone, but the granite masonry and limestone sets of the quay, as far as the East Link

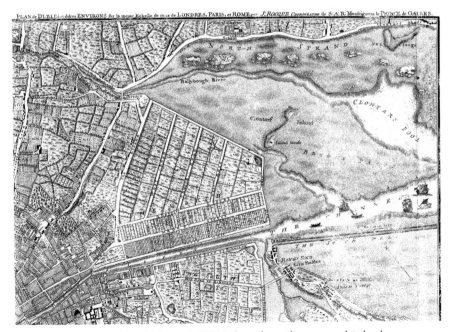

The Lower Liffey as surveyed by John Rocque in 1756. It shows the north quays completed and back-filled as far downstream as the 'Point' where the North and East Walls meet. Amory's Ground to the west would become the site for Gandon's Custom House, while the Lotts downstream would be replaced to a large extent by inner docks and warehouses – including the great Stack A.

The Scherzer lifting bridge at the entrance to the Royal Canal and Spencer Dock, installed in 1912. Its companion upstream was built in 1935.

Bridge, have survived since then with relatively little maintenance or rebuilding required. So the confines of the Liffey between Butt Bridge and the confluence with the Dodder have scarcely changed in the course of very nearly 300 years.

John Rocque's map of 1756 shows an 'East Quay' in two parts running northwards from the end of the North Wall across the river from Ringsend. An unnamed and longer quay continues northwest from the East Quay, nearly as far as the bridge at Ballybough. This has long been known as the East Wall Road and was part of the sea wall built in the first half of the eighteenth century to reclaim a substantial part of the estuary of the Tolka. The North and East Walls formed a point where they met, hence the name that came to be applied to the Point Depot and later the Point Theatre (now the 3Arena). Until well into the nineteenth century this road marked the boundary between tidal flats and reclaimed land. While the right bank of the tidal Liffey came to be defined by the South Wall, the left bank remained as a broad stretch of sand flats merging with the estuary of the Tolka.

The Custom House and its docks

The main structure of James Gandon's magnificent Custom House was completed in 1791, following decades of tension between the Revenue Commissioners for Ireland who wanted it and the Dublin Corporation which did not. Maurice Craig, with his incomparable erudition and charm, gives an account of the building and its generation from both the historical and the architectural viewpoints.

The Revenue Commissioners had three substantial docks created downstream of their headquarters, to the north of the quay. The first of these, completed in 1797, lay beside the Custom House. This, the Old Dock, was filled in in 1927 and is covered by Memorial Road to the east of the Custom House and by some of the buildings of the Financial Services Centre.

Early in the nineteenth century, the next two docks, George's Dock and the Inner Dock, were excavated. Named in honour of the visit of King George IV to Dublin in 1821, the former was supposed to have been opened by the monarch, but a prolonged visit to Slane Castle led to his absence on the occasion. These two docks, originally containing tidal water controlled by a lock system, are now freshwater ponds, providing a beautiful open space, overlooked by apartment blocks and other buildings of the late twentieth century. The redundant Scherzer lifting bridge, installed in the 1930s to give access to the docks, together with its companion downstream at Spencer Dock, have happily been retained as part of the scenery.

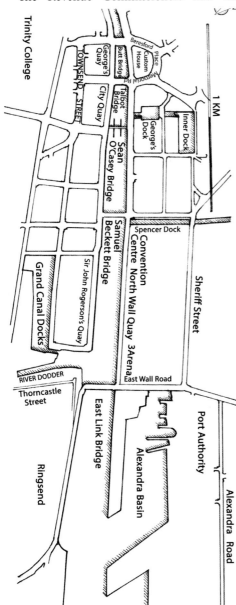

The Docklands and their position in the city.
Ruairi Moriarty.

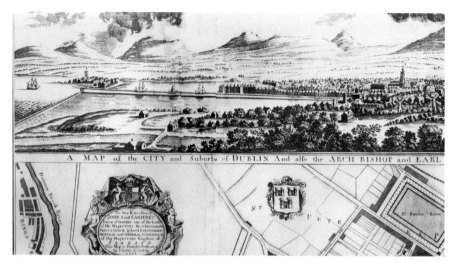

The eastern half of Charles Brooking's sketch *A Prospect of the City of Dublin from the North* included with his map of 1728. The sketch shows the Liffey enclosed as far as Ringsend and the completed East Wall. High tide still covers the sand flats which would soon afterwards be filled in with dredged spoil and sold as 'Lotts'.

North and South Lotts

The name of South Lotts Road recalls the eighteenth-century distribution of reclaimed land. On the Liffeyside, the North Lotts were larger, extending from the Custom House eastwards to the Tolka and northwards to the North Strand and Fairview. In 1682 the City Assembly had this area divided into 152 'lots' which would be distributed by lottery to Assembly members and to favoured officials. The original scheme was not completed, partly because the process of building sea walls and filling in the land beside them took longer than anticipated.

Charles Brooking's map of 1728 shows the completed quays on both banks, but has a legend inside the northern one saying 'This Part is Walled in but as yet over flowed by ye Tide'. Completion of that work was to take nearly seventy years. Brooking's map includes a beautiful engraving entitled *A Prospect of the City of Dublin from the North* which shows water covering the reclaimed area bordering a region of parkland and big houses.

The creation of new land, with its division into properties, made it possible to plan a grid system of roads in a style that could not be followed over the street pattern on the higher ground, which had evolved in the course of the gradual growth of the older parts of the city. The flatness of the reclaimed land also contrasts with the slopes, steep or shallow, of the natural rather than man-made valley of the Liffey. Some of the street names on the Lotts – Mayor Street, Sheriff Street, Guild Street and Commons Street – testify to the enthusiasm of the city fathers for their institutions and offices.

Samuel Beckett Bridge by Santiago Calatrava (2009) and the National Conference Centre by Kevin Roche (2010).

Spencer Dock, flanked by the new and backed by the old.

In contrast to the large area of land reclaimed to the north of the river, the South Lotts were very much more limited in extent. Fifty-one plots behind City Quay were distributed by auction in the 1720s. South Lotts Road itself and a more extensive area of reclamation belong to the Dodder valley rather than that of the Liffey.

Spencer Dock and the Conference Centre

The Royal Canal, begun in 1789, entered the Liffey through a sea lock on the North Wall Quay. The canal itself was widened between the quay and Sheriff Street to provide berthing facilities. This was before the days of the railways that would subsume the greater part of the transport for which the canal had been built. In 1845, some fifty years after the opening of the waterway, the Midland Great Western Railway Company purchased the canal, more in the interests of using its level bankside property than in promoting barge traffic. The canal to the north of Sheriff Street was widened in the 1870s to create a dock for transferring goods, especially coal, to the railway wagons. Opened by the Lord Lieutenant, Earl Spencer, in 1873 and bigger and better than the one it replaced, Spencer Dock never achieved the splendour of the Grand Canal across the river.

There is an element of the romantic in the story of the architect whose design was the winning entry in an international competition and which has left the quayside with one of the most original buildings in the land. Kevin Roche graduated from the UCD School of Architecture in 1945. He worked with Michael Scott, who also claims credit for a notable nearly Liffeyside building in the shape of Busaras a little way upstream. Roche moved to the United States where he established himself as a leader in glass architecture. To return in spirit to Dublin in his 80s and design a fine building which, with Santiago Calatrava's bridge, enhances the entire docklands region is a marvellous achievement.

The most ancient Dubliners

Seven thousand years before the Vikings, Mesolithic hunter-gatherers established a fishery at a spot just a little way downstream of where Spencer Dock now lies. Their ancestors may have done the same for generations before that, but a date between 6100 and 5700 BC was established from archaeological work on a building site in 2005. Melanie McQuade unearthed substantial traces of tidal fish traps made from hazel rods and wattles. Remains of a similar trap constructed 3,000 years later by their Neolithic successors were also found. Although not known in the Liffey in recent centuries, traps of very much the same construction were in use in several Irish river estuaries in the twentieth century.

Bridges of the twenty-first century

In the latter years of the nineteenth century five ferries plied the Liffey within the port. The first operated between City Quay and the Custom House Docks and the fifth between Great Britain Quay and the North Wall. They were in use until well into the twentieth century, the original rowing boats being replaced by substantial motor-driven craft, but still open to the weather. The last of these was retired in 1984.

The ancient practice was revived for two years in the twenty-first century when the Dublin Docklands Development Authority commissioned Liffey River Cruises to provide a service while the Samuel Beckett Bridge was under construction. The service began in October 2007, operating from 7 a.m. to 7 p.m., Monday to Friday. The last passage was made at 7 p.m. on Friday 11 December 2009, the day when the new bridge was opened. More than a quarter of a million passengers were carried during the two years for a fare of €2 one way or €3 return – rather more than the farthing or halfpenny of times long past, but in terms of a proportion of a day's wages considerably better value.

A few years earlier, the first of the twenty-first-century bridges had been completed and named in honour of Seán O'Casey. Annette Black and Michael B. Barry in their *Bridges of Dublin* describe a string of remarkable features in its construction and origins. The architect Brian O'Halloran was selected in December 2002 from 80 entrants to a competition. It was completed in no more than 30 months, which included the commissioning of environmental impact studies and various legal processes. The structure and opening mechanism were pioneering works: the bridge is made in two leaves, each supported by a central pillar on which they swivel.

The Samuel Beckett Bridge was the second of two Liffey crossings by Santiago Calatrava and is described by Wikipedia in these immortal words: 'supported by 31 cable stays from a doubly back-stayed single forward arc tubular tapered spar …' To you and me it is a graceful white-painted structure in the shape of a harp. The form of the bridge, embodying national emblem and Guinness trademark, may well be coincidental, but there is something very pleasing in this symbol of nationhood and conviviality in the modern centre of the ancient capital.

The furniture of the quays

A succession of Guinness cargo ships used to dock either on Custom House Quay or on George's Quay until access was cut off by the building of Matt Talbot Bridge in 1978. Because the Guinness vessels were loaded first from the company's barges by on-board cranes and then from road tankers, these quays had been left free of the cranes and warehouses that occupied the riverside downstream.

LMS railway company offices on North Wall Quay in 2014. Scheduled for redevelopment, their identity is revealed only by a monogram.

LMS monogram.

Seán O'Casey Bridge (2005). The footbridge connects City Quay and Custom House Quay and leads from the south side to the CHQ Building, the huge nineteenth-century warehouse long known as Stack A, which has been transformed into an exhibition centre.

Towards the end of the nineteenth century various shipowners engaged in transporting goods, cattle and people had sheds and warehouses built along the waterfront on the quay downstream of the entrance to the Custom House Docks. These effectively cut the river off from the public roadway and made for a singularly drab waterfront. Some of the shipping companies had in the nineteenth century added good buildings across the road from the warehouses and pleasing remnants of these have been preserved for posterity, while the

The river god carved as a keystone for Carlisle Bridge migrated to a building on Sir John Rogerson's Quay.

quayside buildings, mostly single-storey brick structures, were removed and access to the river restored.

On the right bank along Sir John Rogerson's Quay, a different approach was adopted. Warehouses on the wharves were few and campshires with the giant electrically powered cranes, in service since the early 1900s, left the waterside fully accessible. The warehouses were on the opposite side of the road from the campshires and much of the cargo was transferred to horse-drawn drays and, later, to lorries.

When first built, a strip of foreshore was exposed along the base of both quays at low water. The walls were rebuilt over a long period, from 1870 to 1913 and this work included removing the tidal mud so that vessels could dock at all tides.

Grand Canal Dock and the Dodder

On the right bank, at the eastern end of Sir John Rogerson's Quay, is the breach in the Great South Wall demanded by nature to allow the Dodder, narrowed by eighteenth-century sea walls, to reach the sea and by commerce to provide an entrance from the port to the Grand Canal Docks. The concept of the Grand Canal and its docks was splendid.

Three sea locks, each named in boldly cut lettering in honour of a Lord Lieutenant, were built to admit lighters and even sea-going vessels to the docks so that goods could be transferred to canal barges, to travel through the midlands, on to the Shannon waterway and so to Limerick, with access to the Shannon Estuary and the ocean. The locks are distinguished by superb work in granite by the stonemasons, and also by the carpenters who built the old gates and the iron-founders who made the new ones. Created decades before the rail network provided a faster and more flexible service, the canal system was an exciting and – for the most part – brilliantly planned innovation in transport.

Tragically, the planners had failed to take into account the hidden powers of the Dodder. This wayward river, notorious for its propensity to flood, regularly deposited its burden of silt at the entrance to the canal locks, rendering them almost unserviceable. Britain Quay, on the left bank of the tidal Dodder, did serve for many years as berthage for the craft of the salmon fishermen and for small sea-going fishing boats. A little way upstream of this quay the graceful Ringsend Bridge was built in 1803 to restore the link between Ringsend and the city. It was the last and only successful one of a series of attempts to bridge the Dodder there. Gerard Boate had written in 1643 of a setback in his times:

> Since that time a stone bridge hath been built over that brook (as over Drumconran-water there hath been one from antient times) upon the way betwixt Dublin and Rings-end; which was hardly well accomplished, when the brook in one of those furious risings quite altered its channel for a good way, so as it did not pass under the Bridge as before, but just before the foot of it, letting the same stand upon dry land, and consequently making it altogether useless: in which perverse course it continued, until per force it was constrained to return to its old channel, and to keep within the same.

Those dangerous days have long gone and so, too, have the times of commercial shipping activity around the Grand Canal Docks. The dockland languished for some decades, though treasured by sailboard and other water sports enthusiasts for the space that it provided. Wild flowers thrived in patches of wasteland, old warehouses decayed and, with few exceptions, the area came to be neglected. Then came the Tiger years and a scarcely credible transformation to the bright and beautiful land of the theatre and its plaza and, above all, the calm surface of the sheltered water and its reflections of buildings by day and lights by night.

The last remaining nineteenth-century warehouse on Sir John Rogerson's Quay, overlooked by the pinnacle of Samuel Beckett Bridge.

Replacements and relics

As we have seen, replacement of Dublin's dockland by buildings for commerce or community has been in progress since Viking times, with occasional bouts of major activity, as in the dramatic movement brought about by the building of Carlisle Bridge in 1795. The intrusion of the Loopline railway bridge in 1890 moved merchant vessels a little further down, but substantial craft, most notably those of the Guinness fleet, continued to penetrate far into Dublin's fair city until the 1970s. Two factors contributed to the profound changes that began in the 1980s: one demographic, the other mechanical.

Demographically, the industrialisation of Ireland, which led in the 1960s to the reversal of a century and a half of depopulation, required a great increase in cargo traffic. Mechanically, ships grew bigger and bigger, and the shallow tidal waters of the Liffey of the city centre could no longer accommodate them. At the same time the revolution in the introduction of container traffic and of mechanical handling of bulk cargo led to a catastrophic reduction in the numbers of dock workers employed.

As the shipping moved away, commercial buildings and their population of well-paid workers invaded the quaysides. These quays have been transformed from workplaces to leisure areas, with subtle embellishment in the form of Rachel Joynt's delightful little sea beast lamps sparkling among the paving stones.

East Link: moving the docklands ever further

The East Link Bridge of 1994 – named Tom Clarke Bridge on 3 May 2016 in honour of the 1916 leader – has an opening span, but the removal of cranes and warehouses transposed the quays upstream of it to berthage for visiting vessels of recreation or war, since cargo was no longer to be handled there. So the bridge became the latest in a series of barriers to shipping that had been proceeding downstream from Wood Quay in the course of a thousand years. As Butt Bridge had done a century earlier, the Tom Clarke Bridge marks a boundary between redundant docklands, untenanted by cargo vessels, and an active harbour, thronged with great ships and with leisure craft, seafarers and harbour workers and to some degree intolerant of landlubbers.

The view from the Tom Clarke Bridge is entirely delightful: brightly painted merchant ships to the left; sailing boats ancient and modern to the right; and in the centre a distant view of the open sea, with the harbour tenderly protected by the Great South Wall and the sentinel red Poolbeg Lighthouse.

Gilligan describes the developments demanded by the arrival of steel-hulled

The black guillemot has become a regular summer resident in the tidal Liffey. Normally nesting in crevices in sea cliffs, it has found that drainage tunnels in concrete walls are just as good. At least one pair nests in the fabric of the Tom Clarke Bridge. *Photo: Michael Finn*.

steamers which required deeper berthage than that needed by the sailing ships. In 1836 the Port and Docks Board initiated the building of a timber wharf running northwards from the Point. Dredging beside it produced a relatively deep-water area, 3.6 metres at low tide. It came to be known as 'Halpin's Pond' in honour of the engineer Richard Halpin, Inspector of Works to the Board.

In the days of relatively small merchant ships, it had been possible to beach them for repair work. Early in the nineteenth century 'graving slips' were constructed on which larger vessels could be winched out of the water. By mid-century this was no longer practicable and the 'graving dock' was developed. The ship entered the dock at high tide and lock gates were closed to keep the water out after the tide had fallen so that work on the hull could be accomplished. The first of its kind on the Liffey was opened in 1860 and had been designed to be big enough to accommodate the City of Dublin Steam Packet Company's new mail steamers. A splendid construction of limestone blocks, it lies to the east of East Wall Road and remained in use until 1989.

In 1861 the Port Engineer Bindon Blood Stoney, well aware of the increasing size of the ships using the facilities, proposed the construction of a North Wall Extension, running eastwards from the North Wall Quay and providing depth at low water of 22 feet (6.7 metres). Preparations for the work began in 1864 and included the commissioning of a diving bell. Designed by Stoney, it was built in Drogheda by Grendon and Co. and delivered in 1866. Long since overtaken by diving suits and scuba equipment, the old chamber has for many years been part of the scenery across the river on Sir John Rogerson's Quay. A diving bell,

The diving bell of 1866 raised to sit on a wall in 2018 to accommodate a permanent exhibition of work on the docklands.

when submerged, provides a dry working area on the sea bed. Last used in the 1950s, the bell stood in retirement as a conspicuous feature on Rogerson's Quay. In 2015 work began to give it a new lease of life as an interpretative centre.

At the same time as the graving dock was being built, a retaining wall was constructed running eastwards across the estuary of the Tolka. Now superseded by walls and reclaimed land to its north, its line is that followed by Tolka Quay Road, which brings cars and passengers to the ferry port close to its end. Originally 700 metres long, the road now runs into Dublin Bay for nearly 2 km.

The Alexandra Basin and its environs

Eight years after Stoney's original 1861 proposal, work began on the extension of the North Wall and a parallel wharf was built 250 metres to its north, beginning at the graving dock. These works created the basin which was visited in 1885 by the Prince of Wales and his consort Princess Alexandra, who accepted the invitation of the Dublin Port and Docks Board to name the basin for her. In contrast to the situation on the quays of the right bank with their Grand Canal Docks, the extension and the Alexandra Basin were closed to the general public in 1892 by a wall, with access from North Wall Quay through a pair of fine wrought-iron gates.

Tugboats commissioned in 2010 moored at Alexandra Quay, from the Tom Clarke Bridge. Background bulk storage buildings overlook the Alexandra Basin.

The original timber jetties at the Alexandra Wharf deteriorated over the years and in 1921 the Port's Engineer-in-Chief Joseph Mallagh submitted proposals for their replacement by a masonry quay built to a system of his own design. It was a major innovation in harbour engineering and involved the construction of caissons of reinforced concrete. Measuring 50 feet long by 30 feet wide and 42 feet high (15 x 9 x 12 metres), they were built on a slipway and then launched and floated into position. Once in place the caisson was filled with sand, supplied by the port dredger, and sunk. The sand surface was covered by a concrete slab and the new quayside completed. Begun in 1922, the work was finished in 1931.

The same year saw the beginning of a major landfill project on the part of the Dublin Corporation – a scheme which would convulse any fervent environmentalist of our times. A retaining wall was built in a southeasterly direction beginning at the railway bridge that crosses East Wall Road and meeting Tolka Quay Road.

Now and again the Basin permitted the plain people of Ireland to access it. This happened on such special occasions as visits by sail-training vessels that welcome the public on board. On a summer's day in 2014 Charlie Murphy, Communications Manager of the Dublin Port Company, took me on a tour of the sacred precinct. Public access is forbidden in accordance with two aspects of the worship of the latter-day deity Security. One is the obviously practical consideration that docklands are dangerous places because they need unprotected quays and a great deal of traffic. The other is the international requirement for constant vigilance of cargo handling in the interests of protection from sabotage and the passage of illegal goods.

Some aspects of the environment are plain for all to see, for example the bright colours of the giant cranes. Less obvious to the remote viewer is the fact that the cranes are colour-coded to indicate which of the three stevedoring companies owns them. Another remarkable feature is that these giants have rubber-tyred wheels so that they are free to wander over the level ground, no longer confined, as were their smaller predecessors, to rail tracks. Repair work to these same surfaces is in continuous progress because they were engineered for horse-drawn drays rather than steel colossi.

The second half of the twentieth century saw major developments of berthage and storage facilities on both banks of the river. To the north oil tanks and grain storage silos rose skywards and a power station was built. Apart from the road to the car ferries, public access continued to be severely restricted, but the skyline changed perceptibly decade by decade. The south side of the river saw cargo handling increase between Poolbeg Road and the river, most of it screened from view by mountains of stacked containers. On the other side of the road a succession of new power stations was built on the extensive property owned by the ESB.

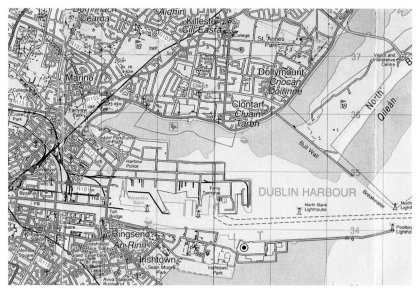

Ordnance Survey *Discovery* map of the lower Liffey from the Loopline to the Poolbeg Lighthouse. Blue gridlines are 1 km apart. The Shelly Banks lie to the east of Irishtown Park, the Wastewater Treatment Works to its north and ESB generating station, with their array of cylindrical oil storage tanks occupy the land to east and west: © Ordnance Survey Ireland Permit No. 9166

The graving dock in service.

Crane 292, dating from 1968, stands above the park surrounding the Port Company Office.

Ships in harbour

The website of the Dublin Port Company (www.dublinport.ie) provides a feast of information. Aimed at mariners and other specialists, it is beautifully produced and full of information fascinating to any casual visitor. To take a few examples: one short blast of a ship's whistle warns it is turning to starboard, two blasts for port and so on. From their high perch on a loaded container vessel, the pilots cannot see any small boat less than half a mile ahead of them. When a large cargo vessel appears on the horizon it may reach the observer in as little as ten minutes.

The website publishes a continuously updated list of ships in port. On a Monday in January 2018, 17 vessels were listed: three 'work vessels', including a dredger, five 'bulk solid', one oil tanker, five 'LoLo' (load-on/load-off) and four RoRo (roll-on/roll-off). Among the latter was the fast ferry *Ulysses* – the name yet another tribute to James Joyce. The numbers fluctuate and in summer cruise liners are a notable addition.

For some years, three vessels were permanently berthed upstream of the East Link Bridge. The *Cill Airne* arrived on 25 May 2007 and now serves as a somewhat exclusive restaurant, forbidden to children and the wearers of track-suits or training shoes. A short but very interesting history is recorded in the website (www.mvcillairne.com) and its preservation is a notable achievement with a very special Liffey connection. *Cill Airne* was one of a pair of vessels commissioned by the government in 1961 to serve as tenders, ferrying passengers from ocean liners in Cork Harbour to the quayside at Cobh. Among the last vessels to be built in the Liffey Dockyard just downstream, they were the very last in Europe to be fashioned from riveted steel before it was replaced by welded plates. The days of the pair as tenders ended with the decline of the liners and *Cill Airne* served as a training vessel for marine engineers before being converted to a sedentary life.

The lightship *Kittiwake* arrived in the port a few months later, on 30 October 2007, and lay just upstream of the East Link Bridge on the left bank at Berth 17B. Named, as were the other Irish lightships, after species of seabird, *Kittiwake* was ordered by the Commissioners of Irish Lights in 1957. Built in Dartmouth two years later, it served to mark the South Rock off the County Down coast. Until 1982 it was manned by a crew of seven, since when its light had been controlled from the shore. The *Kittiwake* retired in 2007 and its successor the *Gannet* was replaced with a buoy two years later.

The third resident of the port is the replica three-masted barque *Jeanie Johnston*, which has occupied Berth 14 on Custom House Quay since September 2008. Wikipedia gives an excellent account of her faintly troubled creation (https://en.wikipedia.org/wiki/Jeanie_Johnston).

Built in Quebec in 1847, the original *Jeanie Johnston* had an impressive career carrying emigrants to Canada and the United States in the wake of the Great Famine. Far from being a coffin ship, thanks to the humanity of the owners and their employment of a ship's doctor, not one life was lost during

Ringsend marina, container terminal and Poolbeg chimney.

her years as a passenger carrier. The replica is two-thirds the size of the original and was built in Blennerville, County Kerry between 1993 and 2002, involving a host of trainee carpenters and others and a serious cost overrun. It was nonetheless a worthwhile achievement and this beautiful ship enjoyed six years of ceremonial visits, sail-training and ocean racing prior to her sojourn in the Liffey. In 2015, the *Cill Airne* had taken up residence a little way downstream of the Conference Centre, the *Jeanie Johnston* had moved to Custom House Quay and the *Kittiwake* had been sold.

Liffeyside ship-building

In 2010 Pat Sweeney revealed a remarkable and half-forgotten aspect of the docklands in his excellent book *Liffey Ships and Shipbuilding*. Sweeney provides a wealth of detail on the very substantial industry that developed in the nineteenth century, peaked during the First World War and finally lost out to distant countries in the second half of the twentieth century. Ship repair was still in operation in 2015 in the single graving dock in the Alexandra Basin.

In addition to a large number of merchantmen destined to sail the world, Sweeney describes two very remarkable Liffeyside ventures: a seventeenth-century catamaran and a nineteenth-century lake steamer. The catamaran was the brainchild of the genius Sir William Petty, better known to history as the director of the Down Survey. His 'double bottom machine', built on the riverside upstream of the Old Bridge (now Father Mathew's) was launched in 1662 and may have been the first of its kind in the western world. It was so successful that three more were built. Sadly, two of these proved unstable and shipbuilding reverted to the single hull.

On the lake steamer, Sweeney quotes an article in the *Illustrated London News* of 8 August 1868 with an illustration of the SS *Faugh-a-Ballagh* built on the North Wall by the Quaker consortium Walpole, Webb and Bewley. Commissioned for the exploration of the great African Lake Nyasa, she was not launched in the Liffey but exported in 80 pieces to be held together by 800 screw bolts. Each piece had to be light enough to be carried over rough terrain by two men and simple enough to be assembled at her lakeside destination by unskilled workers.

Ships were built in the Grand Canal Basin and on Sir John Rogerson's Quay, but the major trade began in the 1860s following deepening of the Liffey and the completion of the graving dock near the East Wall in 1860. Thomas Walpole and William Henry Webb established the first company on the North Wall and were joined later by Thomas Bewley. The group flourished for a few years before being absorbed by various changes of ownership. The final successor, Liffey Dockyard, launched its last vessel in 1969 but continued to function in major ship repair work.

The future of the docklands

Meanwhile, growth continues. Even during the recession after 2008, exports continued to increase. Cargo ships grow longer and longer, and more and bigger cruise vessels visit Dublin.

The Port Company devoted the first years of the recent recession to anticipating a rosy future and in early 2012 adopted a master plan for the period to 2040. Its details were published in a handsome book, notable for being readable as well as providing a fascinating collection of plans and projections.

The planners, possibly under duress from on high, discovered that by demolishing some little-used buildings and making various rearrangements of space, they could actually find 21 hectares of surface within their existing property so that the forbidden reclamation to the northeast would no longer be essential. The plan does foresee an eastward extension of the port to this area, but it will be created where there is permanent water rather than bird-sensitive foreshore. The plan envisages berthing facilities for vessels up to 240 metres in length.

One of the most meaningful developments for citizens and visitors alike was the decision to move the Cruise Terminal to the outer side of Alexandra Quay, immediately downstream of the East Link Bridge, a position otherwise occupied by the company's two new tugboats, built in Spain and brought into service in March 2010. Their names honour two of Ireland's greatest mariners, Francis Beaufort and Ernest Shackleton.

Cruise vessels began to use Alexandra Quay in 2015. This arrangement brings tourists within easy reach of the city centre and exposes them to a combination of bright new buildings and distinguished senior ones. More important for Dublin residents, part of the 4½ hectares of quayside beside the terminal will have an element of public access and an interpretative centre.

A problem facing the giant liners was that the Liffey at Alexandra Quay is too narrow to allow them to turn. The momentous decision taken to remedy this was to widen the mouth of the Alexandra Basin by chopping off a large chunk of the North Wall Extension, which forms the basin's riverside wall. This will allow the biggest ships envisaged to go forwards upstream to East Link, then turn and head downstream rather than make one of the passages in reverse. The wall to be removed has a foundation of granite boulders. These relics of nineteenth-century endeavour will be built into an item of industrial sculpture near the East Link Bridge.

Within the constraints of security, the Company has aspirations to make the port a more welcoming place. On the right bank, while a little more landfill will constrict the river yet more to extend the berthage and cargo handing area, footpaths, cycling paths and 'amenity' spaces have been earmarked. The latter include the City Council's property surrounding the Pigeon House Hotel and former municipal power station – a colossal red-brick shell for which some inspired person is bound to think up a dramatic rebirth. Development plans on both banks contain a very substantial element of public access.

Dramatic decisions have also been taken to open up the left bank docklands to the public. As a first step, the land surrounding the Port Authority's office building – designed by Scott Tallon Walker – was converted to a garden and sculpture park. Not quite sculpture in the accepted sense, the scene is dominated by one of the cranes which had occupied the campshires of the south quays. A pedestrian and cycle path will be constructed around the perimeter of the north dockland, providing new views of the sand flats and their abundant bird life in addition to the more distant scenery. Connections between these routes and their equivalent on the south bank will be provided in the near future by ferry at the East Link. The vessel to be used is the last of the old passenger ferries lovingly restored. At a later stage a ferry downstream will be instituted between Poolbeg and the North Wall so that a circular tour may be made.

A cruise vessel in the Alexandra Basin. The mouth of the basin is to be widened by the removal of part of the quay wall to its left. The stretch of water at the top is the Tolka estuary, fenced in on all sides. The Ringsend Marina is bottom left with mountainous acres of containers downstream to the right. *Courtesy Dublin Port Company*

Ringsend

The community of Ringsend developed as an isolated fishing village on the northern tip of a sand spit far from the city of Dublin. Later, a settlement a little to its south was established and named Irishtown. The sand spit was part of the primeval scene when the Dodder, like the Liffey, entered the sea by way of a broad estuary: the Dodder's with a south–north axis, the Liffey flowing from west to east. While passage by boat from Ringsend to the Ford of the Hurdles was fairly simple, an approach by land demanded a very long walk. So banishing natives from the city, then relatively far upstream, to Irishtown in 1454 was a devastating move.

The former coastguard station at Ringsend.

The degree of separation was eased in the seventeenth century when the first of a succession of bridges was built. By 1756, when Rocque published his map, Ringsend and Irishtown had become popular resorts; Rocque marked two baths, one for men and one for women, discreetly separated by an esplanade. Eastward of Ringsend, the tidal flats of Dublin Bay stretched with only minimal interruption from Clontarf to Booterstown. John de Courcy provides a wealth of historical and modern detail on the region under three headings: Pigeon House, Poolbeg and Ringsend. A concise and convenient description, with helpful maps, has been provided by the Port Company in the form of posters at the Shelly Banks.

Reclamation to the east of the sand spit began in the eighteenth century with the building of the South Wall from the Dodder at Ringsend to a small island known as the Green Patch, 2.4 km out across the sands. This, the first of two sections of the great granite breakwater, was completed in 1755. It obliterated one of a number of 'pools' among the sandbanks in the estuary which had been deep enough for ships to ride at anchor at low tide. A relatively small one was known as the Poolbeg. Small though it was, it gave its name to the lighthouse at the end of the South Wall and to the dry land which arose to east and west of Ringsend, following the imprisoning of Dodder and Liffey estuaries within mighty walls of granite masonry.

The 1838 map shows the South Wall proceeding seawards in a direction slightly to the south of east as far as a point 2.6 km from the Dodder mouth at Ringsend. There the mole curves to the north briefly and an L-shaped wall encloses a 'Harbour' within the Liffey estuary. The curved part of the South Wall itself, however, had been broadened by this time and covered with the buildings of the Pigeon House Fort – created in 1813 to protect the city from a possible French invasion. An 'Intended Wall' is shown on the 1837 map, running from Ringsend parallel to the South Wall for about a kilometre. This marks the beginning of extensive reclamation which continued until the 1960s. The nineteenth-century terrace named Ringsend Park follows the line of this wall.

The road built in the 1980s, which goes by the riverside from the East Link Bridge, is fast and furious, but it does have a footpath that gives a relaxing view of pleasure craft and merchant shipping to the left, with red-brick terraced houses on the right. This road has buried the South Wall, which remains hidden from view from land for the next 2.5 km until it escapes from industrial enclosure at the Shelly Banks. A large roundabout gives access to quieter roads and a variety of attractions nearby.

Viewed from Sandymount, the industrial landscape which developed on the land reclaimed from the South Bull. Dominated for 50 years by the Poolbeg chimneys and since 2017 by the waste disposal unit.

The first exit from the roundabout leads to a container terminal and to the riverside at the Poolbeg Marina. The second allows the Pigeon House Road to reappear and lead to the wonders of the public works that have grown up on the reclaimed land. The third heads past parks and playing fields to Irishtown and so to the suburbs and ultimately to the Dublin Mountains where the Liffey rises. The fourth leads back to town, passing some of the most attractive of all City Council dwellings.

The access road to the marina is a survivor of the Poolbeg Road, most of which has been obliterated by port extensions. The Poolbeg Road runs beside the former Coastguard Station, a charming row of nineteenth-century buildings which include a lookout tower.

Traces of the fort remain on the north side of the Pigeon House Road – limestone masonry with brick surrounds. The Pigeon House Hotel, built in 1798, a decade before the fort was mooted, is the only complete survivor of that period. Nineteenth-century photographs show a number of four-storey barrack buildings within the fort. These were demolished to make room for the Dublin Corporation's power station, the enormous red brick building long abandoned as a source of electricity and patiently waiting for rediscovery.

Two parts of the remnants of the fort were made into beautiful little gardens by the City Council at the instigation of Paddy Higgins, when he was manager of the nearby wastewater treatment plant. The larger of these, where a turret

Part of the entrance gate and boundary wall of the Pigeon House Fort forming a backdrop to the garden created in the twenty-first century by the City Council.

of the entrance gate still stands, marks the southwestern boundary of the fort. The ownership of land in these remote regions enjoys a splendid complexity. The Port Company is a major proprietor – but the road is the property of the ESB, which naturally owns the grounds of the generating stations. But the abandoned red brick power station, together with the Pigeon House Hotel, are the property of the City Council, as are the campus of the wastewater treatment plant and the Ringsend Nature Park.

The Liffey from the shore of Ringsend Marina: merchant shipping uses the left bank; pleasure craft throng the right.

Hidden by these buildings and others, two disused wooden jetties stand in the water. A poster at the Shelly Banks tells the very remarkable story of the beautiful white birds that came to nest nearby:

> The terns initially chose the oil terminal jetties as their nest sites and soon began to defend their nests by swooping at workers. It was decided for safety reasons to identify alternative nest sites. The Port Authority, the ESB and the National Parks and Wildlife Service worked together and found a solution in the form of the disused moorings at the Poolbeg Generating Station known as the ESB dolphins.
>
> Initially the nesting birds lost eggs and chicks over the sides or through gaps in the decking. In order to help these rare birds to breed it was decided to add gravel and a wooden perimeter to each dolphin.

Between 1995 and 2002 this resulted in an increase in nesting birds from 48 to 238 pairs. The ESB dolphin now has a Common Tern Colony whose size justifies designation of the site as a National Heritage Area and as a Special Protection Area under the EU Birds Directive.

Terns protesting at an intrusion of their nesting place on an ESB dolphin. *Photo: Richard Nairn.*

From the Shelly Banks to the Dublin Mountains, where the Liffey rises.

The master plan envisages narrowing the river in this region so that oil jetties and dolphins will be covered over with quays. Birds Directives are not lightly flouted, but the plan gives this full consideration. The two dolphins with their makeshift bird fences will be replaced by three custom-built terneries. Terns are well known to be opportunists, ready to colonise any secure-looking island, making it virtually certain that their rehousing will be a success. The spots chosen for their new homes will, in addition, be birdwatcher-friendly.

Treating the waste

The Wastewater Treatment Plant at Ringsend is supplied with its very raw material from far and wide. The two interceptor sewers that run beneath the city quays merge beneath Burgh Quay; from there the flow is piped to Ringsend. Sewage from the north city passes beneath the river through another spacious tunnel. Excavated just upstream of the present East Link Bridge between 1926 and 1929, it carries electricity cables and water to the north side and sewage to the south. The south access shaft, 32 metres deep, is located at Thorncastle Street and the slightly deeper north shaft is at the former Harbourmaster's Office on the North Wall. In September 2006 work began on a second tunnel. A joint venture of the German firm Ed Züblin AG of Stuttgart and the Wexford contractor Cleary & Doyle, it was completed in October 2008. Measuring 260 metres in length and 2.96 metres bore width, the tunnel descends from 19 metres deep on the right bank to 22 metres on the left, not far from the 3Arena at the Point.

For the first half of the twentieth century a 2.4 metre conduit led from the Ringsend pumping station to the 18 settling tanks that line the roadside to the north of the remnants of the walls of the Pigeon House Fort. The sewage sludge sank to the bottom, leaving relatively clear water above. This was discharged to flow into the river and on to Dublin Bay on a falling tide. These tanks, no longer part of the sewage treatment, are now used for temporarily holding the waste when extreme wet weather poses a risk of overloading the new system.

Until relatively late in the twentieth century, civic authorities in many parts of the world believed that discharge of sewage to the sea, in a more or less treated state, was acceptable. It was assumed that marine currents would provide sufficient dilution to make the waters safe.

After some decades, and with increasingly sensitive methods of monitoring the purity of the water, the danger to public health of discharging to Dublin Bay became apparent. A tunnel was excavated to bring the sewage from north Dublin to a point off the Nose of Howth – perhaps an appropriate location – rather than into Dublin Bay. The sludge from Poolbeg was transferred to the steamboat *Shamrock*, which for more than fifty years carried it to a point northeast of the Baily Lighthouse, far away from the river. Strong currents dispersed the sludge over a wide area of sea bed, where it greatly enhanced the habitat for marine worms. These in due course were eaten by flatfish and so the nitrogen and other elements, duly purified, returned to the people.

With greater technical knowledge and a growing quantity of waste from the expanding city, pressure for improvements came from the scientists and officials of the city authorities, from a considerable element of the public and from some elected representatives. Big Brother, in the shape of directives and funding from the European Commission, played a decisive part.

In the 1970s improvement works began with the diversion of several suburban sewers to Ringsend. Sewage from Dun Laoghaire was brought there by a pipeline buried beneath the sands of the bay in the 1980s. The dumping of sludge at sea had ended in 1999 and the use of the Howth outlet ceased in 2001 when another submarine pipeline was constructed to bring sewage to the Ringsend Treatment Plant.

All these efforts culminated in the commissioning in June 2003 of the huge grey building in whose 24 tanks the foul water is transformed to an astounding degree of purity. The clean water from the tanks is then subjected to ultraviolet radiation, which kills bacteria, after which the water is finally permitted to run away to sea. This battery of 'sequential batch reactors' is unique in being built with two storeys of tanks – the only way such a large plant could be fitted into the available space. One of the biggest of its kind in Europe, the reactors treat the waste products of one-third of the population of Ireland.

Nearby, the sludge, removed from the reactors, is cooked, ground up and transformed into a brown crumbly fertiliser avidly purchased and applied by farmers in the midlands. A by-product of the process is methane gas, which is burned to generate steam that drives a turbine and produces more than half the electric power the treatment plant requires.

The scheme was not an immediate success – foul odours escaped from time to time. The problem came from the Celtic Tiger, which led to an increase in the population of Dublin far beyond any reasonable prediction.

Brent geese breed in Arctic Canada and some hundreds of them spend the winter in Dublin Bay, where they have a preference for mown grass as a food supply. A special safe enclosure has been made for them at the Water Treatment Plant at Poolbeg but they like to swim in the lower Liffey and often fly over the city to forage on playing fields. Conservation led to a notable increase in their numbers in the course of the twentieth century. *Photo: Michael Finn.*

Improvements were made to the existing system and a major extension of the plant was set in motion, creating a huge white structure as a companion to the great ESB chimney stacks.

So much for the liquid waste which can be transported underground, unknown to the great majority of citizens. Safe disposal of the solids, foul and fair, was another matter and one which caused many years of conflict between the authorities faced with the task and many residents who had serious reservations concerning other aspects of the environment. The authorities ultimately had their way and the DWTE Dublin Waste to Energy (Covanta Plant) received its first consignment on 26 April 2017, twenty years after it was first mooted.

Perhaps the most surprising aspect of the development is that the incinerator is a beautiful building, if rather dull when viewed at a distance, as from the Dublin Mountains. From Sandymount its interesting three-part structure makes a pleasing addition to the long-established industrial landscape. But from the docklands the building literally shines, being fronted largely with glass. A gentle stream of 120 lorries each working day deliver more than half a million tons of waste. Their combustion of more than half a million tons of waste each year supplies enough electricity for the needs of 80,000 homes and will heat 50,000.

The redundant 1970s chimneys of the Poolbeg Generating Station, viewed from the Shelly Banks. The ESB announced in 2015 that the chimneys would be preserved. In the same year *The Irish Times* reported that peregrine falcons had nested about a third of the way up the thinner chimney tower and successfully raised two chicks.

The Shelly Banks: back to nature and the past

Close to the treatment plant, a notice gives details of the quality of the bathing water at the Shelly Banks. The usual count of faecal coliform bacteria – a measure of the prevalence of the most dangerous species – is in the region of 9 per 100 ml of water. Anything up to a count of 100 is designated as 'excellent' for bathing. So the waters of Dublin Bay are ten times as pure as the regulations demand. The seaside, strewn with plastic bottles and much, much worse, remembered by most citizens is a thing of the past. In the shadow of the treatment plant the Shelly Banks are as sandy and shelly as nature intended. The restoration of the once-dangerous waters of Dublin Bay to a state of 'excellence' is a truly splendid achievement.

Well known for its contribution to the comfort, health and well-being of the people of Dublin as a complex of electric power and sewage treatment, the Liffeyside at Poolbeg is remarkable too for its wealth of wildlife. With the South Wall and the river on one side and a series of little beaches, confined by angular roadsides on the other, the variety of plant and animal habitats of the Shelly Banks has actually been increased by the harbour works. Far from inhibiting the biodiversity of the spot, the assemblage of concrete and boulders has brought about its enhancement.

The wall of the former garden tended by the custodians of the Pembroke sewage pumping station on the most easterly piece of reclaimed land by the South Wall.

The area has been known to Dubliners for a long time as the Shelly Banks, a good description of the beach, which is liberally scattered with the shells of cockles, occasional mussels, and a great variety of other species. With the exception of the mussels, which live in the open attached to rocks, the shells are the skeletons of molluscs which spend their lives buried beneath the surface of the sand flats, mostly beyond low-tide mark.

The popular name is remarkably hard to find on Ordnance Survey maps or in earlier cartography. This may explain a lack of agreement on its spelling. The Ordnance Survey city map marks a road which it calls 'Shellys Banks'. The nameplate on the road itself appears to believe that the term might commemorate the poet Percy Bysshe Shelley. So the poor shellfish remain unsung except on the Port Company's brilliantly conceived posters at the foot of the South Wall.

One stormy February afternoon in 2014 a band of stalwart members of the Dublin Naturalists' Field Club decided that the high tide and waves breaking over the wall itself made a proposed walk to the Poolbeg Light unduly hazardous. So we spent an hour or two by the riverside in the presence of an unexpectedly large variety of birds. Within the railed-off land of ESB oil storage and City Council treated-sewage discharge, a large flock of black-headed gulls were feeding happily on organisms disturbed by the flowing water. More surprising was the presence of teal and turnstone hunting on a singularly unprepossessing patch of mud and grass. On the Liffey itself were many black-headed gulls and a few common gulls. Notwithstanding its long-established English name, this species is scarce within the city limits. Three other gull species and no fewer than five diving birds were present on that February day: cormorant and shag, black guillemot, great crested grebe and great northern diver.

The teal, a duck which breeds beside Liffey Head and spends the winter at the river mouth. *Photo: Michael Finn.*

Absent on the day was the purple sandpiper, a relatively rare species whose presence in Dublin Bay depends on the man-made habitat of rocky shore created by the boulders that line the breakwaters of Dublin Port and also of Dun Laoghaire. Other absentees were the terns, which are strictly summer visitors.

As it happened, no marine mammals were in sight on the day of that visit. But there are reasonable chances any day of seeing the head of a grey seal or a harbour seal as it breaks the surface for a breath of air. Another frequent visitor is the harbour porpoise, a small species of dolphin which surfaces so quickly that the usual view is of nothing more than its arched back. These common sea beasts pale into insignificance when compared with the list of creatures which a Shelly Banks poster gives for Dublin Bay – and which are therefore theoretically visible from the South Wall. The Minke whale is 'common'; less plentiful are bottle-nosed, common and Risso's dolphins together with fin and killer whales.

The Great South Wall

If the Great South Wall were merely a world-class feat of engineering, it would merit a visit. But, snaking its way along the sand flats of the South Bull to the Poolbeg Lighthouse, far out in Dublin Bay, the breakwater has an atmosphere of pure magic – perhaps coming from the sense of isolation it creates as you walk along it. In total the sea wall runs for 9 km, from Heuston Station to

The nineteenth-century Pembroke pumping station at the foot of the Great South Wall. The left foreground shows the eighteenth-century quarried Dalkey granite surface of the mole.

the Poolbeg Light, but the name 'South Wall' is usually restricted to the mole which begins at the tidal barrage of the drainage outfall at Poolbeg and extends seawards for 2 km.

Details of the building of the mole can be found in Gilligan's book. The problem confronting mariners and, consequently, the harbour authorities had been that the sandbanks of the estuary shifted continuously and ships ran aground much too frequently when attempting to locate the main channel of the Liffey. Moreover, the estuary was extremely difficult and dangerous to navigate in strong winds. The solution was devised early in the eighteenth century, and the City Assembly agreed to fund the building of a wall along the south side of the Liffey, seawards from Ringsend.

In 1715, work began on the first structure, made of wattle and stones and supported by piles. Completed in fifteen years, it made a great improvement, but this barrier was frequently damaged by storms. The present wall is clad on both sides with neatly cut and fitted granite blocks, filled in with sand and rubble. This is capped with paving stones, also hewn from granite, each measuring about one metre long by 30 cm wide. The granite came from Dalkey Quarry, and was ferried across the bay in sailing barges known as gabbards. The wall was begun in 1759 at the seaward end and was completed in 1788.

Construction of the Great South Wall had begun at its outer end in the interests of providing foundations and security for the lighthouse as quickly as possible. The candles were first lit on 29 September 1767, 21 years before the mole was completed. The original tower, designed by the architect John Smyth, was rebuilt in its present shape in 1813. Another era in its life ended when the last lighthouse keeper left the post in 1964, following the installation of remote-controlled equipment. Poolbeg today is a '100 volt, 1.5 kilowatt occulting light showing two red flashes every 20 seconds'. The tower is painted red because you must keep red to your port side as you enter the harbour and sail upstream. Its companion across the way, at the end of the North Wall, is green for starboard.

The wall is wide enough to be safe, but so narrow that there is simply nowhere to walk on either side of it. The distant view on the outward journey is of Howth and the Dublin and Wicklow Mountains. In terms of time, it is a very remarkable assemblage. Howth Head and the two Sugarloaves are derived from seaside and shallow-water sand and mud, very much the same as are being deposited in Dublin Bay today, with the difference that they were laid down in Cambrian times, 500 million years ago, long before birds, beasts and fishes as we know them had evolved. The granite that forms Dalkey and Killiney Hills and the Dublin Mountains – to say nothing of the South Wall itself – was formed at the very roots of mountains that were being built in the Ordovician period, 100 million years after the Cambrian of Howth. And hard by is Bull

Island, the newest dry land in Ireland, which began to rise from the sea all of 200 years ago and is still growing.

On the walk back from the lighthouse, the colourful chimneys, cranes and ships of the port provide an opposite, but equally pleasing, scene. The two walks together illustrate the contrast between concentrated industry and wilderness: the country's lifeline to the goods of the outside world and a lifeline for citizens in search of retreat from the same commercial activities.

The last building at the landward end of the wall is a one-storey house, neatly constructed of limestone with granite door- and window-frames. It contained a pump to raise sewage from the low-lying township of Pembroke. The pumping operation was supervised by the men of two families, over some generations. They lived in two adjacent houses, now demolished but once protected from the sea by the concrete walls that still stand there.

There is a small car park between these walls and the pump house and this is where the great breakwater emerging from the hinterland of power stations and sewage works heads away to sea, welcoming visitors with a warning notice of the inherent dangers of uneven stone paving.

The Half Moon Swimming Club marks a bend in the straight line of the breakwater. It is also the spot where the wall's surface rises to a higher level, providing shelter from the stronger waves of the deeper water. In the early 1990s, a notice told of the perils of submerged rocks, moved in by Hurricane Kay in 1988. A later edition of the notice warned of water quality below the very exacting standards demanded by the regulations of the European Commission. Nonetheless, people swam there and survived. The notice in 2011 warned once again of the potential perils of diving from the pier and striking submerged rocks, the contamination of the water having been brought under control in the intervening twenty years.

The Club's nameplate reads 'Half Moon Swimming and Water Polo Club founded 1898'. It occupies the buildings of a former shore battery, whose guns were supported on half-moon, more or less semicircular, mountings. The inner walls of the shelter are rendered and whitewashed, but the outer wall, to the south, displays its original granite fabric, with a curious insertion of red sandstone.

The power of the sea, even of a shallow sea within the shelter of the hills bordering Dublin Bay, becomes ever more evident as you progress towards the end of the mole. After a storm, its surface is scattered with stones and boulders that have been carried by the waves from its outer defences. Beyond the lighthouse, great chunks of masonry rest among the breakers that have torn them away from the wall.

Major repairs and refurbishment to the South Wall, undertaken at the beginning of the twenty-first century, improved the surface of the breakwater and also provided a footpath around the lighthouse tower. There is a park bench at its base on which walkers can gather their strength before beginning the homeward journey. Attaining the Poolbeg Light gives all the satisfaction of the conquest of a mountain peak – with a small fraction of the effort.

And it ends our encounter with Anna Livia Plurabelle, the River Liffey of many beauties. From that seat, should you lift up your eyes unto the hills, you may see the tall steel mast on the summit of Kippure which overlooks the 'Source of the Liffey' where tradition tells that our beloved river rises.

Anna Liffey, extended by the magnificent eighteenth-century South Wall, leaves for the sea, guarded by the Poolbeg Lighthouse.

References

Aalen, F. H. A., Kevin Whelan and Matthew Stout 1997. *Atlas of the Irish Rural Landscape*. Cork, Cork University Press.

Anon. 1882–83. 'The Liffey from its source to Poolbeg'. *Irish Builder*.

Anon. 1919–1922. Commission of Inquiry into the Resources and Industries of Ireland. National Library of Ireland, Call No. 1B 1549.

Anon. 1950. 'Compact development contributes outstandingly to Hydro-electric power supplies'. *Engineers' Journal* 1950, 1, 1, 18.

Bernard, John 1898 *The Irish Liber Hymnorum* London, Henry Bradshaw Society.

Best, R. I. 1954 *The Book of Leinster*: Dublin, Institute for Advanced Studies.

Black, Annette and Michael B. Barry 2015. *Bridges of Dublin: The Remarkable Story of Dublin's Liffey Bridges*. Dublin City Council.

Buchanan, Colin and Partners 2003. *Chapelizod Village: Urban Design, Conservation & Land Use Plan*. Dublin City Council, Heritage Council.

Budd, Roland 2001. *The Platforme of an Universitie*. Dublin, Particular Books.

Bunbury, Turtle 2009. *Dublin Docklands: An Urban Voyage*. Dublin, Montague Publications Group.

Casey, Christine 2005. *Dublin*. New Haven and London, Yale University Press.

Clarke, Howard 2003. *Irish Historic Towns Atlas* Part 1: to 1610. Dublin, Royal Irish Academy.

Colgan, Nathaniel 1904. *Flora of the County Dublin*. Dublin, Hodges Figgis.

Conlin, Stephen and Peter Harbison 2016. *Dublin: The Story of a City*. Dublin, O'Brien Press.

Corlett, Christiaan 2008. *Beneath the Poulaphuca Reservoir: The 1939 Poulaphuca Survey by the Liffey Reservoir Scheme*. Dublin, Stationery Office.

Costello, Con 1991. *Guide to Kildare and West Wicklow*. Naas, *Leinster Leader*.

Craig, Maurice 1952. *Dublin 1660–1860*. London, Cresset Press.

Craig, Maurice, the Knight of Glin and John Cornforth 1969. *Castletown, Co. Kildare*. Reprinted from *Country Life* 99, 722, 798 and 882.

Cruise, Aidan 2010. *The Dublin and Blessington Steam Tram*. Dublin, South Dublin Libraries.

de Courcy, John W. 1996. *The Liffey in Dublin*. Dublin, Gill & Macmillan.

de Courcy, John W. 1998. 'The Mutual Development of Dublin and the River Liffey', a paper to be presented to the Heritage Society of the Institution of Engineers of Ireland, 27 April 1998.

Dickson, David 1997. *Arctic Ireland*. Belfast, White Row Press.

Donohoe, Patricia (ed.) 2008. *Aspects of Lucan*. Lucan, LPSV.

Fewer, Michael 2007. *The Wicklow Military Road*. Dublin, Ashfield Press.

Frost, Winifred E. 1945. 'River Liffey Survey VI: Results obtained from investigating the food and growth of brown trout (*Salmo trutta*) in alkaline and acid water'. *Proceedings of the Royal Irish Academy* 50 B.

Gilbert, John T. (ed.) 1870. *Historic and Municipal Documents of Ireland, 1172–1320*. London, Longmans, Green and Co.

Gilligan, H. A. 1988. *A History of the Port of Dublin*. Dublin, Gill & Macmillan.

Gregory, Lady Augusta 1904. *Gods and Fighting Men*. London, John Murray.

Grubb, Isabel 2018. *Irish Quakers*. Cork, Risteárd Mac Annraoi.

Gwynn, Edward 1935. *The Metrical Dindshenchas* Part 5. Dublin, Royal Irish Academy.

Harbison, Peter 2000. *Cooper's Ireland: Drawings and Notes from an Eighteenth-Century Gentleman* Dublin, O'Brien Press.

Harty, V. D. 1940. 'Liffey power development 1. Concreting methods'. *Transactions of the Institution of Engineers of Ireland* 66, 1.

Herity, Michael, 2001. *Ordnance Survey Letters Dublin*. Dublin, Four Masters Press.

Hickey, M. D. and J. R. Harris 1947. 'Progress of the *Diphyllobothrium* epizootic at Poulaphouca Reservoir, Co. Wicklow, Ireland'. *Journal of Helminthology* 22, 13–48.

Hogg, William E. 1998. *The Millers and the Mills of Ireland of about 1850*. Dublin, William E. Hogg.

Howley, James 1993. *The Follies and Garden Buildings of Ireland*. New Haven and London, Yale University Press.

James, Dermot and Séamas Ó Maitiú (eds) 1996. *The Wicklow World of Elizabeth Smith 1840–1850*. Dublin, Woodfield Press.

Joyce, Weston St John (ed. Muriel McCarthy) 1994. *The Neighbourhood of Dublin*. Dublin, Hughes & Hughes.

Kenny, Liam (ed.) 1994. *50 Years on the Liffey*. Turlough Hill, Co. Wicklow, ESB.

Kirk, Frank 1993. *Nature in the Phoenix Park*. Dublin, Stationery Office.

Kissane, Noel 1988. *Historic Dublin Maps* Dublin: National Library of Ireland.

Laffan, William and Brendan Rooney 2009. *Thomas Roberts 1748–1777*. Tralee, Churchill House Press.

Le Fanu, Sheridan 1886. *The House by the Churchyard*. Belfast, Appletree Press (1992 edn).

Lennon, Colm and John Montague 2010. *John Rocque's Dublin: A Guide to the Georgian City*. Dublin, Royal Irish Academy.

Lewis, Samuel 1837. *Topographical Dictionary of Ireland*. London, S. Lewis & Co.

MacDonald, J. 1947. 'Liffey hydro-electric (Presidential address)'. *Transactions of the Institution of Engineers of Ireland* 1947, 74, 1.

Maguire W. A. 1972. *The Downshire Estates in Ireland 1801–1845: The Management of Irish Landed Estates in the Early 19th Century*. Oxford, Clarendon Press.

Mallagh, J. 1939. 'City bridges over the Liffey'. *Transactions of the Institution of Engineers of Ireland*.

McAsey, C. (1962) 'Chapelizod, Co. Dublin'. *Dublin Historical Record*, Vol. 17, No. 2.

McConnell, B. and Michael Philcox 1994. *Geology of Kildare–Wicklow*. Dublin, Geological Survey of Ireland.

McCullen, J. 2009. *An Illustrated History of the Phoenix Park: Landscape and Management to 1880*. Dublin, Government Publications.

McQuade, Melanie 2008. 'Gone fishin''. *Archaeology Ireland* Spring, 8–11.

Mulhall, Mary and Joan O'Flynn 2007. *Treasures of Lucan* Lucan, Leamhcáin – Place of the Elms.

Murphy, Margaret and Michael Potterton 2010. *The Dublin Region in the Middle Ages*. Dublin, Four Courts Press.

Murphy, S. 1950. 'Buzzing with business – Stewart's Hospital'. *Ireland of the Welcomes* l0501, 26.

Nairn, Richard and Miriam Crowley 1998. *Wild Wicklow*. Dublin, Town House.

Nairn, Richard, David Jeffrey and Rob Goodbody 2017. *Dublin Bay: Nature and History*. Cork, The Collins Press.

O'Connor, Nessa 2003. *Palmerstown: An Ancient Place*. Dublin, Environmental Publications.

O'Donohue, Patricia (ed.) 2008. *Aspects of Lucan*. Leixlip: LPSV.

O'Donovan, John (ed.) (3rd edn) 1998. *The Annals of Ireland by the Four Masters*. Dublin, Castlebourke.

O'Driscoll, James 1981 (2nd edn). *Cnucha: A History of Castleknock*. Privately published.

O'Keefe, Peter and Tom Simington, revised by Rob Goodbody 2017. *Irish Stone Bridges*. Newbridge, Irish Academic Press.

Ó Maitiú, Séamas and Barry O'Reilly 1997. *Ballyknockan*. Dublin, Woodfield Press.

Perry, Kenneth W. 1986. *The Irish Dipper*. Privately published.

Petty, William 1685. *The Down Survey*. http://downsurvey.tcd.ie/history.html

Philips, Michael and Albert Hamilton 2003. 'Project history of Dublin's River Liffey bridges'. *Proceedings of the Institution of Civil Engineers: Bridge Engineering* 156, 161–79, available at http://www.berthamilton.com/13329.pdf

Reilly, P. A. and J. McCullen 1993. *Wild Plants of the Phoenix Park*. Dublin, Stationery Office.

Rishworth, F. S. 1936. 'Liffey – hydro-electric scheme (Presidential address)'. *Transactions of the Institution of Engineers of Ireland* 63, 1.

Stokes, Whitley 1895. *Rennes Dindseanchas*. Dublin, Royal Irish Academy.

Sweeney, Pat 2010. *Liffey Ships and Shipbuilding*. Mercier Press.

Trant, Kathy 2004. *The Blessington Estate 1667–1908*. Dublin, Anvil Books.

Wallace, Patrick F. 2016. *Viking Dublin: The Wood Quay Excavations*. Sallins, Irish Academic Press.

Warren, William 1993. *Wicklow in the Ice Age*. Dublin, Geological Survey of Ireland.

Went, Arthur E. J. 1946. 'River Liffey Survey VII. Salmon of the River Liffey'. *Proceedings of the Royal Irish Academy* 51 B (2) 9–26.

Wright, G. N. 1822. *A Guide to the County of Wicklow*. London: Baldwin, Craddock and Joy.

Index

Illustrations are indicated by page numbers in bold. Individual streets named in the index are in Dublin unless otherwise specified.

Also from
The Collins Press

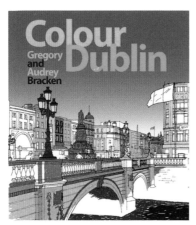

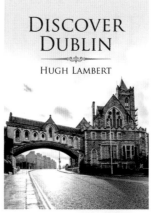

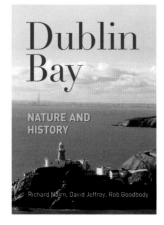

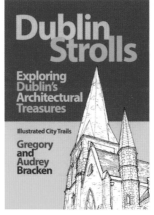

www.collinspress.ie

Also from
The Collins Press

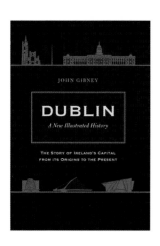
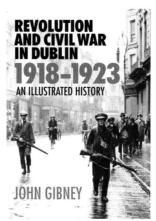
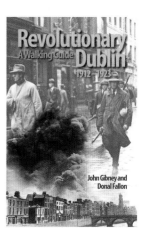

www.collinspress.ie